CAMBRIAN COMPANIONSHIP

A GWR standard 'Dean Goods' locomotive, No. 2447.

An ex-Cambrian Railways 0-6-0 large goods locomotive, No. 855, as rebuilt by the Great Western Railway.

CAMBRIAN
COMPANIONSHIP

T. P. Dalton

Oxford Publishing Company

Acknowledgements

J. H. Russell, the well-known author on the Great
Western Railway, first put the idea for this book into my
head. At the time it seemed a mammoth task but gradually, with his driving force, together with the assistance of
many Cambrian friends, this autobiography began to take
shape. It would be impossible to mention all the names
of those who have contributed, but my special thanks go
to the following ex-Cambrian railwaymen; Jackie Jones,
John Davies, Bob Davies (ABH), Llew Roberts, Gwyn
Roderick and John Roberts (MCH). The majority of
illustrations are those taken by myself, but my sincere
thanks go to Mrs Agnes Walters and I. Melvyn Evans for
their valuable contributions, and to Thomas Hunt for
ferreting out addresses of past friends. Finally my
wholehearted thanks go to Jane Leitch, who profession-
ally coped with my appalling spelling and typed out my
original pencil written manuscript, and her husband Dick,
who read through the proofs. Overall, true friendship is
one of the greatest treasures in life; what more can I ask.

Patrick Dalton
Milford-on-Sea, Hampshire

To Kathleen, my wife, and to Annette and Sarah, my daughters,
for their enthusiasm and encouragement

Typesetting by:
Aquarius Typesetting Services, New Milton, Hants.

Printed in Great Britain by:
Netherwood Dalton & Co. Ltd., Huddersfield,
Yorks.

Published by:
Oxford Publishing Co.
Link House
West Street
POOLE, Dorset

Contents

Preface

Unless one is a student of rail transport within the British Isles, the question mark immediately arises; where and what were the Cambrian Railways? For those not familiar with the territory it is essential to ponder for a while over a map of Mid-Wales, paying attention to the coastline from Aberystwyth in the south to Pwllheli in the north, on the Lleyn Peninsular, the latter stretching out almost to Bardsey Island. The large sweep of Cardigan Bay is backed by a ridge of mountains, from which the railway took its name.

Some very exact histories of the Cambrian Railways have already been recorded; briefly, to refresh one's mind, it was born in 1864 by the amalgamation of a series of little promoted lines such as the Oswestry to Newtown, Newtown to Llanidloes, Newtown to Machynlleth, the Mid-Wales and, finally the Aberystwyth Welsh Coast line, each of which struggled for existence although none of which really materialised. This all took place during a period that could be described as the railway boom years.

Wales is a proud nation, and naturally wanted its own railway. Although predominantly Welsh, the Cambrian headquarters were at Oswestry in Shropshire, whilst on her doorstep the all important LNWR hovered like a hungry hawk, waiting to pounce and take over; however, that was not to be. In spite of the obvious influence of 'big brother' at Euston, she remained independent until the Grouping of our railways took place in 1923. It has often been stated that the LNWR were the rightful owners — yet, contrary to expectations, it was 'God's Wonderful Railway' who finally absorbed the entire running length, together with the Manchester &

Milford Railway which, in the south, ran from Aberystwyth as far as Pencader, for some 56 miles, and which, ultimately, formed the Oswestry District of the GWR, paramount in my memories.

Akin to other lines of similar status the Cambrian had its high noons and years of gloom, yet it survived and served a thin territory well. Although, in 1922, it ceased as such, its name, spirit, and characteristics were to live on through the glorious years of the GWR, on the British Railways (Western Region) and finally British Rail (London Midland Region), now the reluctant owners. Unfortunately I was born during the dying years of the true Cambrian but, happily, still have misty memories of the men and locomotives that served it. Thus my reflections are, more strictly speaking, in its footsteps. In spite of changes in ownership and administration, what remains today is still very much Cambrian. It is important to pay attention to maps Nos. 2 and 3; they are the key to the vault of my story, from whence all began and ended in my personal memories of the Cambrian system.

Finally I must stress that my tale, although containing many facts, portrays my own observations, many of which are conclusions reached through what I saw and the result of conversations with official railwaymen. In certain instances I have denounced BR; idealism is one thing, with time often proving that certain ideas can be dangerous. Persons and personality I respect, but not always their policies, yet I owe BR an immense debt of thanks for their co-operation, which included access to railway departments and the most generous supply of locomotive passes, which has made my story possible.

Chapter 1

Ynyslas and Cambrian Memories

On the edge of the salt-marshes in North Cardiganshire there stood a wooden-constructed signal cabin, its call in life being to control one of the smallest and isolated of stations in the middle of nowhere. Virtually without any shelter, it was subjected to the most diverse weather conditions, which ranged from days of scorching sunshine to winter blizzards and westerly gales, the latter often touching the 100m.p.h. mark. Those were its real foes, yet battered year in and year out by wind, rain and salt spray, it stood the test and faithfully carried out its duties for nearly 100 years. In spite of its solitude it boasted moments of drama and, at intervals, activity, when an express train would thunder past, or two stopping trains would cross on its valuable and lengthy loops.

Too often, however, its lot was one of loneliness apart from the wild geese, the endless wheeling of seagulls and the moan of the wind through the telephone wires. Yet when living alongside it, one was always conscious of its presence — invariably visible while, after dark, the glow of its lights stood out like a beacon on a hill top. Electricity never came its way; the smell of paraffin lamps was just one of its many endearing characteristics. In spite of being scarred by the wrath of storms, age was not its executioner — alas, its light was finally extinguished by man himself, with his blood-stained axe of annihilation. Thus, weary and weather beaten, it finally fell, yet to many it was not only a landmark but something of beauty; such was Ynyslas signal box.

Ynyslas, (translated 'Blue-Green' Island) is the most northerly point of the Cardiganshire coastline — now part of Dyfed. Beyond lie the swift running waters of the Dyfi Estuary, which forms a natural boundary with its northern neighbour county, that of Merioneth which, today, is part of Gwynedd. To the west lies the vast expanse of Cardigan Bay, whilst inshore a high ridge of sand dunes separate the hard golden sands from the great marsh, which stretches inland for miles to the foothills of the surrounding Cambrian Mountains.

My first memories of Ynyslas reach back to the early 1920s — summer days of childhood, when man and his internal combustion engine had not yet commercialised this unique pocket of Cardiganshire. Those were the days that never seemed to end; the sun blazed down from dawn until dusk, on lonely sand dunes that were bleached white. High above, larks sang a continuous song, broken momentarily when they would drop like stones into the rough grass and wild roses that formed a natural border to the narrow fairways of the golf links, located on the lee side of the dunes. It was a land of incredible light, devoid of shadows and eternally bathed in a scent of sea, sand, mirram grass and wild thyme — sheer praise. Of course there were other days, — easily forgotten at that age, — of great storms, when rain beat

down on the windows of our holiday home. Cardigan Bay boiled like a cauldron, while giant waves pounded the beaches, sending streams of spray racing inland, backed by screaming winds, before eventually finding respite, like foam baths, in the ditches and bunkers on the golf course. It summed up all my strength to stand upright against the force of those gales. It was high up on those sand dunes, a land of make believe, while sifting the soft warm sand through my fingers, that I first observed Cambrian and, later, GWR locomotives travelling at a reasonable degree of speed.

A quarter of a mile inland, on the east bank of the Afon Leri, which bisects the vast stretch of bogland from Ynyslas, stood a remote little station. Some sixty years previously Thomas Savin, late constructor of the Cambrian Railways, had ambitious dreams of not only developing a junction at this point but also throwing a massive bridge across the wide estuary to Aberdyfi, lying on the northern bank of Afon Dyfi. Had this scheme materialised, it would undoubtedly have shortened the route from Aberystwyth, the Cambrian terminus to the south, with the northern coastal resorts of Barmouth, Porthmadog and Pwllheli. Happily, and for personal reasons, this never transpired, and a much shorter crossing of the river was by a wooden bridge, six miles upstream at Dovey Junction. Thus Ynyslas Station, in spite of high expectations, and apart from the early elimination of certain riverside sidings, was to remain virtually unchanged for nearly 100 years.

Originally the Afon Leri ran out to the sea, just prior to Aber-Leri crossings. There always existed a backwater at Ynyslas, which extended up into the marshland beyond the present railway bridge which spans the Leri at Ynyslas Station. It is presumed that the original constructors diverted the course of the river into this backwater at Ynyslas, thus eliminating the cost of constructing a further bridge at Aber-Leri. However, there exists some controversy on this point, as old maps indicate that the Leri originally met the sea under the high cliffs some 2½ miles south at Borth, but if one is familiar with Aber-Leri crossings, the original bed of the river is still evident, together with a well-proven legend that it is always an excellent position on the adjacent beach to either drag a net or fish with a rod, as a trickle of fresh water still exists. Personally, I am convinced the plan to eliminate a railway bridge at Aber-Leri is correct, especially so, since the last two miles of the normally winding river just resembles a man-made canal into the original backwater at Ynyslas.

One riverside siding I remember well, even into GWR days, had facing points, with a ground frame leading to a siding which ran alongside the west bank of the Afon Leri, crossing the B4353 by an unmanned crossing and

A 4-6-0 Standard 4MT, No. 75006, stands at the head of the 'up' 6p.m. Aberystwyth to Manchester (London Road) mail train. The train is seen about to leave Ynyslas.

P. Dalton

extending down the river bank to a wharf, whose remains are very much evident today. Indeed, I can well recall those early days, spent watching Jones 0-6-0 goods and Standard Dean engines shunting goods wagons on to that siding.

The second siding obviously came off the 'up' main line, within the bounds of Ynyslas Station; they must have been trailing points, which led on a very tight curve to a timber yard on the east bank of the Leri. Again, the remains are still evident. In fact, the widow of the late Bill Evans, signalman of Ynyslas, still lives in a bungalow perched on the remaining ballast. Obviously the 'up' platform at Ynyslas Station must have been extended later, eliminating the exit to this latter siding.

Returning to Ynyslas Station and placing aside the surroundings of extreme natural beauty, it was by no means unusual. Numerous country stations — even into BR days — could equally have boasted a meagre layout and indeed, many much better. There was the 'up' main line with a 'down' passing loop, the appropriate sleeper-constructed platforms, and the small station

house with a waiting-room; the latter devoid of comfort even in those early days. Facing points on the 'down' loop led to a siding and cattle bay. Last, but by no means least, stood the wooden-constructed signal box, the heart of that lonely station, where my story begins and ends. When the axe finally fell, many years later, it was mine for the asking, and why I never accepted or offered a few pence for that antique, remains a living regret. Its duties in life were to control the home, starter and advance starter on the 'up' main, and the locking bars for the massive level crossing gates which, on numerous occasions, required four men to push open against the force of a severe storm.

Childhood memories are always difficult to recollect in detail, yet turning back many leaves of the calendar to those early days I still recall Ynyslas which, in spite of its status, was a small station yet, at that period, one of reasonable activity. No road transport existed, at least on that route, and it was not an unusual sight to see thirty to forty passengers board a stopping train — especially on market days. It was the only means of transport, and

7

Illfated cutting, between Abermule and Newtown, as seen from the footplate of No. 7800 *Torquay Manor*.

P. Dalton

people would walk for miles, from outlying hamlets and farms, to board trains. There were always cattle wagons and coal trucks in the siding, whilst milk cans and boxes were loaded on and off trains. The station was always clean, firstly in Cambrian livery but later in the well-remembered GWR colours and, never to be forgotten, a beautiful Nestlé's chocolate machine, in red, which, on rare occasions, produced an enormous piece of chocolate for the modest price of one old penny.

In spite of my primitive age, many hours of those endless summer days were spent on the wooden platforms, but always escorted by our faithful nurse. Even at that age, I had elementary ideas from which direction trains would arrive by the movement of the long-armed Cambrian signals. Of course, at that stage of my life, Ynyslas was a large and important station. It certainly provided my first opportunity to watching passing trains moving reasonably fast, especially the express trains, and during those summer months there were plenty of them. Cambrian drivers really whipped through the 'down' loop, never to be repeated in GWR days, and many would appear to have cast speed restrictions to the four winds. A retired Cambrian stationmaster once told me about one particular driver who adopted the crudest of tactics when working 'down' passenger expresses. Once he got the road at Moat Lane Junction to the east he would open the regulator and get his locomotive moving, then give the regulator a massive slam with a small mallet, sending it almost through the cab roof, and away he would go — up the rising gradient without any easing to Talerddig Summit. The roar of the engine's exhaust could be heard right up the valley. It is presumed he either eased or closed it before descending the other side

to Llanbrynmair; surely this was one of the strangest ways of handling a locomotive. One possibility is that he was convinced he could get that extra ounce out of his engine, or maybe this barbaric act was put on to impress the station staff at Moat Lane.

Express trains passing Ynyslas would invariably include through coaches of other companies — the ones I recall especially were those of the GWR and LNWR — while many of the local stopping trains had those quaint little six wheelers, for many years a Cambrian characteristic. There were two six-wheeled observation coaches, which were normally attached to the rear of certain passenger trains, but were confined to the coast road from Machynlleth to Pwllheli; however, on one occasion and for some unknown reason, one appeared at the front of a passenger train to Aberystwyth. As luck had it, I was boarding the train with my father, and was treated to a ringside view of the footplate of the locomotive, its crew, and the road ahead. That was one of my earliest recollections of travelling on the Cambrian.

Freight trains moved much slower through Ynyslas, with a variety of coloured private-owner wagons and trucks which ranged from coal wagons, through food and livestock wagons to gunpowder vans, the latter always painted an unmistakable red. The Cambrian was, at that period, operating an amazing number of through coaches, which arrived and set out to various parts of the country. The station staff would sometimes tell me either where they were going or where they had come from although, at that stage of my life, the information supplied was meaningless — my horizons were far too short, yet that lonely station and its passing trains made a very deep impression. In fact, much later in my life, it became my lifeline on the Cambrian.

In spite of those infant memories of Ynyslas, and my apparent adoption by its staff, I must retrace my steps even further back to Plas-Crug crossings, located east of the locomotive shed at Aberystwyth. It was here that I first smelt Cambrian smoke, and the real seeds of railway fascination were originally sown. How, why and exactly

A small Cambrian Railways 0-6-0 goods locomotive at Llanidloes (Mid-Wales branch), in 1897.

Courtesy L. Roberts

Ynyslas Station, in 1950, showing the 'up' main and 'down' loop lines. The signal cabin, station house, booking office and waiting-room are clearly visible.

P. Dalton

when it all erupted is too far in the past, but undoubtedly three characters were responsible for igniting that vital spark; namely my father, a nurse and a top link Cambrian driver. Each one in different ways amalgamated to lay the foundation stones for this almost lifelong lure for the steel highway.

My father could never be classed as a railway enthusiast; indeed, he was the very opposite. Wisely, he taught me the essentials of my environment at a very early age; how to climb mountains, the art of fly fishing (especially where and when) and to study the weather and the effect of wind and clouds. The latter at that time seemed a pointless bore but, later in life, was to prove dividends. Yet he had sensed my early interest in steam locomotives, and Sunday walks to the riverside would never pass without diverting down the railway track from Plas-Crug crossings to pay a visit to the Cambrian locomotive shed at Aberystwyth.

The Cambrian, so it would seem, never appeared to show much opposition to that form of trespass, although such activities were never attempted in GWR days — in fact, after those early visits, I never visited the shed again until it was rebuilt and, as late as BR days, always with an official pass which was issued annually. However, in spite of a very considerable time lapse, I can still recall that old original red-bricked Cambrian shed and the

associated scents of hot metal, steam and coal, even the old gas lights, as I gazed up at the cleaners at work on those black-liveried locomotives with their tall tapered chimneys.

Cambrian cleaners were always plentiful, and worked throughout the night. In those days it was customary for that particular breed to congregate before duty at some convenient place. Once present and correct they marched round certain streets and sang, before eventually settling for the hours of darkness into the gloom of the locomotive shed, but not before local inhabitants had come to their doorsteps to wish them well.

The sound of water dripping from the waste pipes of dead locomotives, positioned at the western end of the shed, and the odd GWR engine, never under cover, were all early Cambrian memories. Those GWR locomotives worked the ex-Manchester & Milford line, to the south of Aberystwyth, and some still retained polished domes, in spite of it apparently being a pre-World War I practice.

For a youthful railway enthusiast, that period was ripe. In fact, everything 'railwaywise' played into my hands, and even from our home in Llangawsia, a minute hamlet, I could see Cambrian metals. At that time, as a family, we were blessed with a nurse, who must have been collaborator number two; daily, she took my

Lewis Rees (Uncle Lewis), top link Cambrian and GWR driver at Aberystwyth.

Courtesy Mrs Agnes Walters

younger brother and myself for walks alongside Cambrian railway tracks. He was perambulated, whilst I ran alongside his 0-4-0 carriage, possibly visualising myself as a Cambrian thoroughbred; but the all important fact, not appreciated at that age, was her love for a Cambrian railwayman — what an excellent choice! Day after day those walks would include a rest period at Plas-Crug crossings where, protected by heavy wooden fencing, I was able to watch Cambrian locomotives shunting a variety of liveried coaches of different shapes and sizes. Our beloved nurse, who incidentally had the appropriate surname of Bird, hung over the wooden fencing with a different adoration — that of her Cambrian idol. She was the best nurse we ever had.

Lastly, but by no means least, there was the third and vital personality who promoted my railway interest — Lewis Rees, a top link Cambrian and later GWR driver at Aberystwyth. Here was the most lovable of men; kind and gentle, portly, with a big grey moustache and the most penetrating blue eyes. His overalls were always immaculate — a pale denim blue, which contrasted with his highly-polished black boots.

Lewis Rees, or Uncle Lewis as I knew him, was truly one of nature's gentlemen. When setting out for duty he always had one of those fascinating engineman's baskets, which contained his bottle of tea, sandwiches, rule book and emergency working impedimenta. Whenever possible I would always accompany him to Plas-Crug crossings, sometimes being allowed to carry that basket, with youthful pride.

Uncle Lewis lived adjacent to us in Llangawsia, the houses being separated by a privet hedge which had the most convenient hole in it. Night after night I would creep through the undergrowth and sit down beside Uncle Lewis, and listen to endless stories of his days on the footplate — his good runs and his bad ones. Even the walls of his little living room were plastered with framed photographs of locomotives and steam-

ships, all of which built up the most exciting imagination in my mind. The climax of those early days was when Uncle Lewis did a turn for one week as station pilot. His early turns would include shunting duties for the gasworks sidings, which came off the 'up' main road to Llanbadarn. On such occasions — 7.30a.m. would always find me at Plas-Crug crossings — Uncle Lewis never missed that little figure, and would lift me on to the footplate and continue shunting the gaswork's privately-owned wagons. Later, turns would involve footplate rides right down into the station, and in and out of what appeared to me a maze of goods sidings. Sometimes Nurse Bird would take my brother home without me, but Mother never worried, knowing that I was in safe hands with Uncle Lewis who always brought me home, sometimes as black as the ace of spades — beautiful grime I was so proud of because it was that of a railwayman. In his tender-hearted and unpretentious way, Lewis Rees well and truly laid the foundation stones for my railway fascination which lived on, long after him, to the end of steam.

Casting my mind back to that mirror of childhood, there were obviously far greater and more efficient railway companies than the Cambrian. This was a system that was, too often, short of funds while the locomotive stud, with some exceptions, was ancient and underpowered, yet her drivers knew how to get the best out of them and, over the next forty years, no overall faster running was to be seen on that system. It is often said one's first love is the best — thus my special warmth for the Cambrian can be appreciated.

With regard to the locomotives, the passage of time has unfortunately fooled me, in spite of those very early footplate rides. In pushing my memory back to its limits, I recall that my introduction to the footplate was on tender engines, namely the small 4-4-0 Astons and also the 0-6-0 goods engines. Never can I recall having ridden on any of the large Jones 4-4-0 express engines although, many years later, while in conversation with a retired ex-Cambrian driver, he assured me that he could remember seeing me east of the locomotive shed with Lewis Rees, on the footplate of none other than No. 95 — eventually destroyed at Abermule. It is possible, yet I can only accept his word on that moot point. At that stage of my life I had not acquired the art of picking out locomotives of a class by their numbers; however, if the late Dickie Mills was correct, it must surely have been an historic occasion for me.

Somewhere in the misty past I recall a tank engine, possibly an 0-4-2 with an open cab, but certainly not one of the Class 3 Aston 0-4-4 tanks which I can just recollect. Hours of research through Cambrian locomotive lists at that time have not produced the answer. Again, it would appear that the livery of Cambrian locomotives was a very dark bronzed green, although they always appeared black to me. At that age I was neither apace with changes in livery; the main line express corridor coaches were green, whilst some of the small antiquated six-wheeled coaches used on stopping trains were

A pre-World War I Cambrian station scene at Portmadoc. The locomotive in the background is a light Cambrian 2-4-0.
Courtesy Richard Putt

green and white, the original livery.

Before passing on from my personal early memories of the true Cambrian, I have to conclude on a tragic note — a date that every serving Cambrian railwayman was never to forget — 26th January 1921. It concerned Abermule, the scene of the appalling head-on collision which brought the Cambrian to its knees like a boxer on the canvas taking his count. It was more than a nail in the coffin, and a mortal wound from which it was never to recover. Public confidence had been very badly shaken by that ghastly collision, and the ultimate take-over by the GWR in 1922 was naturally welcomed. Even at that age I was aware that something terrible had happened; Uncle Lewis said nothing, people talked in whispers and a special train, unknown to myself, arrived at Aberystwyth conveying the victims. I gathered that two locomotives had been destroyed, but railway accidents were foreign to me, whilst Abermule was a long way off, almost another land.

Later in life, its realities became a very different picture. Time is a great healer and railwaymen, even some who were actually present on that fatal day, told me more and more of what had actually happened. Fireman Owen, who was on the footplate of the 'up' express locomotive, recorded in detail

on many occasions those last dramatic moments before he and his mate finally jumped before impact with the 'down' stopping train.

Abermule, undoubtedly, will go down in railway history as one of the classical head-on collisions, probably the worst of its type in living memory on British metals. The whys and wherefores have already been recorded in great detail, and with remarkable accuracy; Mr Rolt undoubtedly reached perfection in his book *Red for Danger*. A very old friend, the late Arthur Llewellyn, a Newtown passenger guard, returned my copy with the wise comment that it was literature that every railwayman should read, and should be incorporated in the rule books.

Strangely enough, and to the best of my knowledge, no report records the fact that when Owen finally jumped the token accompanied him. History records that he later recovered it from the wreckage, together with the Montgomery to Abermule token from the stopping train. This little detail he has emphatically repeated to me on several occasions, although if my Cambrian recollections are correct, the token was carried by the driver. However, his firsthand description became a very vivid picture in my mind and later, every time I rounded that

11

curve, either on the cushions or the footplate, I was always reminded of the horror of that fatal January morning. Abermule certainly left its scars on Cambrian railwaymen, to the extent that wholesale panic raged up and down the line, especially in signal cabins, with the dreaded fear that a similar catastrophe could happen again. Thus the Cambrian's dying hours saw everybody on their toes.

Abermule, from personal memories, merely amounted to a landmark of changes on the system. Up to that time locomotives had portrayed themselves just as passenger and goods engines, big and small; however, from 1922 onwards, my railway observations became more acute. The familiar black-liveried locomotives associated wih the past became less in numbers, being replaced by the Brunswick Green and polished brass machines which were those of the new owners, the Great Western Railway.

A light Cambrian 4-4-0 locomotive constructed by Sharp Stewart & Co. Ltd.

Locomotive Publishing Co. Ltd.

Chapter 2
The GWR Take-Over : 1922 – 1930

Some of the first GWR engines noted at Ynyslas were the 2-4-0 'Barnham' and 'Stella' classes, the latter being my favourites. To my youthful eye they appeared more refined in design, especially if they had copper caps to their chimneys. There were at least three or four stationed at Aberystwyth, and appeared to have replaced the smaller Aston 4-4-0 locomotives of the Cambrian. However, these newly-acquired locomotives were by no means strangers, because the same class had previously worked the Manchester & Milford line, south of Aberystwyth, to Carmarthen. The larger Cambrian (Jones 4-4-0) express engines continued to run for a considerable number of years but became Swindonised, with GWR type chimneys, safety-valves and unlined GWR green paintwork.

For the railway enthusiast it was an exciting period, as new replacements on the locomotive side seemed to appear quickly. A host of Standard Dean 0-6-0 goods engines arrived, whilst the larger 0-6-0 (Jones) goods, of Cambrian vintage, were retained, but again acquired that GWR stamp as they returned from the factory. Of the two types of goods engines the ex-Cambrian locomotives were then my favourites, possibly due to their relatively high-sided tenders and the brass edging to the wheel splashers. Very soon after the GWR take-over, an 0-4-2 Wolverhampton tank arrived at Aberystwyth with an open cab. I cannot recall her number but, in spite of GWR rules and regulations, I spent many happy hours on her footplate with Uncle Lewis — old habits die slowly.

Undoubtedly, the climax of excitement of this new breed of locomotive was the arrival of the little 4-4-0 Dean 'Duke' class engines. Now, it is an established fact that 'beauty lies in the eye of the beholder' and, in my mind, aesthetically, they were the most handsome locomotives ever to serve on the Cambrian. With their fascinating Cornish names and beautiful proportions, they seemed to fall naturally into Cambrian territory. At first there was only a handful, but more and more arrived and, as far as I can remember, the entire series, at one time or another, saw service in the Oswestry District, with the exception of No. 3286 *Meteor*. No. 3270 *Earl of Devon*, stationed at Aberystwyth, was one of the first I noted, but was quickly followed by *Thames, Cornubia, Tre Pol and Pen, Merlin, Mendip, The Lizard, Isle of Jersey* and an old Aberystwyth favourite, *St. Agnes*. Not all the 'Duke' class carried nameplates and later on, unfortunately, many more lost their christian names on returning to service from overhauls.

Summer holidays were still spent at Ynyslas, but less time was spent in that land of make-believe — the sand dunes. As I no longer required an escort, most of my days were spent on the wooden platforms of Ynyslas Station. The staff were now established friends, but I was always told what not to do and where to stand; law and order existed in those days, and instructions were always abided by. My good behaviour paid dividends. One day, apparently, there was a token failure between Ynyslas and Borth, the latter being the next 'down' station and some 2½ miles to the south. On such occasions the normal procedure was to carry a 'live-man' on the footplate in place of the token, invariably the signalman not on duty, the man in question wearing a red arm band marked 'G.W.R. Pilotman'. On that particular occasion I was standing on the 'down' platform, close to the 'down' starter, when a stopping train drew in headed by one of the newly-acquired 'Duke' class locomotives. Suddenly, without warning, I was swept off my feet by the pilotman, who placed me on that coveted platform, the footplate of one of Mr Dean's engines, with the remark 'You're coming for a ride'.

Even at that early age the footplate was not something new, but rattling along that 4½ mile journey was a new and unforgettable experience. The driver was a very large fat man who, it would appear, could only do up the top button of his jacket. I remember coasting into Borth, past the golf club, and wondering if my father would spot me perched up on what was, to my mind, the highest of all pinnacles.

On arrival at Borth I was lifted down on to the platform, escorted over the footbridge, and placed on the footplate of an 'up' stopping train. Now time has again fooled me although in any case, excitement at that stage

An Aveling Porter steamroller, identical to the Aberystwyth Corporation machine.

P. Dalton

A Dean 'Duke' class locomotive, No. 3260 *Mount Edgcumbe* awaits departure. Of particular interest is the small tender.

A Dean 'Duke' class locomotive, No. 3253 *Boscawen*, carrying the untapered chimney, is seen at Oswestry in the 1930s.

had probably put me way beyond reliable recording. Somewhere in my mind I had visions that the return run to Ynyslas was made on a 'Barnham' or 'Stella' class; however, on reflection, I can still recall the horseshoe-shaped brass facing surrounding the boiler, extending down to the footplate on either side of the firebox. This was a Cambrian characteristic, meaning that the locomotive could well have been a 'Cami' 4-4-0, these still being around at the time.

On arrival back at Ynyslas, flushed with excitement, I never even had the courtesy to say 'thank you', but set off, as fast as my little legs could carry me, away across the fields to our holiday home to record my exploit to my parents. True to form, Father just smiled; however, he was able to assist. In spite of playing a needle match of golf he assured me the name of the 'Duke' on the 'down' run was *Boscawen* — the 18th hole runs parallel to the railway. The mystery of the 'up' run was never solved because, unfortunately, he was already at the 19th hole, either celebrating or drowning his sorrows. I never noted *Boscawen* again until the mid-1930s, when she was stationed at Oswestry. That same afternoon I returned to Ynyslas Station with high hopes; — alas, the token failure had been rectified, and many moons were to pass before climbing aboard again at that little station.

There was, in those days, a batch of smaller 4-4-0 engines that were very much like a 'Duke' at a quick glance, the 3521 class. However, they had straight frames, and never carried nameplates. Again they were not newcomers, as I could vaguely remember the odd one working the Manchester & Milford line in Cambrian days. Records indicate that the Cambrian purchased one of this class to replace 4-4-0 No. 95, destroyed in the Abermule disaster.

As the 1920s progressed so did the 'Duke' class in number, and were not confined only to passenger trains. The 'Barnham' and 'Stella' class engines began to disappear, together with the large Cambrian Jones 4-4-0 locomotives; I was informed that they took over duties on the coast road from Machynlleth to Pwllheli, with which I was not familiar at that period. Some of the 'Stella' class also worked the Mid-Wales line from Moat Lane Junction to Brecon, in company with an assortment of ex-Cambrian and Dean Goods engines. That line always had very severe restrictions beyond Llanidloes, even until the line was finally lifted in BR days.

At this stage in my life I had become highly transport minded, except for private motor cars. I knew all the commercial vehicles operating, which ranged from lorries, steam wagons and rollers to motor buses, and made friends with their drivers; although the railway was my true love and at that stage my sole ambition was to eventually become an engine driver.

Briefly, one must bring road transport into the picture because, as we shall see later, it proved to be a thorn in the side of rail transport. By the mid-1920s road traffic was not heavy — in fact, one could drive mile after mile without meeting any form of road vehicle — but petrol was cheap, and the pirate age of buses had already started. Buses of the GWR were now operating between Aberystwyth and Machynlleth and at Dolgellau, in competition with the blue and white Corris Railway buses. South of Aberystwyth, GWR buses were operating as far afield as Cardigan and Llandyssul, whilst in Aberystwyth a vast privately-owned organisation, Jones Bros, of North Parade, had burst on to the scene and were quickly developing almost a complete monopoly of the Cardiganshire routes. Their fleet was a very mixed bag of all the commercials of the day, including a Lancia with a canvas top and a Star. Nearly all vehicles were second-hand, and many of the bodies were constructed in their Northgate Street garage. In spite of their harlequin appearance, they could well have swept the board with the other operators, but mismanagement finally resulted in liquidation. Crossville Motor Services arrived in 1926, but until the 1930s were the smallest operators until they finally bought out Jones Bros., and absorbed the GWR road services which had since become Wrexham Transport. Crosville now became virtually the sole operators, and in spite of both GWR and LMS interest were eventually to strike a vicious blow to rail passenger services. Strangely enough, in spite of my railway bias, support was not for the ancient AEC railway buses but for those of the outsider, the Leylands of Crosville, which eventually led to further friendship. I knew all their machines from the very start, together with their drivers, and many free rides were subsequently enjoyed. On Sundays their kindness was repaid by my assistance in washing buses at the depot — great fun, squirting water with handpumps from buckets all over the panels and windows.

During the summer months, coach operators ran excursions all over Wales, whilst the GWR had the novel idea of converting a Morris commercial vehicle into a mountain climber. This strange machine, which had no cover, would take hardy passengers from the station at Aberystwyth to the summit of Plynlimon, 2,468ft. above sea level.

Returning to the railway, traffic was heavy, especially during the summer months, which would include numerous cheap excursions. By the end of the 1920s most of the ex-Cambrian engines had disappeared, except for the 0-6-0 goods locomotives, the replacements had gradually settled down to 'Duke' class and 'Dean Goods', whilst occasionally the odd 'Barnum' would be in evidence on a Machynlleth local. Cambrian coaching stock had vanished, except for some of their main line stock which was now adorned in GWR livery. Meanwhile vast changes in track layout and rebuilding had taken place, which I shall mention in another chapter.

Lewis Rees had not been well and had retired, but not before he told me about the massive 4-6-0 'Castle' class locomotives that Mr Collett was building at Swindon, especially No. 4084 *Aberystwyth Castle* which he said was destined to work through to Aberystwyth. Poor Uncle Lewis was obviously getting very tired and divulged this information with his tongue in his cheek, but what a thought; 'Castles' on the Cambrian — that would have set the enthusiasts alight! His retirement was very short, and I can still remember my father tactfully breaking the sad news that my childhood hero had passed away.

For a time my railway activities died with him and, almost in revolt, I turned my affections to the Aberystwyth Corporation steam roller, an Aveling Porter. Her driver, Arthur Morris, became yet another Cambrian companion. Hours were spent on that minute footplate up and down Plas-Crug Avenue, alongside the railway line at Aberystwyth which was being relaid, until one fatal day, an abrupt finish was brought to that particular chapter of steam. The engine was stationary, whilst horse-drawn carts tipped more rubble to be rolled flat. Suddenly, without warning, a water glass blew; the violent bang and steam everywhere frightened me out of my wits. I took a flying leap over her massive driving wheels, and set off for home like a scalded cat. It was some days before Arthur Morris enticed me back on to the footplate, but that was short-lived; Lewis Rees had sown the seeds of my first love, and it was a case of back to Plas-Crug railway crossings.

No. 3254 *Cornubia*, a Dean 'Duke', renumbered to 9054 in BR days, is seen at Dovey Junction with Driver Bob Davies on the footplate. Tidal water lies around the track.

Courtesy Driver Bob Davies

Chapter 3
The GWR Days of the 1930s

By the advent of the 1930s, the GWR was firmly established over the entire ex-Cambrian system; indeed, the new owners wasted no time in putting their new house in order, virtually in all departments. We have already seen that the scrapping of older Cambrian locomotives and coaching stock was one of the first of many swift changes and indeed, the termination of the 1920s saw very few Cambrian locomotive survivors, especially on the main line. Gone were the smaller Aston 4-4-0 and 0-4-0 goods engines; a few of the larger Jones 4-4-0 engines hung on, but were relegated to the coast road from Machynlleth to Pwllheli. Yet the larger 0-6-0 Jones goods engines carried on and were to run for many years, several as far off as early BR days, while one or two odd little Cambrian locomotives, again rebuilt with Swindon characteristics, persisted on some of the minor branch lines such as the Tanat Valley. One glorious example was the ex-Cambrian 2-4-0 No. 1196, a familiar character at Oswestry for many years.

From then on, every decade of steam on the Cambrian saw motive power changes right up to 1968. The beginnings of the 1930s had even seen the removal of some of the early GWR replacements, in particular the 2-4-0 'Stella' and 'Barnham' classes, although one or two remained at Machynlleth, again working the coast road and on the Mid-Wales line from Moat Lane to Brecon. The smaller GWR 4-4-0s, the 3521 class, were now extinct, and the mainstay of the Cambrian were 'Duke' class and Standard 0-6-0 goods locomotives although, as we shall see, within a space of ten years, the picture was to change yet again.

It was almost as if the GWR was determined to make a clean sweep and banish all Cambrian memories, some of which were certainly well overdue. The old Cambrian locomotive shed at Aberystwyth was demolished and on its site a new modern locomotive shed, still with two roads, was built. There were vast track layout alterations and improvements, both up and down the line, with the old and once familiar long-armed Cambrian signals gradually giving way to the more modern GWR lower quadrant type. Also, a vast amount of track relaying took place (Cambrian road was not one of the Company's strongest points), while many bridges were either rebuilt or strengthened. Undoubtedly the most dramatic change at Aberystwyth was the rebuilding of the station itself, which began in the mid-1920s. It was a complete face-lift; platforms and awnings were extended with a most impressive station concourse and, for a brief period, the station acquired an excellent restaurant. The old red-bricked coal offices vanished, and a new row of station shops was built alongside the station frontage. Originally the Cambrian turntable was unsatisfactorily sited north of the locomotive shed, in the carriage sidings, so the GWR temporarily resited a larger turntable south

of the shed, but this again was eventually removed, and reinstalled at Machynlleth. A triangle was subsequently constructed at Aberystwyth, possibly with a view to running trains straight through from the Carmarthen branch on to the main Cambrian line to the north. However, this never materialised, and it was used solely for the purpose of turning locomotives. That particular stretch of track had very personal affections because it was there, many years later, that I learnt of the art of handling a steam locomotive.

The upshot of these changes was the rapid elimination of Cambrian memories, with a completely new look under GWR ownership. It was extremely exciting and, in spite of my initial baptism to the Cambrian Railways, I had at that age already become a true and dedicated disciple of the Great Western Railway. Yet, strangely enough over the next ten years, my personal contact with the Cambrian railwaymen became least of all during the steam era. The reasons were twofold; boarding school days resulted in gaps in my Cambrian observations, although the fundamental reason lay in the fact that I was fortunate to be one of ten small companions who grew up together, a very select band of boys who have always remained the closest of friends. During school holidays we built boats, climbed Welsh peaks and fished the August floods for sewin — yet out of that ten, I was the only true steam lover.

Now, at that age, I had become somewhat conscious of my deep-seated interest and, fearing my companions would consider me childish, kept my railway interests entirely to myself, almost to the degree of a coveted secret. In fact, that policy was continued for many years, and only came out into the open much later and when I was considerably older and a hospital student.

In spite of periods of absence from the Cambrian during school-days, holidays always provided excitement in rooting out changes — especially on the locomotive side. More and more 'Duke' class locomotives saw service in the district, and had become the mainstay of the passenger train workings. One Saturday, during the summer holidays, I recorded 21 separate 'Duke' class engines working through Borth; in fact, the entire series saw service of some sort on Cambrian metals, already mentioned in a previous chapter. There was a batch of regular performers, with well-associated names such as *Boscawen, Cornubia, Excalibur, Mercury, Merlin, Tre Pol and Pen, Mounts Bay, Mendip* and so on; some of the less frequent members worked in from Shrewsbury and Birmingham (Tyseley) during summer months, whilst quite a few of the class began to lose their nameplates.

In spite of their immaculate appearance and apparently reasonable performance, the writing was already on the wall as coaching stock grew heavier. The little 'Duke'

No. 9017 is seen on shed at Machynlleth in August 1959. This is the only 'Dukedog' which has been preserved and can now be seen on the Bluebell Railway in Sussex.

P. Dalton

An ex-GWR 4-4-0 'Dukedog', No. 9025, is seen with top feed and 'Duke' type chimney. Driver G. Thomas and Fireman O. B. Jenkins are in command.

P. Dalton

No. 2298, a BR (WR) 0-6-0, heads a 4.15p.m. Newtown to Aberystwyth local train in August 1955. It is seen approaching Aberystwyth.
P. Dalton

class engines were by no means brand-new when they arrived in the Welsh valleys — many had previously seen years of hard service in Devon and Cornwall, and the GWR obviously had to think of replacements. Unfortunately, at that time, severe problems were still in existence; in spite of a lot of track renewal, the ex-Cambrian lines were still very restricted with regard to axle loads. Mr Collett (Swindon's Locomotive Superintendent) solved the problem by the creation of what today are generally referred to as 'Dukedogs', which first appeared as a series in 1936 as the 3200 class.

The prototype, No. 3265 *Tre Pol and Pen*, emerged from Swindon as early as 1931 with a 'Duke' boiler and frames of a 'Bulldog' — hence their nickname. However, it was many years later before I spotted this change in motive power — pocket money did not run to the luxury of railway periodicals, with their up-to-date news, whilst boarding school days and the fact that she was stationed at Oswestry could be blamed for my missing this obvious and important change. Later on, I gathered that when the rest of the series stepped out of Swindon, there were hoots of amusement from rival companies. However, in spite of their somewhat antique appearance, they were the 'right horses for the course' although in my opinion, they were never as handsome as their predecessors the 'Duke' class. Yet despite this, they were

destined to do some excellent work on the Cambrian lines for the next twenty years.

Once again the old pattern was safe — a predominance of 4-4-0 locomotives. Originally, the first twelve of the thirty locomotives constructed carried nameplates and became the 'Earl' class; unfortunately, their nameplates were very short-lived, and were assigned to a new series of 'Castle' class locomotives. It was stated at the time that the named Earls strongly objected to their titles appearing on such inferior locomotives; anyway, it was a good and feasible excuse.

The 'Dukedogs' were a very mixed bag as a series, almost a bastard class. Some had 'Duke' type chimneys — No. 3202 was always distinguished by her tall narrow chimney, whilst the majority had the more well-remembered thicker parallel stacks with copper caps. Quite a few had top feeds, whilst tenders varied in size. One got the impression that these rebuilds were stopgaps, which was undoubtedly true. Had not World War II intervened, I am certain the Cambrian would have had a very different look, certainly motive power wise.

Surprisingly, timetables for the Oswestry District throughout the 1930s showed little or no change from Cambrian days, and in some cases there were faster timings by the previous owners, especially express trains of which there were far more. However, the GWR

Ex-GWR 2-6-2T, No. 5507 heads the 'down' coastal section of the 'Cambrian Coast Express' between Machynlleth and Dovey Junction, and is seen passing mile-post 77¾.

P. Dalton

An ex-GWR 2-6-2 tank heads the 'up' 'Cambrian Coast Express' along the sea wall between Aberdovey and Dovey Junction in 1950.

quickly rectified the ghastly Cambrian record of local stopping trains, the latter being notorious — not only for their coaching stock but also for poor timekeeping. Having lived briefly with the true Cambrian, an interesting little tale comes to mind. Strictly speaking, the GWR Oswestry District was not exactly the complete running length of the Cambrian Railways, as the latter company ran from Barmouth Junction to Dolgellau, on the ex-GWR Barmouth to Ruabon branch. Cambrian trains were able to run directly on to the Ruabon branch from the south, and again trains were able to use the loop without reversing on the return journey to Dovey Junction and Machynlleth. Apparently, a Cambrian Dolgellau to Machynlleth stopping train drew into Barmouth Junction, and a very tired railway employee dived into a first class compartment and promptly fell asleep. The local train then proceeded slowly, calling at Llwyngwril and Towyn and eventually arrived very late at Aberdovey. A member of the latter station staff spotted the sleeping character, very much out of bounds, in the first class compartment. The guard was duly informed, whereupon it would appear the train was reversed back to Barmouth Junction, and the unfortunate trespasser was either slung out on to the platform or transferred to a third class compartment, and the journey south to Machynlleth began all over again. True or untrue, such was an example of Cambrian local workings — unbelievable yet lovable.

The 'crack' train in GWR days was the 'up' 10.15 a.m. Aberystwyth to Paddington working with two through coaches, for which passengers from Barmouth and Pwllheli joined the train at Dovey Junction or Machynlleth. The 'down' express arrived at Aberystwyth at 5.05p.m. after leaving Paddington at 11.15a.m. with dining cars being operated between Shrewsbury and London in both directions. The latter coaches very seldom penetrated the Oswestry District (GWR) until post World War II days; the first I noted was way back in 1925, on the occasion of the conference of the League of Nations at Aberystwyth. It was a very impressive special train, packed with notable diplomats and hauled by two immaculate little 'Duke' class locomotives, No. 3270 *Earl of Devon* and No. 3291 *Thames*.

In spite of the increased power of the 'Dukedogs' over that of the 'Duke' class, timetables remained the same and most of the heavier passenger trains, especially between Aberystwyth and Borth and the stiff climb from Machnylleth to Talerddig, required an assisting engine. It is interesting to note that an old Cambrian timetable, from as far back as 1904, advertised through coaches from Euston at 9.30 and 11a.m. arriving at Aberystwyth at 4.20 and 5.45p.m., so in spite of a lapse of over thirty years the GWR pre-war express trains showed little improvement.

The Cambrian express trains, in contrast to their stopping trains, really moved. Just before the annihilation of that company I can well remember my father taking me to Bow Street Station, to watch the passing of one of the 'down' afternoon expresses. It was always quite an event, taken at speed and highly appreciated by the village boys who turned out en masse to witness the express negotiate the 'down' loop. They would wave their Welsh tweed caps as the express dashed past, and thundered up the final incline before descending to Aberystwyth.

In spite of the recession during the 1930s, Aberystwyth and the other Cambrian coast resorts enjoyed a vast influx of visitors during the summer months. The real impact of road traffic was still a long way off, and regular visits by ships of the Royal Navy and vast territorial camps on Lovesgrove Flats, near Aberystwyth, all helped to swell railway traffic. Aberystwyth then boasted excellent hotels, each with their own private buses which conveyed guests to and from the London or Northern express trains. Fares were reasonably cheap and the trains were clean, and although somewhat slow, ran to time. Throughout this period there existed an atmosphere of extreme politeness — memorable days.

An old friend of mine recorded an interesting little story which was way beyond Cambrian metals, yet one that typified those stately days of the Great Western Railway. A certain lady of distinction was travelling home from Paddington on one of those renowned two hour express trains to Birmingham, often worked by a 'Saint' or 'Star' class locomotive. The train had just left Leamington Spa when the ticket collector entered the first class portion of the dining car, and almost apologetically approached the aforementioned lady and inquired if he could see her ticket. Having duly punched her ticket, he assured her the train would be on time at Wolverhampton. Just before moving on to the next table the lady passenger asked him if he knew the name of the engine, as her small son would certainly want to know when she got home. The ticket collector assured her he would endeavour to find out, and within minutes returned saying, 'Madame, the name of the engine is *Lady of Quality*'.

Way back on the Cambrian Coast and Mid-Wales, Crosville Motor Services were now virtually the sole operators, and had already started an express service from Aberystwyth to Birmingham. Records of passengers carried included the name of Von Ribbentrop, the arch-Nazi criminal then sheltering under the disguise of a German wine merchant. Western Welsh operated a similar service to Cardiff, whilst the 'Black and White' Leylands ran daily through to London. Neither made any serious impact on rail traffic, whilst the little 'Duke' class engines and a handful of 'Dukedogs' were hard put to cope with the heavier coaching stock and holiday traffic.

Our family holidays, as such, had ceased at Ynyslas but now as young boys, armed with a fleet of canoes, we annually set up camp in bell tents adjacent to the railway line, just north of Borth Station. From dawn to dusk, clad in bathing trunks, we battled through the endless surf and breakers until we reached calmer waters. Turning our light craft inshore we would then race inshore, backed by massive blue-green curling waves. It was an endless sport, highlighted by some fearful pile ups. During this surf riding activity and, unknown to my mates, I was able to keep a precise record of locomotive workings. The 'Duke' class engines all had to have assistance over the severe banks, south to Aberystwyth, with anything over six coaches. The week prior to the original August bank holiday was the peak period, and invariably saw a number of banking engines in the sidings at Borth. These would range from 'Duke' class locomotives to Standard Goods engines, and occasionally the newly-acquired 'Dukedogs'. The Birmingham trains were invariably double-headed and unloaded vast numbers of their passengers at Borth, often nicknamed 'Birmingham-by-the-Sea'. Oswestry men would have appeared to have enjoyed most of the workings, although Aberystwyth men worked twice daily through to Shrewsbury and back and, during summer months, enjoyed a nice double home trip to Birmingham (Tyseley). Often I have heard some of the older drivers reminisce about those runs, especially coming down Wellington Bank with two 'Duke' class engines running fast. Freight trains were heavy during that period — road carriers were few and far between, and when cattle and livestock travelled by rail they were well cared for en route. One special comes to mind, this being the highly important Bass and Worthington working which conveyed the 36 gallon wooden casks of real ale at regular intervals from Burton upon Trent. Whether railway-minded or not, everyone knew the whereabouts of that train, and it was always given absolute priority.

Another feature of the early 1930s was the railway horse. A certain number of very ancient AEC solid-tyred lorries were in existence for delivery of goods to outlying districts, but the town traffic at Aberystwyth was operated by horse-drawn carts. Those beautiful railway Shire horses, which were cared for like human beings and were in perfect condition, with harness and polished brass, hauled some very heavy loads up and down the streets of Aberystwyth, and were the most amazing practical and economic form of transport.

As the 1930s began to draw to a close, a new look in motive power began to make itself apparent, not on the ex-Cambrian main line but the coast road from Machynlleth to Pwllheli. For the first time the Churchward look was to show itself, in the form of those versatile 4500 and 4575 class 2-6-2 tank locomotives, whilst the odd 4300 class (5300 series) Moguls began working into Aberystwyth via the Carmarthen branch line from the south. Further north, on the Ruabon to Barmouth branch (now in the 'blue' classification), larger power was already appearing in the form of 4300 class Moguls, the 2-6-0 'Aberdare' class and even the newly-built Collett 4-6-0s, the 'Manor' class engines.

As we have already seen, the Cambrian Railways ran as far as Dolgellau, but after regionalisation this section was administered by the Wolverhampton Division. An exception was the two little auto tank engines stabled at Penmaenpool, which came under the loving care of Machynlleth Shed in the Oswestry District.

Royal Train workings, especially on a single line system, caused a certain amount of disruption to normal services. In July 1937, King George VI and Queen Elizabeth travelled from the south to Aberystwyth, by rail, to open an extension of the National Library of Wales, the train being worked by two of the cleanest 4300 class locomotives. In spite of traffic curtailments, over 40,000 people arrived by rail at Aberystwyth before 10a.m. for the event. Very soon after that occasion I spotted the first of Mr Collett's 0-6-0 goods locomotives, No. 2298 with 'R.O.D.' tender, which had been assigned to Aberystwyth. Apart from the arrival of a further batch of 'Dukedogs', and the gradual withdrawal of the smaller 'Duke' class, the Cambrian saw no further locomotive changes during that decade. Quite a few repairs were carried out at Aberystwyth Shed, which ranged from valves and pistons to re-wheeling. David Rees, Lewis Rees' son, had returned from Canada, and became an active member of that department for many years.

Up to the beginning of the 1930s, my railway observations had been confined to the bounds of Aberystwyth Station and brief spells at Ynyslas during holiday periods; however, once boarding school days began, my horizon was stretched, as journeys to and from school were always made by rail, which provided a vast assortment of motive power and rival companies — a slight consolation. Reflecting back it is amusing to think of the effects 'up' and 'down' platforms had on my mind at that time; the 'up' was sheer purgatory at first, the gateway to three months' imprisonment, whilst the 'down' was the reverse to extreme, on which even the advertisements were brighter and more cheerful. At first, I was convinced that the station authorities had arranged this as a welcome home benefit. For nine months of the year, from 1930-6, my so-called imprisonment was at Bromsgrove, on the main Birmingham to Gloucester line of the London, Midland & Scottish Railway. To anyone who was slightly interested in steam traction, the name Bromsgrove immediately brought to mind the famous Lickey Incline, just over two miles of double track on a rising gradient of 1 in 37 to Blackwell, at the top of the bank. In those days, everything had to have assistance up the bank to reach the Midland plain beyond. Sometimes as many as four banking engines, working flat out, would push a train up the incline, showering soot and sparks over the surrounding countryside — a truly magnificent sight — but the spectacle that really brought the house down was the famous ex-Midland 0-10-0 banking engine, No. 2290, specially constructed for this task. She had lots of nicknames, but I always knew her as 'Big Bertha'. Now, one will say 'what has this got to do with the Cambrian?' but, as we shall see, a vast amount; in fact, it was the forerunner to further exploits on the Cambrian lines that I had never dreamed possible.

A journey back to school involved the widest range of

A view of Bromsgrove Station showing the Lickey Incline rising from the station.

P. Dalton

No. 58100 at Bromsgrove (South) taking on water prior to a return footplate trip up the incline in November 1955.

P. Dalton

Having just descended the Lickey Incline, and about to cross over on to the banker siding at Bromsgrove (South), are Nos. 47502, 47425 and 58100.

P. Dalton

In November 1955, an ex-LMS 'Jinty', No 47308, is seen at Bromsgrove. It displays the number '5' above the leading buffer.

P. Dalton

An ex-LMS 'Black Five' 4-6-0, locomotive, No. 44813, starts the long haul up the incline between Bromsgrove (South) and Bromsgrove Station, with the banker at the rear.

motive power. At first it was a 'Duke' as far as Welsh-pool, but this was always assisted from Aberystwyth to Borth, and again from Machynlleth to Talerddig Summit. Ex-LNWR engines would take over the joint section from Welshpool to Shrewsbury and then it was the turn of the dirty little Webb 0-6-0 engines, that laboured at a snail's pace up Breidden Bank to Westbury, and ran only slightly faster on the falling gradient to Shrewsbury. Time and again we offered silent prayers that they would fail and prolong our holiday by a few hours, but those little beasts never obliged.

Shrewsbury was one of the most exciting places for the steam enthusiast, there being GWR engines galore together with LMS and ex-LNWR locomotives of all types; never a dull moment. Invariably a 'Saint' or 'Star' class locomotive would haul us forward to Wolverhampton, regular performers being *Saint Sebastian*, *Ivanhoe* and *Talisman* of the 2900 class, whilst on the final lap to Birmingham (Snow Hill) a 'Castle' or perhaps the greatest of them all, a 'King', would do the honours. The latter were very restricted engines, and in those days never worked west of Wolverhampton. The final part of our journey from Birmingham (New Street) to Bromsgrove was invariably worked by an LMS or ex-Midland Compound 4-4-0 locomotive.

As I grow older, I find it difficult to be convinced that carriage of materials by rail today, in spite of High Speed Trains and the so-called massive sorting departments, is more efficient than the methods employed in my youth; indeed, to my mind, it is the reverse. Way back in the 1930s, a third class ticket from Aberystwyth to Birmingham was approximately 15s. The usual practice was to purchase our railway tickets the day before we returned to school, then wander off to the parcels office where a green form P.L.A. was duly completed, for the reasonable surcharge of 3s. Later the same day, an express GWR parcels van would collect our trunks, originally a horse-drawn vehicle which was eventually replaced by a petrol-engined Thorneycroft. This particular task was always carried out by a well-known Aberystwyth character, Driver J. B. Jones who, incidentally, performed the same duty for my daughters after World War II when we lived at Ynyslas. The following day, at about 8p.m., our trucks were outside our dormitories at school and, what is more, were already unpacked by Matron. Our seniors had travelled ahead of us, crossing Birmingham from Snow Hill to New Street Station, and finally transported from Bromsgrove Station up to school, quite unbelievable today.

Another classic feat was performed in the reverse direction. During term I once constructed a 12ft. canoe, the complete framework, but uncovered. The day before we broke up I tied on two labels, and bid farewell to my skeleton craft. We reached home at about 2.30p.m. the following day and, sure enough, that same evening, a GWR van pulled up at the gate. A railway official with a wonderfully waxed moustache carried my boat up the drive with a remark 'You won't go far in this, it will

sink'. There was not a trace of damage; we certainly have something to learn from our forefathers.

On returning to Bromsgrove, my first Sunday walk took me to the first overbridge to watch the great engine push a passenger train up to Blackwell. The deep Derby bark of her exhaust was in complete contrast to that of the little 'Duke' class engines on the Cambrian. Completely enthralled by such a sight I patiently waited to see her run back on the 'down' line, not realising that I was committing the cardinal mistake of being late for my first Sunday lunch. That same afternoon I returned to the lineside at Bromsgrove South, the home of the banking engines. I had very tender hindquarters, but the great engine had made a far bigger impression than the first of many schoolboy hidings.

Over the next five years, Bromsgrove South became a regular visiting spot. My frequent excursions over the years did not go unnoticed by men of the banking engines and eventually I was invited into their lineside cabin, but the climax was a ride to Blackwell and back on the great engine. The all-important point was that my railway fascination could well have died at that stage; there were so many other distractions, but after a long lapse since the days of Lewis Rees, I was back on the footplate, and that early fire of enthusiasm had been re-kindled.

As the years rolled by, the 'perks' of becoming a prefect and receiving a school rugby cap included the use of a bicycle. There were two ways of looking at that privilege. From an academic point it very nearly spelt disaster yet, from the more pleasant angle of steam, it was the 'goose that laid the golden egg'. One of the many amenities of such status included not having to assemble in the hall for prep. Thus, during the dark evenings, once my mates were settled down to two hours work I regret to say, I was in full cry for Bromsgrove South, to ride the 0-6-0 tank engines or the great old lady herself, in the company of now well-established companions.

Those nocturnal excursions, a closely-guarded secret and divulged here for the first time, taught me a great deal about locomotives. After playing rugby football regularly I was a strong lad with a good back, useful for when I began the noble art of firing. At that age I quickly picked up the essentials of the footplate and the working of signals which was, all in all, a perfect grounding. By 9p.m. I was always safely back in my study, unknown to my closest friends.

Naturally it came as no surprise, when my school-days ended in 1936, that I unhappily found myself nowhere near to School Certificate standard. Therefore it was a case of going back to 'Dukedog' country for some hard labour, with my nose to the grindstone until I was eligible to enter university and on to Guy's Hospital as a student. One lives and learns by experience, so there was no more falling behind because of steam engines; however, between my studies, I frequently wandered over to Paddington. My railway affections were no longer a secret, and many happy hours were spent on platforms talking to drivers, these being magnificent men who invited me up on to their footplate, took me round the wheel and described their runs up from the West Country in detail. On occasions I even pushed my interests to their limits in escorting selected members of Guy's Nurses Home to the end of platform 1 to watch GWR steam. Those ministering angels certainly lived up to their call in life — not only dedication, — but that of long suffering.

Trains continued to arrive and depart on time, yet underneath the apparent calm there existed an air of uncertainty. Air raid shelters were being dug in the parks, barrage balloons floated above and the drums of war were beginning to beat. Thus what I had looked up-on as the 'golden days' of the 1930s were drawing to a close.

No. 6371, a 2-6-0 ex-GWR Mogul, is pictured on the triangle at Aberystwyth in May 1956.

P. Dalton

The driver of an empty stock train, hauled by ex-GWR Mogul No. 6383, exchanges the token at Ynyslas.

P. Dalton

Chapter 4
War Years on the Cambrian

As the humid days of August 1939 were drawing to a close, eight young men on summer vacation decided, one early morning, to play eighteen holes of golf as a double foursome — or even an eightsome. Four balls were driven off the first tee at Aberystwyth Golf Club; the course was clear, and all had agreed that such a combination was possible under the conditions. However, before the next four members had time to play their second shots, the professional, Joe Robson, came running out of his shop with radio news that the Nazi Air Force had bombed Cracow in Poland. No further golf was played and our steps were retraced. Packed into one car, our next stop was the local drill hall, and within a very short space of time the Territorial Army was enlarged by eight. The rest is history. It was one of the quickest unanimous decisions we ever made, but we were determined to stick together.

On 3rd September 1939 war broke out; it came as no surprise, as the die was already cast. In a way it was a sense of relief, because it provided the end of eighteen months of uncertainty. We were now gunners in the North Cardiganshire Battery, together with a host of Cambrian companions which ranged from signalmen, clerical staff, bus drivers and conductors. The drill hall was in close proximity to the railway whilst our parade ground, the municipal car-park, was positioned alongside the railway station at Aberystwyth. Thus, between struggling with the elementary fundamentals of an 18 pounder field gun, I had virtually a ringside seat in observing the abrupt change from peace to war on the Cambrian. Normally the traffic, especially on the passenger side, would tail off in September, apart from some late excursions. However, these were all cancelled, and passenger traffic increased, yet of a type unfamiliar to our way of life. Train load after train load arrived at Aberystwyth at regular intervals, conveying the little evacuees from the industrial areas of Liverpool, Manchester and the Midlands — potential targets for the enemy bombers. Each child had a label tied to his or her arm, indicating their name and home address. It was a fantastic operation, especially at such short notice. Probably, if I had been older, it would have been a moving sight, yet somehow it got through and made me feel proud of my homeland and nationality.

Petrol rationing soon put cars off the roads, and express bus services were curtailed. At first many buses and coaches were de-licenced, whilst on the railway through coaches to Paddington ceased. A journey to London now often entailed changes at Welshpool and Shrewsbury, with a much later arrival time. However, at first, apart from these passenger train revisions, outwardly there appeared to be little difference but, as the dust of war and change in way of life began to settle, one became aware of its realities and what it entailed, es-

pecially during the hours of blackout. The regulations of train travel after dark resulted in white lines on the platform edges and, in some cases, unlighted stations, whilst the unfamiliar spectacle of female guards and ticket collectors became more and more apparent. The 'down' 11.05a.m. passenger train from Paddington did not arrive at Aberystwyth until 6.30p.m., whilst freight trains grew heavier and were given priority. It was no unusual occurrence for a passenger train to be shunted into a loop to permit a freight working to thunder through on the main line, headed by two hard-working 'Dukedogs'.

The 'Phoney War' came to an end in the summer of 1940, and again the Cambrian was to play her part in conveying large numbers of the weary British Expeditionary Force to rest camps. Many of the remaining 'Duke' and the more recent 'Dukedog' locomotives were now well over mileage repairs, and were hard put to keep these very heavy trains moving. In spite of the increased military traffic, normal passenger services were often duplicated during the summer months. Towards the end of August 1940, the 'up' 10.05a.m. service from Aberystwyth ran in three parts; the particular portion I travelled upon was made up entirely of green Southern Railway coaching stock, something I have never witnessed before or after on Cambrian metals.

Once the heavy air raids began, more and more vital war traffic was diverted where possible on to minor lines, and here again the Cambrian was to play an important part. The remote Carmarthen to Aberystwyth branch had been classified as a 'blue' route, but the main Cambrian line from Aberystwyth to the north was still in the 'yellow' category. The little 'Dukedogs', in spite of being less than ten years old, were no match for this heavier traffic, which ultimately led to the easing of restrictions, and 'blue' engines with outside cylinders were permitted to work north of Aberystwyth. This move saw the advent of two very special daily munitions trains, both 'up' and 'down', from Llandeilo in South Wales to Saltney Junction outside Chester. These vital warmongers, known as the 'Saltney Goods', were given absolute priority, together with a range of motive power — the complete Churchward look.

This move resulted in the first appearance of the 'Aberdare' class engines, and the more recently familiar 'Manor' class 4-6-0s. The first I noted was No. 7806 *Cockington Manor*, working an 'up' Saltney goods train near Borth in June 1942. Also, 4300 class locomotives became very regular performers on this task. On one occasion, Aberystwyth was nearly razed to the ground, happily unknown to her inhabitants. A very heavily laden 'down' Saltney train, headed by a 4300 class locomotive, experienced brake failure while descending Fronfraith Bank into Aberystwyth, and only finally managed to come to a halt just in front of the stop blocks on platform 1 road at the latter station. Both 'up' and 'down' trains had to reverse at Aberystwyth, as there existed no run through on to the Carmarthen branch. Very soon after this change in motive power, Oswestry acquired two 'Manor' class engines, Nos. 7807 and 7819, transferred from Neyland. Both started work on the heavier passenger trains and gave some respite to Machynlleth Shed, who had to provide banking engines for virtually everything to Talerddig Summit.

Vast military and air force camps had sprung up along the Cambrian coastline and, not surprisingly, the remote Dovey Junction took on a very different look — during the hours of daylight it became a hive of activity, especially with service personnel. Also, around this time, there was a certain curtailment in road repairs. During World War I the Cambrian installed a goods loop at Clatter, between Carno and Caersws, but unfortunately it was lifted prior to World War II and, in spite of the increased traffic, was not reinstated, but several War Department sidings were constructed on the Coast Road. Traffic was not only heavy by rail, but also on road motor services; Crosville had already lost a number of its garages as munition factories, and had to resort to open yards as depots. Vast numbers of second-hand vehicles were either borrowed or bought; Caledonian, Western National, and Yorkshire United buses all saw service in Mid-Wales, whilst coaches were converted into buses. It was now an all out effort to keep the wheels turning, and how wonderfully it was achieved.

Throughout the years my visits to the Cambrian Coast were very few and far between, but during one of those rare visits a chance meeting with a railwayman put me back into the picture, so that I was reasonably up to date with the state of affairs on the Cambrian. He was the late George Francis, a passenger guard from Welshpool who I believe at that time was a goods guard. When returning to Aberystwyth from the south, on 48 hours' leave, I had developed the practice of travelling on the 10.55p.m. Euston to Crewe (non-stop), then catching the York to Swansea mail train as far as Whitchurch. The coaching stock of the 'up' mail from Aberystwyth travelled as far as Whitchurch, and would then form the 'down' mail back.

Later, as the air raids got heavier, there were the inevitable delays, and to ensure catching my connection at Whitchurch, when possible, the 5.30p.m. ex-Euston service was a much safer bet. The first time I travelled by this earlier train we were hauled to Crewe by an unrebuilt 'Royal Scot' class, *The North Staffordshire Regiment*, still in maroon livery. I made friends with the crew and we had an excellent run to Crewe, and had no difficulty in reaching Whitchurch long before the 'up' mail from Aberystwyth was due. It was a beautiful June night, with the last rays of double summer sun fading. Standing alone on the platform, in the comparative peace of Whitchurch, a goods train rumbled in and came to a halt, headed by a Collett 2251 class locomotive. Incidentally,

this class of locomotive had now become a fairly familiar sight on the Cambrian. George Francis the guard, unknown to me at that stage, called out 'Where are you going soldier?', and having explained that I was waiting for the mail train from Aberystwyth he then suggested I rode with him in his brake van to Oswestry, where there was more comfort and the chance of a warm drink. It is the only time I have ever ridden in one of those comfortless wagons, but George and I were to become great friends. Over the odd few miles to Oswestry we very quickly dropped on to the right wavelength — that of railwaymen. Despite the violent bumps as we checked at every 'down' loop (freight trains were not vacuum-brake connected then, certainly not on Cambrian metals), George really put me back into the picture in almost all departments. I think we crossed the 'up' mail at Ellesmere, but I cannot recollect whether my freight journey was rewarded with the promised warm drink and comfort at Oswestry. However, I can remember walking along the 'down' platform while watching a 'Manor' class engine coming off shed and sitting in the middle road, waiting to work the 'down' mail forward to Aberystwyth. Overhead the drone of friendly fighter planes, returning to their home base, heralded the break of dawn. The rest of that journey was a blissful blank until I woke up while running alongside the sea at Borth, bathed in brilliant June sunshine. That 'down' mail was to convey me home several times during World War II, latterly from Catterick, with LNER engines as far as York and invariably an LMS 'Black Five' via Crewe to Whitchurch.

In spite of such superior motive power, the sight of a little 'Dukedog' waiting to head the last lap home from Whitchurch always gave me a deep sense of satisfaction, a real home-coming. There existed a massive ordnance depot at Catterick, and the railway ran right into the heart of the camp. Going on duty entailed crossing some of the sidings which, when occupied, meant that we would crawl between wagons, even when shunting was taking place — sheer stupidity. Occasionally I would climb aboard the massive NER 0-8-0 locomotives and chat with their crews, invariably Darlington men.

One Saturday evening I went into Darlington, where a troop special left the station at about 11p.m. for Catterick. It was packed to capacity and vast amounts of North Country ale had been consumed by all, and in those days it really was beer. Arguments went on up and down the platform, between British and American forces, as to who was going to finish the war. I wandered up to the front, and had a few words with the crew of the NER 0-6-0 locomotive in charge. It was with no surprise that they passed a few caustic remarks concerning the condition of their passengers, and having agreed, and not being very anxious to join them on the train, I suggested they might like a pilotman as far as Catterick. My request was accepted, and there followed an amazing trip through deep snow on a bitterly cold night. Readers who have ever ridden those trains must surely remember the unmanned crossings beyond Catterick Bridge. I know not the names of the crew or the number of the locomotive, but they were three Northern gems. Shortly after that pleasant little event I was posted overseas, and from the sands of the desert and the hills of Italy, the Cambrian and its 4-4-0 locomotives seemed a long way off.

The next time I saw the Oswestry District was when the war was over; vast changes, locomotivewise, had taken place. Three further 'Manor' class engines had been allocated to the district — No. 7808 *Cookham Manor* was stationed at Oswestry, whilst No. 7802 *Bradley Manor* and No. 7803 *Barcote Manor* had arrived at Aberystwyth. The latter shed had also acquired two of the 4300 class, Nos. 6371 & 6383. A few 'Duke' class engines remained faithful to the system whilst the 'Dukedogs' reigned supreme in numbers, but the main passenger services were now operated by the larger 'blue' engines, shared by Oswestry and Aberystwyth sheds. The Cambrian era still lingered on, with a few Dean 0-6-0 engines remaining, while on the coast road there was an abundance of 4500 class 2-6-2 tank engines, which worked both passenger and goods trains.

The end of hostilities resulted in the closing down of a large number of military camps, especially as demobilisation got under way, and the Cambrian began to take on more of its familiar peacetime role. There was naturally a marked shrinkage in traffic, especially in the size of passenger trains, the most affected section being the Aberystwyth to Carmarthen branch. The line, in spite of its gallant war effort, ran through the thinnest of railway territory, and was already being severely stabbed in the back by road motor services. The writing must have already been on the wall, not unnoticed by the GWR, as the latter carried out a series of clearance tests with diesel rail cars, although nothing materialised. Its future was bleak; vast changes were already on the horizon.

A Labour Government had swept the boards, and with it came the impending gloom of nationlisation. A date that was to register the beginning of great changes on the railway system of our island, 1st January 1948, saw the end of the four old companies; personally, to coin a popular title, *Gone with Regret*. 'Dukedog' No. 9017, drew the last 'down' GWR passenger train out of Oswestry, and from midnight the Great Western Railway ceased to exist, yet in spirit, like its predecessor, the Cambrian, was to live on for many years.

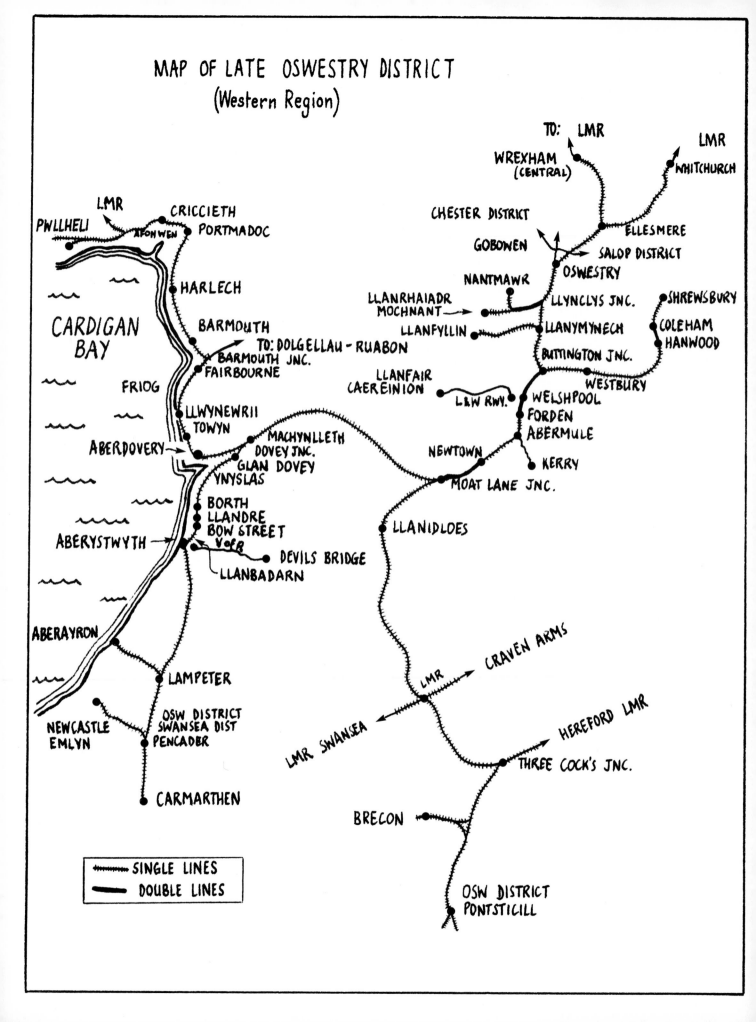

Chapter 5
Post-War Borth and Ynyslas Stations

New Year's Day 1948, a memorable date, saw the beginning of public ownership on our railway system in Britain. Apart from the odd jubilant whistle at midnight, outwardly there was no visible changes on the Cambrian for a considerable period. GWR locomotives, in the old familiar colours, continued to haul the well-established chocolate and cream coaching stock but inevitably, as time progressed, changes, very minor at first, began to take place. These were most noticeable, especially by senior railwaymen who had grown up in railway families. One was aware of the nods and shakes of the head from such men, together with remarks such as: 'The old company would not have done things this way' or 'If I had my time over again I would not change, they were good bosses.' Comparatively so early into nationalisation, such comments were naturally 'food for thought', especially from older railwaymen who seemed not quite sure of the ground that lay ahead. Indeed, I have heard similar remarks from the older bus drivers, whose companies were not nationalised at this stage. Crosville would send a bus to some remote depot involving one man, one bus and one route; they would look after themselves, the job was secure and they took a pride in it, in spite of the low standard of remuneration. Today, alas now too often, it is the case of book off — beer and bingo.

As those early days of state ownership showed little changes, I began to console myself that, after all, the new administration would not be as bad as I had previously anticipated; however, little did I realise at the time that within twenty years, butchery would take place on the Cambrian, resulting in an almost virtual annihilation of its original railway system. It was an ill wind, yet over that period I was to become more closely associated with Cambrian railwaymen than ever before. Familiar figures of the past, both up and down the line, were to become the greatest of friends — especially the men of Aberystwyth and Machynlleth and the intermediate stations.

At that stage my battle dress had been cast aside and temporarily I began married life at Borth, that long straggling village perched precariously on a shingle bank — forever at the mercy of the waves of Cardigan Bay. However, Borth was but a stepping-stone before setting up home at Ynyslas, 2½ miles to the north, back to where my tale began. Of course, my daily journey to and from work at Aberystwyth was made by rail, and my brief stay at Borth paid dividends; it was the beginning of the build-up of Cambrian companionship. There I met two magnificent stationmasters, Messrs Williams and Hughes, the former being in charge of Borth and Ynyslas to the north whilst the latter had command of Llandre and Bow Street to the south. Both, in a nutshell, were the railway enthusiasts' dream; it took no time for either of these gentlemen to discover my lifelong interest, and every day I was

called into their office and furnished with first hand railway news. When Mr Williams eventually retired, Mr Hughes took over and so it went on.

Undoubtedly, the hallmark of Borth was her little signal cabin, kept in almost drawing room condition. Levers, brass and other metal all shone brilliantly, whilst one could safely eat a meal off the lino floor. The greatest credit goes to George Faulkner and Harry Woolham, the signalmen. Mr Hughes' original station at Llandre had the most unusual architecture, and was always highlighted with an excellent floral display; he was a keen and great gardener. Within two years Ynyslas, to the north, became my home. The war had preserved this most northern point of Cardiganshire, except for the remains of a military camp, while the sand dunes, the golf course and the great marsh were still there and unspoilt, almost the case of a pipe dream coming true. Ynyslas Station structure-wise was the same, but aged and very shabby. The September sun shone with a slight autumnal chill the first morning I set out to board the 'down' 8.10a.m. passenger train for Aberystwyth.

Nearly a quarter of a century had passed since I had stood on those wooden platforms. At first it was a shock; was it really always as quiet and so deserted in my childhood days? Peeping into the waiting-room, familiar objects I had forgotten almost greeted me with a smile. The red GWR fire buckets, the old GWR role oil cloth map, looking the worse for wear, and damp patches everywhere on the walls. Suddenly a bell rang, and a woman came out of the station house. She obviously looked surprised to see me then, in Welsh, said 'Good morning', closed the crossing gates and vanished again quickly. My train was approaching the 'down' home signal, preceded by the familiar figure of signalman Bill Evans who was walking down the platform with the token under his arm. I remembered him and, what is more, I like to think he recalled me too. 'Welcome back' he said, as he shook me warmly by the hand. 'I'd heard you had come back to live in Ynyslas, we need more passengers. Come up to the box tomorrow.' Then, as he bundled me into an empty compartment, he continued 'Marshall will be on tonight, remember the mail doesn't stop here.' Finally, 'It's good to see you again.'

That same evening my return journey terminated at Borth, and Mr Williams adjusted my season ticket. Happily, the following day was my Saturday off, so I took the opportunity of accepting Bill Evans's invitation up to the signal box, and spent two happy hours reminiscing over the distant past. It was the first time I had ever been in the box, and its interior presented the sharpest contrast to that of the Borth cabin. The paintwork on the levers was almost indiscernible; no spit and polish here. The Swindon grate was drawing well, but had obviously not seen black lead for many moons, whilst what remained of

A view of the rebuilt Dovey Junction Station, showing the station offices and new sigal box. An 'up' coast train arrives on the coast loop, and the wooden bridge spanning the River Dovey is seen on the extreme right.

P. Dalton

A view of the north-eastern end of the rebuilt Dovey Junction Station, showing the coast loops and the new buildings.

P. Dalton

The original station at Dovey Junction, as seen in January 1950, showing the 'up' main platform, the coast platform (left) and the Aberystwyth loop (right).

P. Dalton

The original station buildings and signal box at Dovey Junction, photographed in January 1950.

P. Dalton

A view of Borth Station, looking north.

In this 1950 view of Bow Street Station, looking north, the 'up' main and platform shelter are seen on the left, and on the right are the 'down' loop, station house, booking office and signal box. Clarach road bridge is in the centre background.

P. Dalton

A view of Llandre Station, looking north.

P. Dalton

the lino on the floor had seen better days. The fumes from paraffin lamps, cigarette smoke and a coal fire had combined to change the GWR standard cream to a subtle shade of orange. Yet, in spite of her obvious neglect, beneath all the grime she was beautiful and romantic, and personally she will always remain the box of boxes.

Subsequently, for six days of the week over the next twenty years, she was my waiting-room, and I became familiar with all her idiosyncracies. In a westerly gale her sides would open and close like an accordian, with only the weight of the levers and framing preventing her from taking off across the bog in a gale. Had the occasion arisen, I could have worked that box blind-folded. Within her weather-beaten walls lay a wealth of information that included old rule books, timetables, traffic appendices etc. — nothing went on the bonfire, as every scrap of railway information was passed on to me. Under her slender roof I met, at intervals, railway-men from all departments, many of which became very close friends and who always knew where and when my next photographic expedition was planned, or when the next footplate trip was imminent; in short, she became the focal point of my railway activities in South Cambria. It would be impossible to mention all those I met in the cabin over the years, but three must not go unpassed. From a personal point of view, they were the brick arch of Ynyslas.

Bill Evans, the senior man, was undoubtedly 'king of the box'. He was a Montgomery man, who virtually served all his railway life at Ynyslas. He was a good sig-nalman, quiet and confident, and was blessed with a vast knowledge of the floating bog that surrounded his box. His mate Marshall Phillips, who was equally competent,

never let anything get him down. Come storm, tempest, frozen points or token failures, he took all in his stride with a constant smile and a whistle. Marshall was a happy man, a born comedian and superb mimic. The third member of the trio was Jack Caffrey, an ex-goods guard who tragically lost a leg on duty. Owing to the mis-fortune he was obliged to terminate his railway life as crossing keeper, residing in the small station house along-side the booking office on the 'down' platform. Despite his disability, which often resulted in a great deal of pain, he still managed to enjoy life. He was a notorious leg-puller, too often at my expense.

My return to Ynyslas presented a personal problem at first, due to the 'up' 6p.m. mail train not calling at the latter station. Bill Evans suggested writing to Oswestry, with the possibility of the mail train calling to set down. It was a good idea and could well attract some more pass-engers; the aforementioned were badly needed, as there were some ugly rumours afoot concerning the future of Ynyslas. I wrote off the same day and got a reply by return regretting that it was impossible, as the 'up' mail was a fast Post Office-controlled train which only called at stations where Post Office mail was taken on — then further pointed out that alternative trains and road trans-port were possible. Bill Evans read the letter the next morning and just shook his head, finally commenting 'You would not have had a reply like that from the old company. It's the damned same with everything now.' I must admit that, as an outsider, this was the first instance of State-owned stupidity which I had come across. As a season ticket holder my request had been most reason-able but now, however, armed with a working timetable, I wrote a personal letter to Mr T. C. Sellers, an ex-

A general view of the terminus station at Aberystwyth. On the left is the Carmarthen bay, and on the right, the main line platforms and goods depot. A BR Standard 4-6-0 awaits departure with the 'up' 6p.m. mail train.

P. Dalton

A view at Aberystwyth, looking east from the Carmarthen bay platform. The signal box and carriage sidings are seen on the left of the picture, the locomotive shed in the centre, and the coaling stage to the right.

P. Dalton

Cambrian man, who was coming up to the end of his reign as District Traffic Superintendent at Oswestry. I pointed out that the so-called fast mail train stopped at all stations to Welshpool except Ynyslas, Commins Coch Halt and Talerddig, also tabulating the stations where no Post Office mail was taken on. I also reminded him that at least ten minutes was allowed for the loading of milk at Forden, and finally concluded that the 'up' mail had a reasonable wait, at Dovey Junction, to cross the 'down' 3.55p.m. ex-Shrewsbury passenger train. Under the circumstances, would he inform me from what date the 'up' 6p.m. mail would call to set down at Ynyslas. By return post I got a short but very polite reply: 'From the following Monday', signed T. C. Sellers.

Gossip spreads quickly in remote areas, and virtually overnight Ynyslas gained five extra daily passengers. Subsequent timetables stated that the train called to set down only but, however, both Bill and Marshall booked boarding passengers — many from way beyond Cambrian territory. Naturally I was delighted with the outcome, and was convinced that I had prolongd the agony of Ynyslas, as Dr Beeching's surgery plans were still not close at hand. However, sadly, the hideous spiral of rail fares had already begun, and one by one my fellow travellers sought cheaper means of transport so that I became the sole little niggerboy, at least at Ynyslas.

At this stage quite a few years had slipped by, and I was now firmly established at Ynyslas and regarded not only the station herself as a personal one, but even myself as a railwayman. Subconsciously I knew it could not last, in spite of her valuable lengthy loops which were precious during the height of summer holiday traffic. Both Bill and Marshall were coming up to retirement, and both finally reached that goal early in the 1960s, shortly

followed by Jack Caffrey. Ynyslas was never the same, and as a station she finally fell in 1965.

I shall always remember Bill's last night on duty. I climbed down from the locomotive working the 'up' 6p.m. mail, and made my way up to the box to bid my farewells to him as a railwayman. Fortunately he had a smallholding alongside the Lerri, so it was not a final goodbye. He told me he was looking forward to his retirement, then quietly handed me his set of ex-Cambrian Railway buttons. Later, as I walked down the wooden platform, I showed Jack Caffrey my newly-acquired treasures saying 'Look what Bill has given me.' Jack never liked to be outdone, so he replied with the request 'Wait a minute, you do the gates', and vanished into the station house. He was not gone long, and on his return handed me an equal number of Corris Railway buttons.

When walking home across Tycanol Fields I could hear the boom of the breakers on the beach; an offshore breeze was blowing, it being one of those days when great blue-green swells came rolling in in threes, with the spray streaming off their backs. We used to call them curlers when we were young — a bass fisherman's delight. However, my thoughts were not those of a surf caster that evening but of the generosity of two more of my Cambrian companions, which finally carried me back some forty years to days of extreme childhood, when Cambrian 4-4-0 locomotives with express head-lamps would ease but slightly for Ynyslas, a smart token exchange, with regulators opened, and belching clouds of black Cambrian smoke as they sped onwards across the bog to Borth and the south. Yes, those were the days.

A two coach train, headed by a BR 2-6-4 tank, is pictured in the coast loop at Machynlleth. In this view, looking east, the locomotive shed, coaling stage and goods depot can be seen on the right, and on the left, the 'up' main platform, water tower and new signal box.

P. Dalton

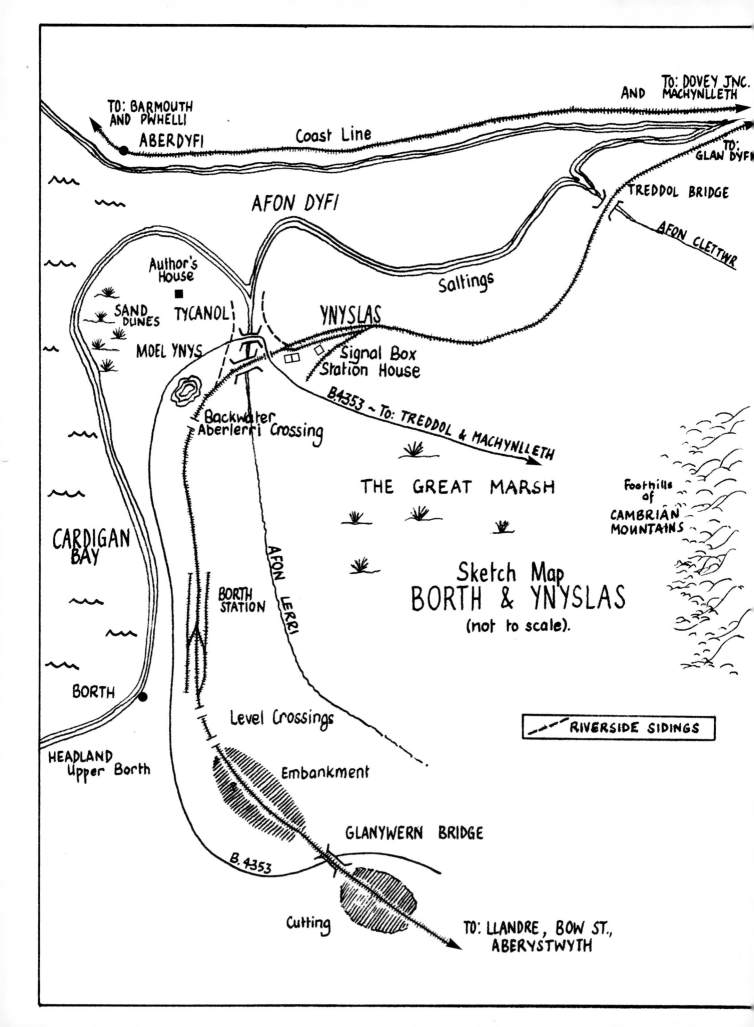

TO: DOVEY JNC. MACHYNLLETH

AND

TO: BARMOUTH AND PWHELLI

ABERDYFI

Coast Line

TO: GLAN DYFI

TREDDOL BRIDGE

AFON DYFI

AFON CLETTWR

Saltings

Author's House

TYCANOL

SAND DUNES

MOEL YNYS

YNYSLAS

Signal Box
Station House

B.4353 ~ TO: TREDDOL & MACHYNLLETH

Backwater
Aberlerri Crossing

THE GREAT MARSH

Foothills
of
CAMBRIAN
MOUNTAINS

CARDIGAN BAY

AFON LERRI

Sketch Map
BORTH & YNYSLAS
(not to scale).

BORTH STATION

RIVERSIDE SIDINGS

BORTH

Level Crossings

HEADLAND
Upper Borth

Embankment

GLANYWERN BRIDGE

B. 4353

Cutting

TO: LLANDRE, BOW ST.,
ABERYSTWYTH

Chapter 6
The Road to Ynyslas

Golden October or Indian summer, call it what you may, but the autumn of 1947 was such a time, with long days of warm sunshine and a light north-westerly breeze, backed by a deep blue sea flecked with tiny white waves. These were days when the mountains of Cambria stood out a bluish purple and, as the sun went down over Cardigan Bay, the sky would change minute by minute from pale pink to deep orange-scarlet and purple.

It was one of those evenings when I walked up platform 2 at Aberystwyth to board the 'up' 6p.m. working, or 'second mail' as she was locally referred to. The hands of the station clock stood at 5.50p.m. and a handful of passengers hung around open carriage doors, whilst Post Office officials mingled with the platform staff and chatted as mail bags from trollies were hurled into open vans, with the familiar cries of 'Salop', 'York', 'Crewe' etc. The train was made up of four passenger coaches and three mail vans, whilst up in front, attached and just under the platform awning, stood GWR 4-6-0 No. 7807 *Compton Manor*. She had recently passed through the factory and was painted out in unlined green, with the post-war GWR insignia on her tender. A thin trail of blackish smoke drifted southwards from her chimney over the station. She had no visible copper cap; it had been painted over black, a wartime practice. Dai, her driver, leaned against the reversing gear, idly rolling himself a cigarette, whilst Billy, his mate, hung over the fireman's cabside, possibly watching the last rays of sunlight vanish. Up in front these two were in a different world and were oblivious to the platform activity, being so accustomed to their natural surroundings that neither were conscious of that fascinating and indescribable aroma of hot metal, steam and burnt oil, topped up with the scent of a paraffin lamp — it had simply become a way of life. Boiler pressure stood at just under the 250lb. mark, which gave that distinctive sizzle from the brass polished safety-valve. The layout of the footplate and bunker full of coal was clearly visible from the reflected light of the half-open firebox doors, within which burned a beautiful thick clean fire which sent out a warm and comforting glow.

Promptly, at 5.55p.m., the stocky platform starting signal came 'off' with a bump, and showed a clear blue-green against the fading light. Billy woke up from his sky gazing, wound up the handbrakes, checked his injectors and returned to his cabside, now with his eyes fixed on his train length and the platform. Momentarily, far below, Roger, the station foreman, appeared and called out the load. Dai then acknowledged with a wave of his hand, his cigarette now well alight. Doors slammed and a whistle blew, followed by another, whilst way back down the platform a clear green light was visible. Billy then called out 'Right away, Dai' and at once the scene changed. Bent over the reversing gear, Dai gently

opened the regulator and, without the trace of a slip, No. 7807 moved quietly forward with the softest of beats from her exhaust. No. 7807 *Compton Manor* had the original draughting, the thicker prototype chimney and jumper ring and, when worked lightly, gave almost the soft whisper of a bark. Billy, now satisfied that his train load was following, returned to his footplate duties. A diehard Swindon enthusiast once told me 'Swindon engines never slip'; I cannot blame his over-patriotism but, personally, I found the 'Manor' class extremely sure-footed. No. 7807 had now got hold of her load, and quietly moved out on to the 'up' main line.

The signalman on late turn waved a lever cloth from his open cabin window, and a sudden darkness descended as the locomotive passed between the shadows of the locomotive shed and carriage sidings. A couple of crew whistles rang out as the light from the east end of the shed showed a 2251 class 0-6-0, with her Oswestry crew, ready to move off shed and follow the 'up' mail with the 6.20p.m. goods.

Dai sounded a sharp blast on the Swindon whistle as Plas-Crug Crossings were approached, but there was still only the softest of beats from No. 7807's exhaust while her speed was no more than 15m.p.h. Way ahead on the straight road Llanbadarn Crossing signal stood out red, in the 'on' position, so Billy called out and Dai acknowledged with a wave of his hand. The speed then dropped, slower and slower, past the gasworks — a sudden glow of light within, and No. 7807 was now moving virtually at walking pace.

Normally the 'down' 'Cambrian Coast Express' reached Aberystwyth at 5.55p.m., but that night she was running late and the 'up' mail had been given the road to Llanbadarn. Suddenly, a white light appeared ahead briefly; it seemed almost stationary, but then it swung to Dai's right followed by the reflected light from the coaches as it entered the facing points for the 'down' road. There was always a pronounced 'kick' when these points were negotiated, especially when running a bit fast. Dai did not bring No. 7807 to a standstill as No. 7803 *Barcote Manor* thundered past on the 'down' road with her six lighted coaches. Almost immediately the 'down' outer home changed to red and then there was a slight pause, and Llanbadarn showed a 'clear' green in the quickly failing light. Once more, the wave of Dai's hand acknowledged Billy's call of Llanbadarn off. Again there was a whisper of a bark from No. 7807 as she slowly gathered speed but ever so gently with Dai, as always, being very light on the lever. Billy leant out as they approached Llanbadarn box and swept up the tablet like a slip fielder. Quickly he reviewed his catch while clearly the light from the firebox showed him the required words 'Llanbadarn to Bow Street'. Dai again acknowledged.

The 'up' 6p.m. mail train leaves Ynyslas on the 'up' main line.

P. Dalton

The approach to Ynsylas Station from the south, as seen from the footplate of 'Manor' class locomotive No. 7802 *Bradley Manor*. Mr Caffrey, the crossing keeper, stands in front of the station buildings which are beside the 'down' loop.

P. Dalton

Fireman Ward picks up the token at Llanbadarn Crossing from the 'up' 6p.m. mail train.

P. Dalton

Ahead lay 2½ miles of Fronfraith Bank, a steady climb of 1 in 75, so Dai opened the regulator and adjusted the reversing gear. A clear exhaust beat was now apparent, together with a slight vibration of boiler plates and the momentary rattle of the reversing gear, before No. 7807 settled down to a steady beat. Boiler pressure stood at just under the 250lb. mark, while the lights of Llanbadarn and the already distant Aberystwyth disappeared as the 'up' mail rumbled over Factory Bridge, and entered the deep cutting of Fronfraith Bank. Dai was briefly able to see the silvery River Rheidol, away down below his cabside, and spotted a fisherman silhouetted against the twilight. He then called Billy's attention and pointed far below, possibly spotting one of his mates. Aberystwyth and Machynlleth locomotivemen were class fishermen, and despite it being the tail end of the season the sewin were still running. Momentarily, Dai's thoughts wandered to one of his favourite pools after dark, but quickly returned to the road ahead. The lights from the coaches reflected against the high sides of the cuttings, while clean white smoke billowed around the cabside as No. 7807 passed under the first overbridge. The firebox

doors were open, with the flap plate down, so Billy pulled some coal forward and, with that familiar scrape of the shovel, sent in about half a dozen well-judged shots, followed up by the corners, with the flap plate being dropped between each shovelful in true GWR style. Quickly the footplate was swept and hosed down, with a final spray being directed over the bunker coal. No. 7807 was in 'good nick', as little or no steam was apparent at the front end as she beat her way up the bank with ease.

Suddenly it got lighter, as the road turned to the west, with the train running under the second overbridge and then the third, the latter heralding the top of the first bank. The road ahead then dropped dramatically, while the exhaust beat became noticeably quicker as the speed rose. The locomotive was still steaming well, and when passing under Ffynnon-Caradog Bridge, Dai closed the regulator and Billy the firebox doors. The cylinder exhaust was now very clear, and the 'click' of the rail joints got quicker and quicker as No. 7807 leant into the right-hand curve and passed over the Aberystwyth to Machynlleth road bridge. Lights of moving traffic were

No. 7808 *Compton Manor* leaves Llandre with the 'up' 6p.m. Aberystwyth to Oswestry mail train. The author can be seen on the footplate behind the driver.

Courtesy I. Melvyn Evans

visible far below, first on the fireman's side then on that of the driver. The short bursts of the vacuum brake hissed out and Billy called out 'Bow Street off' as the green light of her home signal stood out against the distant station lights. Suddenly, Bow Street platform started to race by and Gwilym, the ever-hatless signalman, snatched up the token from Billy, and the 'up' mail ground to a halt. They were two minutes late and Dai replaced his watch, but Bow Street were on the ball and no time was lost.

Gwilym then appeared, far below on the platform, and handed up the token for the next section; 1 mile and 47 chains long, again at 1 in 75, but on a winding road up the valley. Billy then checked his tablet verbally with Dai, after which he called out 'right away.' Dai, who was satisfied, opened the regulator and, with no trace of a slip, No. 7807 burst away under Clarach Road Bridge with a sharp, clear blast. Billy put on another half dozen shovelfulls of good South Wales coal for the uphill climb

to Llandre, but *Compton Manor* made easy work of this bank whereas a 'Duke' or a 'Dukedog' would be really labouring here with a similar load. At the top of the bank the line turned westward and now on the level, Dai kept No. 7807 steaming until the Llandre distant signal and a small level crossing was passed; somebody waved a dish-cloth from inside the crossing keeper's house. The home signal stood at green and *Compton Manor* coasted into Llandre Station, coming to a standstill off the platform but astride the next level crossing gates to Upper Llandre. Smart token work saved another half minute.

Ahead lay 2 miles and 53 chains of falling road at 1 in 60. It was quite dark now as No. 7807 got away with the quietest of exhaust beats, but quickly gathered speed on the falling gradient. The train then passed under the first road bridge and into the deep cutting on a left-hand curve, quickly followed by the second overbridge. Most drivers would close the regulator here but Dai kept her open, even over the next Dolybont overbridge. There was a very sharp kick there as the locomotive entered the reverse curve; Dai closed the regulator with a slam, and speed increased as she ran freely down the straight road ahead. Once again he could hear the exhilarating sound of the cylinder exhaust mingled with the hiss of the safety-valve as she blew off, topping the 250lb. mark. With a speed of between 50 and 55m.p.h. they entered a short cutting and gave a long blast on the whistle, then passed under an overbridge and over Glan-y-Wern Road Bridge, topping 60m.p.h. Here the long boiler of No. 7807 seemed to sway as she leaned into a long gentle right-hand curve.

Away to the left and far below, the lights of Borth were clearly visible, whilst further afield a distant twinkle picked out Aberdyfi far beyond across the estuary. Borth home signal stood out clearly in the 'off' position and suddenly the lights of Borth appeared, almost level with the footplate on Billy's side of the cab. No. 7807 was still running fast, while all the time the hiss of the vacuum-brake application resounded in short bursts. Borth Station lights appeared very bright as Billy leaned out of the cab, and sent the token slithering along the tiled platform. Harry Woolham, who was on late turn, was not going to try and grab at that daisy cutter. There were several passengers here, and some mail bags on a trolley. It was always an exhilarating run down the bank from Llandre, even freer when running on a 4-6-0 Standard Class 4 engine accompanied by their characteristic rattle. For real appreciation of speed, on this sudden drop to sea level, there was nothing to beat the small wheel running of a 'Duke' or 'Dukedog'.

Dai then checked his watch — they were on time — but Borth would give nothing away and stuck to the allotted station wait. It was a draughty station, where one could smell the sea for the first time, and in a westerly gale it could be a bit uncomfortable up in front. Promptly, at 6.21p.m., Billy called 'right away'. The

next two miles to Ynyslas were easy going, as the line ran on a slightly falling gradient. The line then skirted the edge of the great expanse of marsh, running parallel to the sea, and just prior to Ynyslas the road turned inland at Aber-Leri Crossings. Both the distant and the home signals stood out clearly, and No. 7807 rumbled over the wooden River Leri bridge and dropped abruptly into Ynyslas Station. Dai had taken this last stretch very quietly and now brought No. 7807 to a halt at Ynyslas, just off the end of the 'up' platform; it was a long climb down. There was no station time loss at Ynyslas and again the blast of No. 7807's exhaust rang out as Dai and Billy set off on the next six miles, over the open bogland to Dovey Junction, where they joined the coast mail train and travelled on to Machynlleth. Here their 'up' journey ended as they handed No. 7807 over to the Oswestry men; Billy had left the fire in good trim for the long climb ahead to Talerddig Summit. They now had two hours to wait before they worked the last 'down' passenger service home to Aberystwyth on a 'Dukedog'. When they arrived back on shed they booked off, and perhaps consumed a welcome pint apiece.

Back at Ynyslas all was quiet, as the tail lamp of the last mail van vanished across the bog; the little station oil lamps flickered, and a slight breeze blew in from the sea. High above, the stars stood out in a darkened sky, whilst from the marsh arose that fascinating cry of a distant curlew or plover.

Over the next twenty years, this was to be my home. I was to see it under a variety of climatic conditions, and was destined to ride thousands of miles on the footplates of a variety of locomotives, many way beyond the Oswestry District. Despite my wide travels, no stretch of road was to be more familiar, and above all appreciated, than those 10 miles and 36 chains of uphill and downdale road from Aberystwyth to Ynyslas.

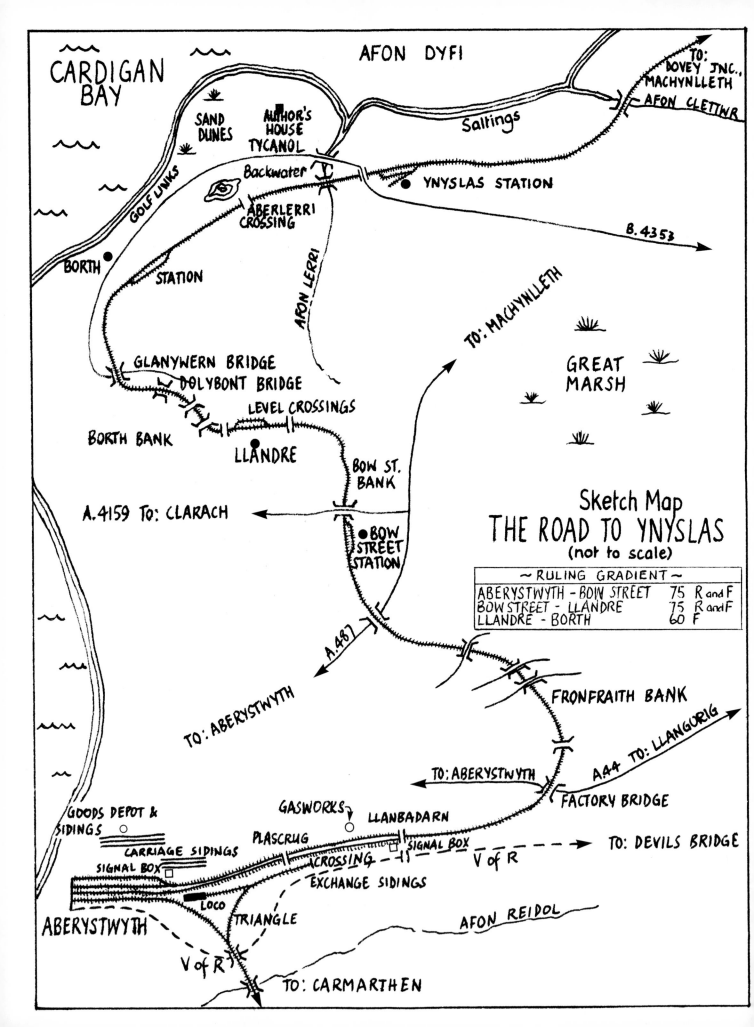

Chapter 7

'See How They Ran!'

Steam on the Cambrian in BR Days

Ex-GWR Mogul No. 6342 gets away from Bow Street with the 'up' Aberystwyth to Machynlleth local train.

P. Dalton

Six years of war had pushed our railways to their limits. Both big and small sections alike had suffered from lack of normal track maintenance, although this did not include masses of war-weary locomotives and rolling stock. Fortunately, the Cambrian as a district did not come out of this too badly, because on the locomotive side it was the reverse. The so-called dark days of war had brought a new healthy look on the motive power side, presenting quite a different picture to the final days of pre-war peace, days when the most powerful locomotives were the 'Dukedogs' and, on rare occasions, the odd 'Bulldog' from Shrewsbury. These machines were now at the bottom of the power ladder, restrictions had been eased, and the larger and more powerful 2-6-0 Moguls and 'Manor' Class 4-6-0s were the prime performers of Aberystwyth and Oswestry sheds.

As already stated, at first the change of ownership appeared to make no difference; day-to-day routine went on as usual. However, after a while, changes gradually began to take place in all departments but, reflecting back, some of the greatest were possibly on the motive power side, changes that could be described as a see-saw pattern and were devoid of any ultimate goal. The whys and wherefores of some of these dramatic changes were sometimes explained or even excused; however, I am convinced that partisanship, which was still rife, played a vital part, especially on the ex-Cambrian lines. Locomotive Superintendents from foreign camps wanted things their way, whilst continual regional changes were again a vital factor in this ever-changing picture.

Not long after nationalisation, Oswestry acquired three further 'Manor' class engines, Nos. 7820-22, virtually brand-new and constructed at Swindon. Carmarthen Shed was allocated Nos. 7825, 7826 and 7829, all of which worked in and out of Aberystwyth. These locomotives, completed in the early days of public ownership, never carried true GWR livery, with the modified green appearing later. Originally they emerged from the factory in BR black, fully lined out in LNWR style. With very slight exceptions, this latter series resembled the original

One of the last of the ex-GWR 0-6-0 pannier tanks stationed at Aberystwyth was No. 7428. She still carries 'GWR' on her side tanks in this post-nationalisation view. Aberystwyth signal box, seen in the background, is now closed, and what remains of the station is controlled by Dovey Junction box.

P. Dalton

locomotives constructed in pre-war days. Not surprisingly, this influx, together with the versatile 6300 class engines, resulted in the majority of passenger and goods trains being worked to and from Aberystwyth, both to the north and south, by locomotives in the 'blue' category.

After being given something larger and stronger, locomotivemen naturally frowned upon the little 'Dukedogs', many of which had already gone into store at various points. Quite a few were relegated to the coast road, whilst a few went off on trial as banking engines in Devon and Cornwall — the original home of their predecessors, the 'Duke' class. However, they failed to impress, and one wondered if their days were already numbered.

The back road at Aberystwyth was full of 'Dukedogs' in store, together with the odd 2251 class Collett Goods engine. Machynlleth Shed was later allocated a 'Manor' class engine, No. 7806 *Cockington Manor*, the intention being to utilise this locomotive on the coast section of the 'Cambrian Coast Express' from Pwllheli to Dovey Junction — in fact, Paddington was anxious at that time to diagram a 'Manor' class locomotive to work through from

Pwllheli to Shrewsbury. However Douglas Sinclair, Locomotive Inspector at Oswestry, had different views. He knew only too well the problems of Talerddig Bank, which was just after Machynlleth on the 'up' run. Wisdom prevailed and he won the day, whereupon No. 7806 was considered a waste of power on the coast road and joined her two sister engines, Nos. 7802 and 7803, at Aberystwyth. Carmarthen Shed was allocated a further 'Manor' class, No. 7804 *Baydon Manor*, which also worked over late Oswestry District metals into Aberystwyth from the south. The 'Manor' class now well and truly 'ruled the roost', and were becoming the hallmark of the Cambrian lines. They were highly popular with enginemen, they coped with loads with ease and cut down banking requirements. With regards to motive power, everything was all that could be desired, the only fly in the ointment being the poor quality of coal.

For some considerable time, Swindon had been carrying out exhaustive experiments to improve steaming rates. A couple of 'Dukedogs' emerged from repairs with the improved draughting; the orifices of their blast pipes

'Dukedogs' lie in store at Aberystwyth in February 1957. The line-up comprises Nos. 9018, 9017, 9015, 9013, 9022 and 9016, and they are standing on the 'back road'. The refuge siding is seen alongside whilst part of the triangle for the turning of locomotives is seen on the left of the picture.

P. Dalton

Ex-GWR Mogul No. 7329 hauls a ballast train along the sea wall between Gogarth Halt and Aberdovey.

P.Dalton

No. 6371, an ex-GWR Mogul, enters the single road at Llanbadarn with an Aberystwyth to Shrewsbury stopping train.

P. Dalton

With a 'down' Birmingham to Aberystwyth (SO) summer express, an ex-GWR Mogul, No. 6368, stops at Dovey Junction.

P. Dalton

An ex-GWR Mogul, No. 6335, returns with a Saturday 'down' Birmingham special, having spent a week in the Midlands. It is pictured climbing Borth Bank.

P. Dalton

had been opened up. The results were quite amazing and ultimately, more and more came out of store and went through similar surgery — new life for the old ladies and back into service. It is a well-known fact that the majority of GWR engines underwent similar modifications, even to the extent of double blast pipes and chimneys. Already 'Manor' class locomotives Nos. 7803-8 had acquired the new look and bark, but rumours were already afoot that a motive power change on the Cambrian was about to take place. All kinds of wild talk went on up and down the line; the permanent way men said that the 'Manor' class were knocking the road about, especially the crossovers, whilst enginemen stated that the well-tried and new improved 'Dukedogs' were to take over. Eventually, Swindon gave me confirmation that the 'Manor' class could be utilised to better purposes elsewhere. Almost overnight Oswestry was relieved of her 'Manor' stud, with the exception of No. 7819 *Hinton Manor*, undoubtedly the best of her class and on which I shall further elaborate in a subsequent chapter. The reason for retaining her was for the purpose of working ballast trains from Llynellys; however, she remained the pride of Oswestry Shed, and the chargemen always saw that she was in splendid condition.

The replacements for the 'Manor' class were the new BR Standard Class 4 (75000 series) locomotives. Standard engines were not new to the district, as some Class 2 (78000 series) 2-6-0 locomotives had already started service from Oswestry and Machynlleth; nicknamed 'Mickey Mouse' engines, they were not popular. Their counterparts, the Ivatt 2-6-0 locomotives, were more favoured, especially when they had received the improved draughting. The latter class took over the role of operating the light traffic on the Mid-Wales line to Brecon. In spite of Swindon's explanation for the first of these motive power changes it was not easy to digest, as the changes were not universal throughout the district. Aberystwyth remained truly Swindon, whilst 'Manor' class engines also worked in from Carmarthen and Shrewsbury; but, even stranger, Oswestry's exiled 'Manor' class engines now appeared almost en bloc over the Barmouth to Ruabon branch.

This picture remained unchanged until approximately the mid-1950s. Locomotivemen gradually began to get the hang of the new Standard Class 4s although they were generally not popular, particularly on goods workings and more especially pick up goods, which entailed a certain amount of shunting in and out of sidings and loops. Generally, they were stated to be clumsy, and very prone to slipping.

The next minor change came as no surprise, that of the down-grading of power classification of the 'Dukedogs' from a 'B' category to that of 'A', in the 'yellow' classification; but the decision that freight and local passenger trains were to be operated by the 2251 class 0-6-0 locomotives was indeed something right out of the blue. This move saw an influx of this class of locomotive to the district; five were allocated to Aberystwyth, Nos. 2200, 2217, 2260, 2271 and 2298, all of which remained very faithful to that depot until they were gradually withdrawn

No. 6335 heads towards the reverse curve at Dolybont Bridge with a Saturday 'down' Birmingham special.

P. Dalton

Moguls in action. No. 4377 pilots No. 6378 on an 'up' excursion from Aberystwyth to Shrewsbury. The train is seen entering the single road at Llanbadarn Crossing.

P. Dalton

No. 6371 approaches Dovey Junction with a 'down' Birmingham to Aberystwyth express in August 1962.

P. Dalton

towards the end of steam. However, their new role of working freight and local passenger trains on the main line was short-lived; they could never be classed as ideal passenger engines.

Regional changes were already in the pipeline, with Chester having been earmarked to be handed over to London Midland rule. Under the latter administration GWR engines would not be tolerated, as partisanship was obviously not dead. No sooner had the Cambrian men become accustomed to the Standard Class 4 engines then the next motive power change took place; virtually overnight, the latter class vanished from Oswestry. The replacements, to the delight of enginemen, were 'Manor' class engines Nos. 7800, 7801, 7807, 7822 and 7827, now in green livery and fully lined out, a refreshing sight especially when hauling chocolate and cream coaching stock, which had given way to the original BR plum and cream. The pendulum had really swung this time — Oswestry's banished Standard Class 4s now appeared 'lock, stock and barrel' on the Barmouth to Ruabon route. Somehow this did not tie up with Swindon's original explanation, especially when Oswestry very soon claimed three further 'Manor' class engines, Nos. 7809,

7810 and 7812, whilst to the south Aberystwyth gained Nos. 7814, 7815, 7818 and 7823 of the same class but lost her four Moguls, Nos. 6335, 6371, 6378 and 4377. The latter was originally a replacement for No. 6383, which had been condemned. No. 4377 worked her way up from Truro in a shocking state, and was almost immediately accepted for a heavy general overhaul at Swindon; but, on re-entering service, she proved to be one of the best of her class ever to work the district. When she finally left the district, in February 1959, I believe she was the sole survivor of the 4300 class.

'Manor' class engines Nos. 7811, 7824 and 7828 were also regular visitors to Aberystwyth from Shrewsbury. In fact, the whole district at this period saw 'Manors' galore, which seemed to work everything everywhere. It was appreciably noticeable that 'Dukedogs' were very much in the minority now because in fact, towards the end of the 1950s, only Nos. 9004, 9013-15, 9017, 9018 and 9021 were in steam, the remainder of the class having been either cut up or were sitting dead, awaiting their fate.

Sam Pugh, for many years the Aberystwyth supervisor, had retired and was replaced by two GWR men

'Dukedog' No. 9018 is pictured on the 'back road' at Machynlleth Shed.

P. Dalton

No. 9021, a 4-4-0 'Dukedog' stands 'in store' at Moat Lane Junction in February 1957.

P. Dalton

from Abercynon in South Wales, Jack Harris and George Hinton. These two really made the sparks fly; out came the scrappers — bags of bull everywhere. Only two 'Dukedogs', Nos. 9017 and 9021, remained in steam at this depot, both being beautifully turned out and regularly working the 'up' 9.55a.m. stopper to Shrewsbury, returning on the 'down' 3.55p.m. passenger working. The South Wales supervisors were not long at Aberystwyth, moving on up the ladder to higher promotion.

After a series of short appointments Danny Rowlands, an Aberystwyth driver, was appointed to the post. Danny was a remarkable man, and if one did not know him he could well have passed as Superintendent of the line. He was always very well-dressed, most polite and a real enthusiast. During his reign he was fortunate to have an abundance of cleaners, a bonus of which he took full advantage. The best Aberystwyth 'Manor' was always assigned to the 'Cambrian Coast Express' and was turned out almost too clean to be true; it would have done justice to any Royal working. Copper and brass flashed in the sunlight, with smokebox hinges and baffles being picked out with white paint.

The diagram for the 'Cambrian Coast Express' during that period was shared by Aberystwyth and Shrewsbury engines, and enjoyed the most complicated of crew working arrangements. For example, an Aberystwyth engine manned by Machynlleth men would work the 'up'

express to Shrewsbury, from where the locomotive would then do a short trip to Welshpool and back before spending the night at Shrewsbury. Then, before returning on the 'down' express to Aberystwyth the following day, it would work as far as Baschurch and Welshpool and back. Shrewsbury men worked the 'down' express as far as Welshpool, with the last lap home to Aberystwyth being completed by men of the home depot. The Shrewsbury engine would spend the night at Aberystwyth with no further duties, as hers would start the following day on completion of the 'up' run. Shrewsbury Shed was not going to be outdone by the Aberystwyth spit and polish, and entered into the battle of pride. Danny Rowlands always had the Shrewsbury engine cleaned at Aberystwyth but, unfortunately, Shrewsbury did not respond when entertaining a visitor. Their engine thus had a wash and brush up daily, whilst Danny's had his done every other day. Both looked immaculate but, to split hairs, Danny's engine would, so to speak, win a photo finish.

A new Locomotive Superintendent had been appointed at Oswestry, the late Danny Goodman, an ex-LMS man who had spent a large portion of his railway life at Paxton Street, Swansea. I first met Danny when the District Engineer invited me to join a select group of railwaymen aboard an engineer's special on the Vale of Rheidol Railway. During that happy occasion, Danny

No. 9014 drifts down Borth Bank with a summer evening local train to Machynlleth.

P. Dalton

With a 'down' Machynlleth to Aberystwyth local train in August 1956, 4-4-0 No. 9012 enters the reverse curve at Dolybont Bridge. This particular locomotive was always recognisable by the missing portion of chimney.

P. Dalton

'Dukedog' No. 9013 leaves Llandre Station whilst heading an Aberystwyth to Machylleth local train in 1956.

P. Dalton

A 'down' morning local train from Machynlleth approaches Bow Street headed by 'Dukedog' No. 9005.

P. Dalton

openly admitted to me that he had little time for GWR engines. I could not blame him for his personal feelings because, after all, he was a dedicated LMS man, and why not. For hours that afternoon we argued humorously on the merits of certain locomotives and, as an amateur, I voiced the feelings of my locomotive friends, also pushing the views of Inspector Sinclair, that an Aberystwyth engine should work both the 'up' and 'down' 'Cambrian Coast Express' in both directions, using the same engine and same crew — pride in the job.

Strangely enough, but by mere coincidence, it all happened two weeks later. Obviously this move had been in the pipeline for some time, but Danny Goodman gave nothing away. From the moment of its inception the 'Cambrian Coast Express' became a closed book; there were no problems and in fact, one could set one's watch by the train. Unfortunately, towards the end of steam, the rota reverted almost to the previous working, possibly due to the fact that Aberystwyth Shed had been closed.

Danny Goodman's LMS partisanship was rife, because already some of the nine 4500 class tank engines operating the coast road had received the death sentence. Their replacements were the BR Class 3 (82000 series) 2-6-2 tank engines, which proved to be excellent little

locomotives for such a line. I was most impressed with the ones I rode. They were designed at Swindon with, not exactly LMS policy, virtually a No. 2 boiler. It is purely surmising on my part but, reflecting back on past conversations with Danny Goodman, it would have appeared that his influence played a large part in the introduction of the Stanier Class 3 2-6-2 tank engines. In spite of my GWR loyalty they were, in my eyes, handsome little locomotives but, again, Stanier engines always were nine-tenths Swindon. One Machynlleth driver remarked to me 'What next? It wouldn't surprise me to see a 'Royal Scot' on a Portmadoc local!' For some reason, the Stanier 2-6-2 tanks put up a miserable performance, and were removed. Even a BR Class 2 2-6-2 tank was tried out, but this got no further than the water-column at Llwyngwril; she too was promptly dismissed. However, this was not the end, as it was the case of 'third time lucky' which was igniting a spark for yet another motive power change.

BR Class 4 (80000 series) 2-6-4 tank engine No. 80104 arrived at Machynlleth and was highly popular, even to the extent of being the most favoured class of Standard locomotive ever to work on Cambrian metals. For some unknown reason Oswestry appeared to be the main target for locomotive changes, possibly due to her status. However, her entire stud of 'Manor' class engines

An 'up' Aberystwyth to Birmingham Sunday excursion is pictured at Borth in August 1957. 'Dukedog' No. 9018 pilots 'Manor' Class 4-6-0 No. 7818 *Granville Manor* on this occasion.

P. Dalton

Class 2251 0-6-0 No. 2264 leaves Llandre with a 'down' local train on a frosty morning.

P. Dalton

No. 2235, an 0-6-0 Class 2251 locomotive, is seen between Glandyfi and Dovey Junction on an 'up' passenger train.

P. Dalton

were transferred to Shrewsbury, which had become the new headquarters of the Cambrian, and in return Oswestry received five BR Class 4 tank engines.

Aberystwyth Shed also was not to escape this sudden change of policy. She too lost her 'Manor' allocation, the replacements being Standard Class 4 (75000 series) engines and Class 4 (80000 series) tank locomotives. The pendulum had swung again. Truck load after truck load of GWR spares were despatched to Oxley whilst BR No. 75004, now with a double chimney, took over the role of working the 'Cambrian Coast Express'. There were grumbles and grouses everywhere. I later met Danny Goodman and, with tongue in cheek, said 'You've made a right mess of things now.' Unknown to me he was a very sick man, and had not long to live. Danny was a great friend, a man blessed with a round chubby face, coupled with a great sense of humour. As a professional railwayman he had the incredible knack of always listening and never once told me, as an amateur, to shut up or mind my own business. Strangely enough, in spite of his LMS devotion, he had the highest respect for his 'Castle' class stud at Shrewsbury, although it was

not easily extracted; but on occasions he would reel off the entire list and, most unengineerman-like, by their names and not their numbers.

A few weeks after meeting Danny for the last time I met Bill Neal, late Shed Master at Machynlleth. He approached me with a broad grin on his face and, in his deep voice, said 'What have you been saying to the Guvnor?'

'Nothing,' I replied. 'Why?'

'The Standard engines are going, and we are getting 'Manors' back, and the only spares we have got are a few brake blocks.'

Nos. 7803, 7819, 7821 and 7828 were destined for Aberystwyth; surely this was the most violent swing of the pendulum yet, especially in so short a space of time, not forgetting the fact that the Cambrian was now London Midland Region, and the palacial offices at Shrewsbury were to become vacant, as headquarters were to move on to Stoke-on-Trent. Changes were coming so quickly that it was difficult to keep pace with them.

No. 2202, a Collett 0-6-0, climbs Borth Bank with a 'down' local train for Aberystwyth.

P. Dalton

Collett 0-6-0, No. 2275, with headlamp missing, heads an Aberystwyth to Machynlleth local train as it leaves Glandyfi for Dovey Junction.

P. Dalton

Class 2251 Collett 0-6-0, No. 2298, approaches Llandre with the'down' 8.10a.m. Machynlleth to Aberystwyth passenger train in June 1960.

P. Dalton

Ex-GWR Mogul No. 6368 is pictured on shed at Machynlleth.

P. Dalton

An ex-GWR 2-6-2T, No. 8102, heads an 'up' Aberystwyth to Carmarthen passenger train near Abermad Bridge.

P. Dalton

An Ivatt 2-6-0 works a typical Mid-Wales train between St. Harmons and Rhayader.

P. Dalton

A 2-6-2T locomotive, No. 5556, heads a Machynlleth to Barmouth local train along the sea wall between Dovey Junction and Aberdovey.

P. Dalton

Two 'Dukedogs', Nos. 9021 and 9017, double-head the 12.45p.m. Aberystwyth to Whitchurch express on 11th April 1956 and await departure from Aberystwyth Station. A dynamometer car is attached to the rear of the train.

P. Dalton

Ex-GWR Mogul No. 5322 passes Dovey Junction with a 'down' Birmingham to Aberystwyth express in August 1963. The train has just used the Aberystwyth loop line.,

P. Dalton

An ex-GWR 'Dukedog' 4-4-0, No. 9024, is pictured near Llandre, with the 8.10a.m. local train from Machynlleth to Aberystwyth in August 1955.

P. Dalton

No. 7825 *Lechlade Manor* attacks the 1 in 42 climb out of Aberystwyth as it heads the 12.05p.m. Carmarthen passenger train in February 1958.

P. Dalton

Danny Rowlands, Shed Supervisor at Aberystwyth, was delighted. Out came the polish and white paint, whilst locomotivemen openly stated 'Well, what next? Possibly Gresley engines next week.' 'Manor' class engines Nos. 7821 and 7828 were in reasonable condition, but No. 7819 was run down and went through the factory. The latter eventually returned looking beautiful, and coped with the 'Cambrian Coast Express' for months. Even the old faithful, No. 7802 *Bradley Manor*, returned from the Midlands to carry out stalwart duties.

Steam by this time was in the evening of its life on the Cambrian, as diesel multiple units and diesel locomotives had already penetrated her network. 'Manor' class No. 7803 *Barcote Manor*, the last to pass through the factory, worked the 'Cambrian Coast Express' for a few months, then suffered a fractured connecting rod at Coleham. She limped into Shrewsbury and remained dead for two weeks, before being transferred to Swindon for repairs. She eventually returned to Aberystwyth for a short while, prior to the shed being closed, at a time when most of the remaining 'Manor' class engines, now minus name and number plates, were being transferred to Shrewsbury. Their final hours created the saddest of spectacles; they were left run down and uncared for, with their once proud numbers now chalked upon their cab sides.

In spite of my Cambrian baptism I had become a devoted disciple of the GWR, and personally will always associate the ex-Cambrian lines with the 'Duke' class, the 'Dukedogs' and the 'Manor' class engines. The latter were most appreciated by my many locomotive friends whilst a few have been saved from the flame throwers of Barry, especially the pick of the class *Hinton Manor*; but those that have gone will live on forever in the Valhalla of steam engines, if such a place exists.

Engines of the GWR were now being withdrawn at alarming rates although in fact, members of the 'Manor' class outlived many of their superior sisters; but it came as no surprise when they were equally sentenced, and stood silent in Shrewsbury awaiting their fate. The final swing of the pendulum had taken place and the Cambrian, for its last hours of steam, was operated by an assortment of Standard engines; it was the end of the see-saw pattern.

The last return of the 'Manor' class to Cambrian metals was the strangest of motive power changes, especially so under London Midland control. I never fathomed the reason but the end was nigh, and my interest had died with them. Probably my good friend Danny Goodman would have supplied the answer, but he had already moved on to a new and richer life.

Already the revival of chocolate and cream (Western Region) coaching stock had given way to LMS maroon. Titled trains no longer carried smokebox headboards, and the familiar carriage roof boards were also something of the past. For two days the 'Cambrian Coast Express' carried the newly-designed continental type destination boards, but I pointed out to the stationmaster that Aberystwyth was even incorrectly spelt 'Aberystwith'. They were immediately removed, never to reappear.

Earlier, every locomotive had holes drilled in their cab sides so that drivers could display their names for the benefit of passengers! I only ever saw one adorning a cabside, when the late driver E. G. Kenny set out for Carmarthen with two coaches, and that was for the sole purpose of raising a laugh from his mates as he passed the locomotive shed. I wonder who the bright boy was at headquarters or in the House of Commons who thought up that absurd gimmick. Overall it must have cost a considerable amount.

The gloom was descending, as Dr Beeching's slaughter plans were already in action. The Mid-Wales line had gone whilst flood water, the arch-enemy of the Cambrian, had put paid to the Barmouth to Ruabon and Aberystwyth to Carmarthen branches. On the main line to Shrewsbury, an assortment of grimy Standard Class 4 4-6-0s and Class 4 (76000 series) 2-6-0s worked the remaining steam service; the latter were newcomers to the Cambrian. Finally, one Shrewsbury locomotive completed a very heavy daily duty — she would work the 'down' mail to Aberystwyth, have a breather, then return to Shrewsbury with the 'up' 'Cambrian Coast Express'. However, that was not the end; she then returned to Aberystwyth on the 'down' afternoon express, turned round, and worked the 'up' mail back to Shrewsbury. Quite a tall order for a run down locomotive.

Oswestry's running shed, the mecca of the Cambrian, was closed early in January 1965, to be followed by Aberystwyth the following April. Much speculation followed concerning the future of this relatively modern locomotive shed, and once again rumours were rife. It was to be bulldozed down or converted into a road motor transport depot; however, somebody thought up the brilliant idea of utilising it for the Vale of Rheidol narrow gauge purposes. Today, the Vale of Rheidol has a much more direct approach to the original Carmarthen Bay in the main station, and eliminates the problems of crossing Park Avenue. Porthmadog and Pwllheli locomotive sheds struggled on until 1966 and, finally, Machynlleth fell in December of the same year. These were the saddest of times — it was as if the evil hands of the strangler were at the throat of the Cambrian, and very

naturally it now became a struggle for existence, with every man for himself. For some considerable time Aberystwyth Shed had lost a lot of her previous priorities; valves and pistons and other repairs had long since ceased whilst even boiler washouts were carried out at Machynlleth, in her dark ancient shed. Finally, when the axe fell on Aberystwyth, a Machynlleth locomotive and crew were sent daily to Aberystwyth to shunt the yard, whilst sets of local men sat idle in the cabin. I was not to witness the finality of steam on the Cambrian, but a few weeks after Aberystwyth Shed closed a real pantomime commenced.

The curtain raiser was the renewal of the pump house fittings the very day Aberystwyth Shed closed. Ynyslas, which I now regarded as my own property, was doomed but had not yet fallen. One morning, when I was sitting in the box waiting for the 'down' d.m.u. from Machynlleth, the telephone tinkled. The signalman on duty picked up the receiver, listened, then raised one finger in a gesture of silence and handed it to me. Aberystwyth Shed had now been closed for two weeks. Eventually a voice came through 'Is that Aberystwyth Loco? Control speaking. What steam have you got on the shed?' Not surprisingly, the Aberystwyth reply was 'The only - - - - - - steam here is in the kettle.' The expressive word used by the Aberystwyth gentleman was extremely rude but, under the circumstances, I could not blame him. Ynyslas as a station eventually fell, which compelled me to transfer my support back to Borth. About this time, Shrewsbury, for some unknown reason, had run short of locomotive coal while a vast dump existed at Aberystwyth, which stretched back to GWR days. A crane was duly sent to Aberystwyth, and wagon load after wagon load of coal was transferred to starving Shrewsbury. Later, I returned to Borth one evening on the 'up' 5.15p.m. d.m.u. and there, sitting in the 'down' loop, was a Shrewsbury Standard Class 4 with a string of loaded coal wagons.

'What have we got here?' I remarked to the signalman.

'Wait a minute, I'll see the passenger away.' Then, having completed his duty, he returned and said 'The best yet, a train load of coal for Aberystwyth Loco.'

The coal dump was never removed from Aberystwyth and it was finally bought by the local boys, who sold it at a handsome profit. It is now a well-known fact that the order of the day was to eliminate steam as quickly as possible from all over British Railways, and one shudders at the thought of similar performances being repeated all over the country. Gradually the dust of change began to settle; timetables were revised, and steam traction was gone forever. Double roads vanished quickly, together with a host of stations, until the 'streamlined' route finally became Aberystwyth – Borth – Dovey Junction – Machynlleth – Newtown – Welshpool and Shrewsbury. Aberystwyth locomotivemen now enjoyed the major turns whilst poor Machynlleth had virtually nothing, except for an odd trip up the coast and the occasional outing to Shrewsbury during summer months.

It has often been stated that Euston always wanted to get control of the Cambrian; this may well have been the case in LNWR days, but certainly not in BR's time. The London Midland Region never had anything further from their mind as any form of closure was welcomed and in fact, it would appear that under London Midland rule the Cambrian system was purposely run down. However, they were to acquire something new which, happily, they have really strived to preserve — the Vale of Rheidol narrow guage line, the only steam service operated by BR today.

A 'Dukedog' with a 'Duke' type chimney, No. 9025, approaches Llandre with the 8.10a.m. Machynlleth to Aberystwyth train.

P. Dalton

Chapter 8
The Vale of Rheidol Railway

The Vale of Rheidol narrow gauge shed at Aberystwyth, on 7th September 1955, housed the entire stock of three locomotives, Nos. 7, 8 and 9. No. 7 *Owain Glyndwr* receives attention outside the shed and No. 8 *Llywelyn* can be seen inside the shed building on the right.

P. Dalton

The Vale of Rheidol narrow gauge railway, known locally as 'Lein Fach', takes its name from the parent River Rheidol, whose course it follows from Aberystwyth for about twelve miles to Devil's Bridge. Since its inception in 1902 it has come under four ownerships, originally the Vale of Rheidol Light Railway, Cambrian Railways, the GWR and finally British Rail — will there ever be a fifth owner? Certainly it is food for thought. Some very exact histories of this little line have already been written, therefore I do not wish to repeat these facts; however, it would be of interest to review the mixed and changed fortunes of this sole surviving BR steam passenger service.

Over the years, I have had the good fortune to ride all three Vale of Rheidol locomotives existing today on numerous occasions. My debut was as a very small boy, way back in Cambrian days, on none other than locomotive No. 9 *Prince of Wales*, in its original form as No.2 Cambrian Railways. Naturally the details of that initial trip are now a very misty picture, yet certain incidents are still very clear in my memory. I recall being

lifted on to the small footplate, and remember the intense heat and the fact that the locomotive did not ride as smoothly as the larger engines on the main line. Yet the last three quarters of a mile of the uphill climb to Devil's Bridge is as clear as yesterday. Here the line twists and curves around jagged rocks, on the sharpest of curves. The sanding gear on Vale of Rheidol locomotives has never been one of their strongest points; I can well remember the fireman temporarily vanishing, to sit in front of the smokebox door to pour ashes from a bucket on to the slippery rails. This section can be very treacherous; in fact, locomotives have been known to slip themselves to a standstill at this point, when caterpillars have invaded the track from the heavily surrounding undergrowth.

In 1922, when the line became the property of the GWR, changes took place very quickly. Locomotive No. 3 *Rheidol* was withdrawn, and the new owners quickly constructed two further locomotives, GWR Nos. 7 and 8, which were very similar to the original engines, Nos. 1 and 2, constructed by Davies & Metcalfe. Lein

A view from the footplate of No. 7 *Owain Glyndwr* as it hauls a morning train from Devil's Bridge down the Rheidol Valley to Aberystwyth.

P. Dalton

Vale of Rheidol locomotive No. 9 *Prince of Wales*, having traversed Park Avenue Crossing, sets out for Devil's Bridge with Driver Jackie Jones on the footplate.

P. Dalton

On 25th July 1957, Vale of Rheidol's No. 9 *Prince of Wales* returns from the 'showground' to Aberystwyth with No. 8 *Llywelyn* at the other end of the train.

P. Dalton

Fach was in the happy position of possessing four loco-motives although, in 1931, No. 1 *Edward VII* (GWR No. 1212) was withdrawn, both original engines having been rebuilt at Swindon.

The GWR carried out rebuilding and renewal of coaching stock, although this made no real improvement to the number of passengers carried. It is a well-known fact that the GWR paid great attention to her branch lines because they were, in her eyes, feeders for the main line, yet strangely enough Paddington never really went out of its way to publicise the line. Between the two wars, it must surely have been the most stable and best main-tained of narrow gauge railways in Wales. Throughout the 1920s and 1930s, the Vale of Rheidol ran passenger services during the summer months only. Trains were never overloaded, and that strange familiar rocking sound transmitted through the rails would herald another journey to or from Devil's Bridge. To me, their running was just a sign of summer, in so much that the smell of new mown grass or the distinctive thud of a cricket ball against a willow bat portrayed the same picture. At that time I regarded the Vale of Rheidol as a novelty which only came to life in the summer. Obviously, during World War II, such a system became a dead man, and no further trains ran until the war in Europe was over.

Once again it was very much the same picture; a rather grimy little train with a mere handful of passengers, that pounded its way up the Rheidol Valley to Devil's Bridge. It appeared to have become almost a nuisance value; succession after succession of stationmasters cursed it and one even said to me, when a main line train was being held, 'That damned Devil's Bridge, the sooner they close it the better. Why don't you buy the line?' Tragically this was the attitude, whilst the poor little line struggled and lost money every year right into BR days. One shudders to think how near its fair neck came to the axe of annihilation, yet at the eleventh hour the unbeliev-able happened.

Around this time three vital things occurred which, ultimately, were to alter the entire destiny of the Vale of Rheidol Railway. Mr Sellers, an ex-Cambrian man, had retired from Oswestry as District Traffic Superintendent and was succeeded by Oliver Veltom, an ex-GWR man. He was a remarkable person, not only young and vigor-ous but gifted with an intense knowledge of all railway departments. It was with no surprise that these qualities were very quickly absorbed by the entire district, and in no time it was established that one did not try to pull a fast one over the 'new Guv'; he knew all the answers. Suffice it to say that, at this stage, he immediately took the Vale of Rheidol to his heart.

Secondly, narrow gauge history was being reincarnated. The ancient Tal-y-llyn Railway had been reborn, whilst further north the Ffestiniog Railway was also in the process of resurrection; both had started operating virtually from scratch. It was, therefore, no surprise that Paddington suddenly sat up with a start; here were these little lines, devoid of funds and faced with gigantic engineering problems, that were actually carrying more passengers than their own established line. Indeed, one wondered if the powers that existed had ever realised that they were in possession of probably, at that time, not only the best maintained and possibly the most scenic of railways of its type, but further, that such a line even existed.

The third point was the appointment of the late Lewis Hamer as stationmaster at Aberystwyth. Here was a true railwayman, one who started his railway life on the Vale of Rheidol in Cambrian days. He was already a well-known character, highly respected throughout the district, and had served on Control through the difficult days of World War II. Now, in the evening of his railway life, he was destined to return and take command at Abery-

stwyth, the birthplace of his railway career. Naturally, the little Vale of Rheidol Railway was his baby.

Oliver Veltom and Lewis Hamer, incidently the closest of friends, immediately set to work on the rejuvenation of the little line and gradually coaxed the dying embers back into flame. How near to destruction the line came we shall never know but, without a shadow of doubt, the two railwaymen, with their influence and enthusiasm, not only snatched the railway from the jaws of death but played, as we shall see, a vital role in putting her back on her feet again. From 1950 to 1954 there was an annual average of approximately 15,000 passengers carried, but 1955-6 showed increases from 25,000 to 26,000 — a very marked improvement; nothing sweeps cleaner than a new broom.

British Railways were now within a decade of ownership but, in spite of the ambitious dreams of the politicians, public ownership overall was already under severe criticism from both the press and the public (least of all our railways). The previous pipe-dreams were not bearing fruit yet Aberystwyth, in sharp contrast, had become the cleanest of stations; there was no litter, while gone from the platforms were the old fish boxes. Daily an

No. 7 *Owain Glyndwr* heads the 'Royal Welsh Show' 'up' working to Llanbadarn and is banked by locomotive No. 8 *Llywelyn*.

P. Dalton

A member of the Board suggests to Mr Grand that they should have their photographs taken in front of locomotive No. 7 *Owain Glyndwr* on 17th May 1956.

P. Dalton

immaculate 'Cambrian Coast Express' set out for and arrived from Paddington, whilst Vale of Rheidol trains, above reproach, highlighted the scene. Their new commanding officer was ever present, personally recording daily the ever-increasing number of passengers carried. It was Lewis Hamer's enthusiasm, together with his ability to pass it on to all who served under him, that had performed the miracle, and twice daily I was fortunately able to witness this amazing transformation.

The year of 1955 was one to remember, one that certainly saved the Vale of Rheidol from her previously impending death-bed. On 5th August that same year HM Queen Elizabeth II and HRH Prince Philip visited Abery-

stwyth by rail to open a new wing of the National Library of Wales, and many high ranking railway officers were present. Oliver Veltom and Lewis Hamer did not lose the opportunity of pushing the prospects of Lein Fach to their seniors; the telegraph system to Devil's Bridge was in an appalling state so together they proposed to re-lay a cable up the centre of the track, a vast saving which is still in operation today. Overall, the outcome of these discussions was the backing of Paddington, who was now prepared to widely publicise the line. Nothing succeeds like success; the following year saw a further 4,000 passengers carried.

Early in May 1956, the Western Area Board visited Aberystwyth in force. Again, many high ranking railway officers were present, led by the Chairman Mr Hanks and Mr K. W. C. Grand, General Manager. A special train conveyed the party to Devil's Bridge, so that the Board were able to see for themselves the possibilities. It was a happy occasion; locomotives were now restored to Brunswick Green and fully lined out, whilst the ageing coaching stock looked sparkling in the afternoon sun with a new coat of chocolate and cream. Motive Power Superintendent Mr H. E. A. White and Mr Smeddle, Chief Mechanical Engineer, chose to ride the entire way to Devil's Bridge seated in front of the smokebox door of locomotive No. 7; both being attired in immaculate dark suits. Unfortunately, time did not permit my taking a further photograph of their arrival at Devil's Bridge, somewhat begrimed. A great deal of good came out of that little touch of pageantry, as the Board had seen for themselves not only the natural beauty of the Rheidol Valley in spring but the future potential prospects for the line. Rightly so, she was given their long-awaited blessing.

An engineer's special is photographed between Aberffrwd and Devil's Bridge in July 1960.

P. Dalton

No. 8 *Llywelyn* takes on water at Aberffrwd Station, July 1960, whilst on an engineer's special.

P. Dalton

A private charter train takes on water at Aberffrwd in June 1956.

P. Dalton

Vale of Rheidol locomotive No. 7 *Owain Glyndwr* sets out from Aberystwyth, with two members of the Board seated in front of the smoke-box door during the BR (WR) Board visit to Aberystwyth in May 1956.

P. Dalton

An exceptional year for the Vale of Rheidol was 1957, being that of the Royal Welsh Show workings. Today the show has a permanent site at Builth Wells, but in 1957 was sited at Aberystwyth. At that time a permanent site was being debated, and Aberystwyth was very much on the shortlist; however, that year was to prove two things. The proposed Aberystwyth site was not considered suitable but it was to be the little Vale of Rheidol's golden hour, as she had turned the corner of doubt and uncertainty and was at last on firm ground. The show ran for three days, and was sited just beyond Llanbadarn signal box where the double main line ended. Paddington had been anxious to erect a temporary platform, and operate a push and pull service on the main line. Lewis Hamer was horrified; here was his baby running right through the showground where the potentials were enormous, especially so had the site been chosen as permanent. However, he was a law unto himself; he got his own way and, what is more, insisted that the fare should be 6d. and no more.

Naturally, with no passing loop at Llanbadarn (Vale of Rheidol line), operational problems arose. However, the two maestros had worked this out to the finest detail; they operated an engine at both ends, something which had never previously happened on the Vale of Rheidol Railway. During the show operation, the Devil's Bridge service still operated, but was slightly curtailed. It was a gamble, because it involved all three engines being in steam, leaving no standby engine. For those who lived within the sound of the Vale of Rheidol whistles it was a

unique occasion. For three days, from dawn until dusk, those little engines propelled train load after train load to and from the showground.

There were two set-backs, the first occurring on the second day. Locomotive No. 9, working the restricted Devil's Bridge service, developed a fractured hanger spring, but she limped home and the fitters worked well into the night to ensure that she would be in steam the following day. The third and final day was more serious. The River Rheidol burst its banks with a vengeance and the entire showground became aquatic, thus eliminating Aberystwyth's prospects of becoming a permanent site. In spite of this appalling bad luck, the Vale of Rheidol Railway, during those three memorable days, had carried 53,000 passengers, creating an all-time record. It was not only a personal triumph for Lewis Hamer and Oliver Veltom, but reflected the highest credit on all railwaymen concerned, for the smoothness of the entire operation. A few days later I called upon one of the architects, Lewis Hamer, to offer my congratulations. He rose from his desk with the broadest of grins, brim-full of confidence, and characteristically replied 'Yes, we took them there, and we brought them back.'

Lewis Hamer retired from railway life in 1957 but, in a relatively short space of time, had really set the ball rolling. His successor, Ernie Roberts, an ex-mayor and alderman, continued to carry the torch and, year after year, the number of passengers rose. Finally, when the latter retired, Relief Stationmaster Harry Rees stepped into the breach. The flame of the Vale of Rheidol was

No. 9 *Prince of Wales* heads a private charter train round horse-shoe curve between Aberffrwd and Devil's Bridge in June 1956.

P. Dalton

now fanned to firebox heat; he worked tooth and nail for her continued prosperity, even to the extent of visiting surrounding holiday camps, in off duty periods, exhibiting films of the Vale of Rheidol. Such was the spirit of the Vale of Rheidol, to continue her life when steam throughout the British Isles was already doomed.

Under London Midland rule, some interesting changes took place on the locomotive side. Originally Vale of Rheidol engines had been fed on South Wales coal, large Orlivie; the practice was to build up a thick fire at Aberystwyth, and away they would go to Devil's Bridge with no further attention. Naturally, this entailed expert attention and preparation. For years Johnny (Mostyn) James, son of an ex-Aberystwyth driver, had coped with this delicate operation and had become the master; unfortunately, he later left the railway service.

There were coal problems during the 1950s, so Danny

Goodman decided to experiment with hard coal. This move resulted in a much thinner fire, with the added problem of firing the engines on the climb to Devil's Bridge. The locomotives do not carry bunkers, with the result that coal had to be carried on the footplate with reserves on the side tanks — not exactly an ideal arrangement.

After exhaustive trials it was established that locomotives steamed very well, and that the wear and tear on grates was considerably reduced. At first black smoke was a problem, causing discomfort to the passengers riding in open coaches. Small, washed Rossington cobbles were the substitute which, I understand, are still the order of the day. At the time I could never make up my mind if the changed technique was due to Danny's LMS heritage, or the tragic departure of Johnny Mostyn.

Recently, severe pressure has been brought to bear

Vale of Rheidol locomotives Nos. 8 and 9 prepare to head 'up' afternoon trains to Devil's Bridge from Aberystwyth.

P. Dalton

upon the London Midland Region by the Forestry Commission and private landowners adjacent to the Vale of Rheidol's long-established right of way. It would appear that the Lein Fach has been accused of causing serious fires, from sparks emitted from their locomotives. I have been very familiar with this line for over fifty years, and cannot recall any fires except in the summer of 1976 when the whole country was alight. There were far more serious fires in the South of England, where no Vale of Rheidol exists, although many of those counties would give their right arm for such an asset. The majority of these fires in the South were started by irresponsible sun-soaked members of the public; cigarette ends, glass and, in some cases, sheer vandalism. I suspect the same happens in the Rheidol Valley, as those little engines are not spark throwers. Surely the Forestry Commission and landowners should be compelled to keep their own gardens in order; year after year they are gradually en-

croaching on the line, blanketing out the natural scenery. BR have made a valiant effort to keep this line alive; it is a vital tourist attraction, not only for Aberystwyth but for the surrounding district and Wales. The 'goose that lays the golden egg' should not be slain or sabotaged for the sake of a few dank plantations, devoid of bird life and a breeding ground for foxes. Steam would still exist, even if oil-fired, but much of the hitherto glamour would be lost whilst there would be the unnecessary expense of conversion. This issue should be fought tooth and nail; surely these little locomotives should not be allowed to become the scapegoats.

Happily, the Vale of Rheidol continues to carry a very healthy number of passengers, even to the extent that some unfortunate would-be travellers have to be turned away through lack of seating space. Some of the coaching stock is being rebuilt; this is long overdue, especially if compared with the comfort of her northern neighbours, but one thing must be taken at a time, with the cost of overhauling a locomotive now being such a massive figure. The all-important fact remains that in spite of closures everywhere, BR have kept this little railway alive. Long may it continue, as they are the rightful owners. The Great Little Trains of Wales are now firmly established, of which the Vale of Rheidol is an important member.

Personally, and I am sure I voice the feelings of many, may I suggest that the livery of this fascinating line should once again be restored to that of its original form, or that of the long-proven Great Western Railway. Holiday passengers on such a line do not wish to be reminded of the ever-rising fares of blue electric trains, with their crude insignia, because somehow it does not blend with the Rheidol Valley. Those three stalwart little locomotives can possibly claim the distinction of having received, in their lifetime, more forms of livery than any other locomotive within the British Isles. Indeed, they would appear to change each year in some detail or other. Several years have elapsed since my last visit to the line, but I gather from railway periodicals that locomotive No. 7 has been restored to green livery, whilst the original locomotive No. 9 has acquired the most unusual mustard colour, undoubtedly a work of art but certainly not Vale of Rheidol. Whatever next? Possibly Midland Crimson Lake, with coaching stock in LNER apple green!

Finally, as one born within walking distance of the Vale of Rheidol Railway, whatever the future holds never let this little line die. There are many beautiful routes to Devil's Bridge, but none is fairer than the 11 miles and 70 chains of her single 1ft. 11½in. gauge track. Long live Lein Fach!

Chapter 9
The Cambrian Lines from the Footplate

The Cambrian running length, in my childhood memories, never really extended further than the gasworks sidings at Aberystwyth. Naturally, I realised that trains arrived from and set out for such places as Oswestry and Whitchurch, while through coaches went further afield; but they were all magical places, and the real picture never came alive in my mind until GWR days. The late GWR Oswestry District eventually incorporated the total running length of the Cambrian, together with the addition of the ex-Manchester & Milford Railway, which ran from Aberystwyth as far as Pencader. The section from the latter station to Carmarthen was assigned to the Swansea District.

An old BR Western Operating Area working timetable (Oswestry District) shows a very concise map of that area. Stretching one's imagination, it could be described as rugby football posts that had suffered a severe electric shock. The two uprights represent the lines from Pwllheli in the north to Pencader in the south, and again Whitchurch to Pontsticill. The horizontal or crossbar represents the section between Dovey and Moat Lane Junctions. The total running length of the district was approximately 214 miles of single track, the exceptions being 23 odd miles of double road, that is Aberystwyth to Llanbadarn crossings, Moat Lane Junction to Newtown and Forden to Buttington Junction. On the coast road there existed a very short section between Pwllheli East and Pwllheli, the northern terminus.

In order to familiarise oneself with the ex-Cambrian line, a gradient map of course is invaluable. Briefly, the main line to the south from Whitchurch rose and fell at intervals, with no gradients greater than 1 in 80 as far as Oswestry. It was virtually a falling gradient for the next sixteen miles to Welshpool, while the odd nineteen miles from Welshpool to Moat Lane Junction were a series of slight rises and falls along the Severn Valley, always in close contact with the river. However, from the latter junction, the main line rose abruptly with a maximum gradient of 1 in 80 just prior to Talerddig. The little station here is now closed, and the line fell sharply with a maximum of 1 in 52 for the next fifteen miles to Machynlleth. Without doubt, this stretch was the severest on the Cambrian. Westwards from Machynlleth to Borth, via Dovey Junction, the running was easy along the banks of the River Dyfi, and finally along the seashore at Borth. Once again, in sharp contrast, the last 8½ miles to Aberystwyth were by no means an easy section, very much a switchback affair with gradients which ranged from 1 in 75 to that of 1 in 60.

Turning to the coast road, this line rose north of Towyn through Llwyngwril and on to the famous Friog Ridge, before plunging down to Barmouth Junction and across the wide estuary to Barmouth itself. The line continued to rise right through to Harlech with a maximum

gradient of 1 in 75, and a sudden drop to Monfford prior to crossing the Glaslyn Estuary to Porthmadog. The road then wound its way up the Wern Bank, before another sudden drop through Black Rock and on to Criccieth. The last eight miles north to Pwllheli were on a falling gradient, via the now extinct Afonwen Junction.

The Mid-Wales line from Moat lane to Brecon presented a varied picture, characterised by short rises and falls. It was easy going to Llanidloes then rose suddenly to 1 in 60, prior to Tylwch Halt, but after Pantydwr the line fell gradually at 1 in 75 to well beyond Builth Wells, then rose again via Three Cocks Junction to that of Tal-y-llyn, before finally falling to Brecon.

Finally, the Aberystwyth to Carmarthen branch line presented possibly the most varied nature of all the late Oswestry District. Right from the word go at Aberystwyth it started climbing at 1 in 42, with another four miles of 1 in 41 from Trawscoed to Strata Florida and with a series of rises and falls, not of the same severity, as far as Pencader. From this point the line fell again, at 1 in 60, to just short of Carmarthen.

I have but touched briefly on the Cambrian terrain, yet it would clearly indicate that it was not the easiest of routes to operate, apart from one or two sections of reasonable running. The whole system was characterised by short passing loops and very tight curves. Undoubtedly the toughest section, which really put locomotives and their crews to the test, was the formidable nine miles from Cemmaes Road to Talerddig Summit, 650ft. above sea level. Here the mountains sweep right down to the line side, and if one relished the sound of a wide open regulator echoing around the rocks there was no better vantage point. Naturally a system of this sort does not call for spectacular footplate commentaries, especially if one considers all the restrictions imposed, yet there were moments of great thrills when descending some of the banks which, when added to the scenery, to my mind are unrivalled.

My greatest number of runs on the main line were made between Aberystwyth and Shrewsbury, invariably on the 'Manor' class 4-6-0 engines. These were constructed in the traditional Churchward style, originally designed for mixed traffic and minor lines yet, on a system such as the Cambrian, they were regarded as big and powerful.

During the 1950s, vast experiments were carried out at Swindon on improved draughting, with the result that the majority of GWR engines underwent changes, especially in their blast pipes. The 'Manor' class were not excluded; the first I rode with these modifications was No. 7803 *Barcote Manor*. My journey on that occasion had started at Paddington, in the company of the late Inspector George Holland, who rode the entire route to Aberystwyth with me. The initial section to Shrewsbury

A view of the winding single track which runs along the sea wall between Dovey Junction and Aberdovey, as seen from the footplate of BR 4-6-0 No. 75002.

P. Dalton

was on the footplate of 'Castle' class No. 7001 *Sir James Milne*, an Old Oak Common engine. It was an excellent run, but that is another story outside the Oswestry District. Our 'down' journey from Shrewsbury to Aberystwyth did not produce anything spectacular; *Barcote Manor* coped with her load of seven coaches with ease, and arrived at Aberystwyth two minutes on the right side of the clock. She was never worked hard, having only just returned from the factory, yet the one thing that really stood out on that run was the blast of her exhaust.

There is a rising gradient all the way from Shrewsbury to Westbury, and as we passed Coleham Shed there were the most unmistakable jeers and rude signs from her enginemen on the way our engine was being handled. At the time I was standing behind her driver who was highly embarassed. However, it was a case of bark and no bite, but certainly not that of ham-fisted driving. In fact, if she was opened up on a bank it became one continuous roar with no audible beat, while locomotive No. 7802 *Bradley Manor*, a stronger engine, was indeed a close second. Over the years, I was fortunate enough to be able to ride the entire 'Manor' class, with the exception of Nos. 7813 and 7816, neither of which have I ever set eyes upon. Overall, the 'Manor' was an excellent class, and certainly the most favoured to work the ex-Cambrian metals.

The majority of my footplate trips were made with very old friends, men of Aberystwyth and Machynlleth locomotive depots, accompanied by Inspectors Douglas Sinclair and Glyn Taylor, and latterly with another old friend, Inspector Bill Parcell of Stafford Road, Wolverhampton. Bill was on loan to Shrewsbury, when headquarters were at the latter station before they finally

moved on to Stoke-on-Trent. Previously I had spent many hours in his company running fast on the 'King' and 'Castle' class locomotives between Wolverhampton and Paddington. Possibly I was fortunate, especially on long runs, to invariably pick good engines. On one occasion, when climbing down at Wolverhampton from 'King' class No. 6001 *King Edward VII*, after an incredible run down from Paddington, Bill Parcell remarked, 'It's about time you rode a bad one.'

Towards the end of steam on the Cambrian that opportunity arose. I rode the 7.35a.m. ex-Aberystwyth stopping train as far as Welshpool, on the footplate of 'Manor' class No. 7801 *Anthony Manor*, with an Oswestry crew accompanied by Inspector Sinclair. She was a pathetic sight, being both rusty and filthy with steam escaping everywhere, and how that poor old lady struggled up Talerddig Bank with a meagre load of approximately 214 tons tare behind her tender I will never know. It has often fascinated me how locomotives of a class could vary — not necessarily for limited periods, but overall. The 'Manor' class was no exception; certain members, in spite of routine visits to the factory, would develop their old distinguishable characteristics after a certain mileage. No. 7803 *Barcote Manor* was a strong engine but, after a period, started to run rough, especially on the fireman's side. On one occasion she became too rough for passenger work and was relegated to goods traffic, eventually ending up on the 'back road' at Aberystwyth where she awaited an appointment at Swindon. No. 7807 *Compton Manor* was tarred with the same brush; her rough riding was not just confined to one side, but overall, and only after a considerable mileage under her belt. No. 7806 *Cockington Manor*

The approach to the Friog Rocks from Barmouth Junction. The avalanche shelter and parapet can be seen in the distance; the site of two fatal disasters. The view is pictured from the footplate of GWR 2-6-2T No. 5510.

P. Dalton

The 'up' 'Cambrian Coast Express' approaches Shrewsbury with 'Manor' No. 7802 *Bradley Manor* in charge. The avoiding lines are to the left.

P. Dalton

was a good engine until she received the improved draughting, and then became nobody's friend. She was then tried out several times on the 'Cambrian Coast Express', with little or no success. Because of internal steam pipes bursting, drivers cursed her, and it became the case of 'give a dog a bad name'. Eventually, she left the district. Two years later I rode behind her from Kidderminster to Birmingham (Snow Hill), and inquired from her driver what she was like.

'Won't steam' was his reply.

The next thing I heard about her was that she was on the condemned list.

From my personal experience, the best of the class constructed in pre-World War II days were Nos. 7802, 7804, 7810, 7811 and 7815, while Nos. 7818 and 7819 were exceptional locomotives, especially No. 7819 *Hinton Manor*. The latter was undoubtedly the best of her class; she was the last to receive the improved draughting and the post-war GWR green livery. The later series (Nos. 7820-9) showed slight variations. No. 7823 *Hook Norton Manor* was always considered on the weak side and was very heavy on water. I would say the best of the later batch were Nos. 7821, 7825, 7826, 7828 and 7829.

I have often heard it stated that the 'Manor' class engines were considered poor steamers. The only ones I rode prior to receiving the improved draughting and new look were Nos. 7802-7, 7811, 7819 and 7822 but to

me, they all appeared to steam well; I'm certain the crux of the matter lay in the poor quality of coal available at the time. With regards to appearance, my preference lay with the prototypes and thicker chimneys.

Despite their age, the 4300 class (5300 and 6300 series) Moguls were excellent locomotives whilst the original 9300 series, then on the 'red' classification, saw service in the Oswestry District, but not until they were altered and renumbered as the 7300 series and reclassified as 'blue' engines. None were stationed at Aberystwyth, but several of the class worked in and out of the latter station to and from both Carmarthen and Shrewsbury. On one occasion, one one of the 7300 series headed the 'up' 'Cambrian Coast Express' and an alert relief signalman at Llandre spotted the 'red' route mark on the cabside of the locomotive and immediately rang the motive power depot at Machynlleth, stating that an unpermitted locomotive had passed his box. The locomotive was withdrawn at Machynlleth, and a standby engine was attached. All was well, however, as it later transpired that a young and very enthusiastic cleaner had really set to, and had cleaned the fireman's cabside with such vigour that the original 'red' route spot had reasserted itself from layers of grime.

Except for banking or piloting duties, the 4-4-0 'Dukedogs' were never assigned to the 'Cambrian Coast Express' during the post-World War II period, although once, in the 1950s, 'Dukedogs' Nos. 9017 and 9021 headed the 'down' 'Cambrian Coast Express' from Shrewsbury to Aberystwyth. On this occasion Jack

No. 7818 *Granville Manor* approaches Rock Cutting above Commins Coch (Talerddig Bank) with the 'down' 'Cambrian Coast Express'.

P. Dalton

Thomas, late Locomotive Inspector at Oswestry, was present on the leading engine. The following day the same pair headed the 'up' 12.35p.m. express to Whitchurch, this being a trial operation prior to the first withdrawal of the 'Manor' class engines.

When looking back through my logs on the main Cambrian line, the running would appear very similar, but two 'up' and 'down' runs to Shrewsbury and back aboard 'Manor' class No. 7818 *Granville Manor* appear the most interesting. Of the smaller-wheeled 9000 class 4-4-0s, I have selected a run to Welshpool on the footplate of 'Dukedog' No. 9018.

It was a bitterly cold January morning in 1960 when I climbed aboard No. 7818 *Granville Manor*, which was scheduled to work the 'up' 'Cambrian Coast Express' from Aberystwyth. On both 'up' and 'down' runs I was accompanied by my old friend, Inspector Glyn Taylor, whilst at the regulator was Driver Bill James, whom I stood behind in both directions. The locomotive had only recently returned from the factory and looked superb in the pale watery sunshine which, once we left Aberystwyth, we were not to see again. In fact, conditions to Shrewsbury were appalling the entire way. For nearly 48 hours there had been torrential rain, so that the Severn Valley between Moat Lane and Buttington junctions had virtually become a lake. The wind had veered to the north-west bringing overnight snow and finally, adding insult to injury, a damp wet fog had descended, which obliterated almost everything en route.

Probably, it was fortunate that the occasion was not my introduction to the footplate, otherwise it could have been 'once bitten, twice shy.' Inspector Glyn Taylor had

already travelled down on the early morning mail train from Oswestry to accompany me, and we have often laughed about that bleak day. Apart from firing periods, his entire 'up' and 'down' journeys were made standing with his back to the firebox doors, clad in two dust-coats and a heavy mackintosh.

Our train consisted of a light load of four coaches from Aberystwyth to Dovey Junction, which included one brief stop at Borth. Now, for the first time, we really felt the intense cold when running across the open bogland from Ynyslas to Dovey Junction. The surrounding hills, although white, were no longer visible through the thick mist and, unprotected, Dovey Junction was not the best of places to hang around under those almost arctic conditions. Fortunately, the coast section of the 'Cambrian Coast Express' was on time, but we had to draw forward and then set back to couple up with its three through coaches from Pwllheli. This little operation was completed smartly, and we were away on time with no regrets.

Over the first twenty miles to Machynlleth, No. 7818 had not been pushed. She smelt of new paint and was not running freely, but had no difficulty in keeping to the booked time. The fog really descended on the long uphill climb to Talerddig, and it became quite impossible to pick out familiar landmarks. In spite of her new condition, No. 7818 put up a fine effort, and topped the stiff climb two minutes under the booked time. She was one of the first of her class to receive the improved draughting, but her bark was nowhere near that of No. 7803 *Barcote Manor*.

It was noticeable, on the falling gradients to Moat Lane Junction, that she was not running freely; in fact, she was very much at a running in stage. Unfortunately, we were held at Caersws to cross a 'down' goods, and lost our gained minutes during the ascent of Talerddig Bank. We were four minutes late leaving Moat Lane Junction, and a further check at the home signal at Newtown did not help matters. When we got down almost to river level in the Severn Valley, the fog descended even more, resembling a dirty white blanket which swirled around the footplate, whilst water, which was just visible through the murk, lay on either side of the track. Indeed, we could well have been at sea.

It was the 41st anniversary of the Abermule disaster, and my thoughts went back again to that terrible day as we rounded that memorable curve and descended into her little station. Handing over the correct token for the section, we made a brief stop at Montgomery but, in spite of the appalling conditions, we managed to snatch back nearly two minutes of lost time before drawing to a halt at Welshpool. Normally we should have had a clear run through to Shrewsbury, but the fog now got thicker and even colder, adding to the fact that there existed ahead a stiffish climb from Buttington Junction up Breidden Bank to Westbury, with an engine which was not at her best.

Fog is nobody's friend, particularly enginemen, although happily it was a condition that was compara-

The 'down' 'Cambrian Coast Express' passes Moat Lane Junction headed by No. 7818 *Granville Manor*. Seen from the footplate is an Ivatt 2-6-0 locomotive on the shed road.

P. Dalton

No. 7818 *Granville Manor* approaches Welshpool with the 'down' 'Cambrian Coast Express'. A Collett 2251 class is seen on the 'up' road preparing to leave with a local train for Shrewsbury.

P. Dalton

tively rare on the Cambrian, especially on my home territory near the coast line. Give me snow, ice or even water — at least one can see those hazards. On a single line system such as the Cambrian, distant signals are set in the 'on' position so that the Automatic Train Control system does not come into operation. I recall one very memorable day spent riding one of Worcester's 'Castle' class locomotives from Worcester (Shrub Hill) to Paddington in very thick fog. Both the 'up' and 'down' runs were made in the poorest visibility; in fact, I was just able to see beyond the length of the locomotive's boiler, but the sound of that audible siren or bell ringing when passing distant signals was most reassuring.

Returning to the 'up' 'Cambrian Coast Express', and Bill James's intimate knowledge of the road, and the way he handled the locomotive, resulted in our being on time at Shrewsbury (Abbey Foregate). Unfortunately, adverse signals now brought us to a standstill for three minutes until we finally got the road, and crept into a damp and cold Shrewsbury Station four minutes late. It did not take the same number of minutes for Glyn Taylor and myself to dive into the comparative comfort of the refreshment room. Never has a warm drink and a pipe full of tobacco tasted better.

Considering the climatic conditions, it was a surprise when the 'down' Paddington portion of the 'Cambrian Coast Express' ran in on time, so that we were able to get away on booked time. Bill James and his mate looked revived but, alas, the fog now appeared thicker, and it became very difficult to pick out signals. Nevertheless, our crew were the complete masters, and even No. 7818 appeared to run down Breidden Bank more freely, with our arrival back at Welshpool being dead on time. It was the same picture along the Severn Valley up to Moat Lane Junction, but as we got colder we still stuck to the booked time. The uphill climb to Talerddig Summit was made in spectacular fashion, and as Bill James closed the regulator, in the famous deep rock cutting prior to the long descent to Machynlleth, the entire picture suddenly changed. Gone was the past gloom and all around the mountains stood out white with snow; a refreshing sight. Bill then let No. 7818 run as freely as she was capable, with little brake application. There was a slight easing for the 'down' loop at Llanbrynmair, and again prior to the deep rock cutting just before Commins Coch Halt, which we appeared to shave. We continued to run reasonably freely along the banks of River Dyfi to Machynlleth, now bathed in pale sunshine, two minutes on the right side of the clock.

There was a nice recovery period on the next easy section to Borth, with no stop at Dovey Junction, so that with a moderate load of only four coaches, having shed the 'coast' portion at Machynlleth, there were no problems. The uphill and down dale road from Borth to Aberystwyth was again taken with respect for the new engine, and our final arrival back at Aberystwyth was on time. Accounting for the weather conditions, both crew and locomotive had put up a most creditable perform-

ance. The locomotive, in spite of not running freely, had steamed well and had ridden almost like a car. This was most noticeable on the 'down' run, especially when negotiating the loops.

Four months later, I was privileged to make the same footplate journey. It was most interesting because it was upon the same locomotive, now with quite a few miles of running behind her. Once again I had the pleasant company of my old friend Inspector Glyn Taylor and, contrary to our previous outing, the weather was all that could be wished for — it was mid-May and brilliant sunshine. Appearancewise, No. 7818 *Granville Manor* was again beautifully groomed; Danny Rowlands had obviously not let his daily spot of spit and polish slip up. As on my previous run, I once again stood behind her driver, on both the 'up' and 'down' trips, with yet another old friend, Jackie Jones, with whom I had previously ridden many miles. Unfortunately my log has become slightly obliterated, but I am certain that his mate was Trefor Davies. Anyway, he fired most intelligently throughout, and both Jackie and himself made their task a very easy affair. In sharp contrast, Glyn Taylor was clad in a light dust-coat, and kept well clear of the firebox doors.

Throughout my experience on locomotives, although they were a mass of metal, I have always regarded them with an element of humanity; possibly, on this occasion, No. 7818 wanted to prove a point to me. From the very first bank out of Aberystwyth, and during the descent to Bow Street, it quickly became apparent that she was a very different locomotive to the one on my previous run, in spite of her good behaviour. She was now a very free runner and steamed freely, being very strong at the front end and riding to perfection. The techniques of drivers vary of course, but Jackie never hammered an engine and was inclined to forfeit a minute or two on the uphill climbs, yet kept to time by allowing the locomotive to run freely downhill. Obviously, this method not only made an easier passage for his mate, but paid dividends in fuel and water consumption. Glancing through my logs, an interesting run appears in sharp contrast.

The locomotive was No. 7800 *Torquay Manor*, hauling a similar load under good conditions to Shrewsbury. In all fairness to the engine, she was a little on the run down side, but not over mileage. Her driver was one of the 'wide open regulator' types; in fact, she was thrashed the entire way to Shrewsbury. The unfortunate fireman worked his guts out and, on arrival at the latter station, the tender was virtually devoid of coal, and water consumption had been very heavy, all at the expense of being one minute late with an almost white-hot smokebox door.

On my more recent run on *Granville Manor*, she drew into Shrewsbury as fresh as a new coat of paint, promptly on booked time. Cool drinks were available in the refreshment room on that occasion, whilst Glyn Taylor remarked '7818 is a very different engine since you last rode her — she's one of our best'. We were then joined

Driver Jackie Jones inspects the front end of No. 7818 *Granville Manor* at Welshpool before leaving with the 'up' 'Cambrian Coast Express'. An ex-GWR Mogul is seen in the distance heading a 'down' goods train.

P. Dalton

by Inspector Bill Parcell, who was on loan to the Shrewsbury Division due to headquarters having been moved to the latter station from Oswestry. Bill's presence was more than welcomed because he said to me 'You're coming with me down the Central Wales on Thursday to Swansea and back. I've got a pass for you. I think I've walked every inch of the track from Craven Arms to Llandeilo on the C.T.C. lark. Only one box between the two stations at Llandrindod Wells, that's the idea, but it will be nice to ride the section for a change.' Naturally, to me, such an invitation was more than welcome. That day, with the sun's rays pouring through the originally covered roof, Shrewsbury was one of the most pleasant of stations.

Our return journey on the 'down' 'Cambrian Coast Express' to Aberystwyth was made in equal style to the 'up' run, arriving at the latter station dead on time, with no effort. Once again I was treated to a classic descent of Talerddig Bank, the latter bathed in spring sunshine and providing a fleeting glance of the distant Cader Idris, one of the renowned Welsh mountains. No. 7818 *Granville Manor*, apart from brief rests for valves and pis-

tons, boiler wash-outs, etc., coped with the 'up' and 'down' 'Cambrian Coast Express' for the next eighteen months — no wonder she became a real favourite with the men of Aberystwyth Shed.

My run, although typical, was an excellent example of correct working; same engine and crew throughout, pride in the job, and copy-book running. Briefly, mention must be made of No. 7818's sister engine, No. 7819 *Hinton Manor*, overall my favourite of the entire class. She was an incredible locomotive, always very strong, even when run down, and enginemen always relied upon her. It is a nice thought that she has been rescued from the Barry slaughterhouse, and is proving her reprieval on the Severn Valley Railway. I have had the good fortune to ride her on numerous occasions, but always recall one particular night spent working the 'up' 6p.m. mail train from Aberystwyth. It was a nasty night with a sticky road, and a train load of seven bogies. True to form she regained four minutes of lost time, due to a late start over the none too easy section between Aberystwyth and Ynyslas, with intermediate stops at Bow Street, Llandre and Borth which all gave nothing away.

81

A view of the Cambrian goods loop at Clatter, which was installed in World War I and lifted just prior to World War II. It is seen from the fireman's side of No. 7807 *Compton Manor*. The old signal box at this time was still standing.

P. Dalton

It was one of her many excellent performances and, at the time, she had the original prototype chimney and jumper ring.

I was never as familiar with the 'Duke' and 'Dukedog' 4-4-0s as I was with the 'Manor' class. The former were being withdrawn whilst many of the latter were being put into store when I really started my footplate running in earnest. This, of course, was due to the fact that locomotives with outside cylinders in the 'blue' category worked express trains. Although both classes were regular performers on the 'Cambrian Coast Express' in pre-World War II days, I can only recall one instance after the war when 'Dukedogs' were operative on such trains. In fact I have only ridden two of the famous 'Duke' class; the first instance was as a very small boy (already mentioned) and finally, much later, which I shall mention in another chapter.

The 'Dukedogs' were originally numbered as the 3200 class, but became the 9000 class just prior to nationalisation with the advent of the 2251 class (3200 series) Collett type 0-6-0 mixed traffic engines. The 9000 class were again a very mixed bag; those that I had some experience on were Nos. 9004, 9012, 9017, 9018, 9021 and 9025, the latter differing from the rest with a 'Duke' type chimney. My running on them was short, merely between Ynyslas and Aberystwyth and occasionally on pilot engines to Talerddig Summit. In my opinion the best engines were Nos. 9017-9021, the former happily

still preserved and operative on the Bluebell Line in Sussex, but no longer superheated. Cambrian enginemen never referred to the 9000 class as 'Earls', the names of which some of the class originally carried, but just 'Dukes' and, on numerous occasions, latterly adding the word 'damned', or often something stronger. Overall, they were very similar to the original 'Duke' class, apart from their frames and slightly increased weight. Momentarily I must divert and mention a distinguishing characteristic of railwaymen who had originally served with the true Cambrian Railways. When quoting the London Midland & Scottish Railway they would never say LMS, but the old LMNS. I only discovered this in post-war days but, no doubt, it stemmed from the close ties between the LNWR and the Cambrian Railways.

Returning to the 'Dukedogs', my longest run on a 9000 class (or a 'ninety') was on No. 9018 working the 'up' 9.55a.m. stopping passenger train from Aberystwyth to Welshpool. At that period, the complicated crew workings and locomotive designation (already mentioned) was in existence; it was most unsatisfactory, a glaring example of which we shall see later. Once again, Inspector Douglas Sinclair accompanied me, whilst the late Bill Baker was at the regulator. Bill was a rum character, a rough diamond from the Black Country, who was possessed with the most vivid stretch of imagination and addressed everybody as 'kid'. He once told me that he had worked trains in South America, but possibly never went further afield than Blackpool. Anyway, addressing me as 'kid', he described in detail those far away freight trains, which apparently were so long that you were quite unable to see the guard's brake van. The latter, he informed me, had a little form of Gyser apparatus with a whistle attached, so that the guard could give the distant enginemen the 'right away'. It was a well-known fact at Aberystwyth Shed that Bill and his mate never spoke to each other, yet pulled together in silence and carried out their respective footplate duties without reproach. Douglas Sinclair already knew the situation but showed no concern, his sole concern being that footplate duties were carried out satisfactorily. However, during our run to Welshpool, within his right, Douglas pointed out something to the fireman. Typically, Bill Baker turned to Douglas and, breaking silence, said, 'Leave the kid alone, he's doing his best.' That was Bill Baker.

It was late September 1955 when I climbed aboard No. 9018 at Aberystwyth. She was, at that time, a Machynlleth-based engine, having previously worked the 'down' 8.10a.m. local train from her home depot. Our load of 114 tons tare for four coaches was relatively light, but to counteract this a strong north-westerly gale was blowing together with frequent hail showers, which combined to make the road ahead treacherous. We were away promptly on time with a couple of short slips. These little engines, together with their forerunners the 'Duke' class, were very prone to this little form of mis-

BR Standard No. 75002 passes the 'down' 'Cambrian Coast Express' with a Pwllheli to Machynlleth train. On this occasion No. 7822 *Foxcote Manor* headed the 'CCE'.

P. Dalton

Two sister locomotives cross at Abermule, No. 7818 *Granville Manor* with the 'down' 'Cambrian Coast Express' and No. 7819 *Hinton Manor* with the 'up' Aberystwyth to Whitchurch express.

P. Dalton

No. 7827 *Lydham Manor* prepares to leave Montogomery Station whilst working a 'down' Oswestry to Aberystwyth stopping train. It waits as No. 7818 *Granville Manor* approaches with the 'up' 'Cambrian Coast Express'.

P. Dalton

chief. We reached 35m.p.h. at Llanbadarn box, where the double road ended, and set about the first bank, Fronfraith, which we topped at 28m.p.h., with the needle dancing on the 180lb. mark. On the next climb, which was a gradient of 1 in 75 to Llandre, our speed dropped to 26m.p.h. while the boiler pressure fell to the 170lb. mark, but on the 2½ mile drop to Borth I was again reminded how freely this class of locomotive could run. In spite of meeting the full force of the gale head-on, the little engine touched a maximum speed of 56m.p.h. I was struck with her smooth riding, but Inspector Sinclair and Bill Baker both thought otherwise.

Thank goodness our stay at Borth was not delayed, and we set off swiftly across the wide open bogland to Glandyfi after a brief call at Ynyslas. Normally this is a beautiful stretch of line, but that day was not one in which to feast one's eyes on the surroundings. I was riding behind Driver Baker, and in spite of the storm sheet which had been erected, together with being on the lee side of the gale, fine particles of dust were flying around the footplate. Fireman Davies put in some valiant efforts with the hose, but the coal dust got the upper hand. Speeds had risen from 49½m.p.h., between Borth and Ynyslas, to a maximum of 56½m.p.h. just prior to Glandyfi, the next stopping station. Some relative shelter was granted from Dovey Junction to Machynlleth by the surrounding hills, but the home signal at the latter station held us for half a minute. However, we had covered the 26 miles 42 chains from Aberystwyth in an overall time of 41 minutes, the booked time being 41 minutes 30 seconds.

Our departure from Machynlleth was half a minute late and, in spite of some nice easy running along the banks of the River Dyfi, we were checked again at the next crossing station, Cemmaes Road, due to BR locomotive No. 75028 running late with a 'down' passenger train. The great bank starts in earnest here, and rises at 1 in 60 through Commins Coch Halt to Llanbrynmair, but the really tough section winds and twists up the valley from this point to a maximum gradient of 1 in 52 at Talerddig. Driver Bill Baker worked No. 9018 at 30 per cent cut-off and finally emerged through the deep rock cutting at the summit at a modest 22m.p.h., with the needle down below the 170lb. mark, but we must not forget the two intermediate stops on the uphill climb. The little engine ran very freely down to Moat Lane Junction via the stopping stations of Carno, Pontdolgoch and Caersws, but we continued on booked time.

The comparatively easy section between Moat Lane Junction and Welshpool presented no difficulties, in spite of the fact that we were four minutes late leaving Newtown due to signal checks and platform activity. The last firing took place at Forden and now, with cut-off back to 25 per cent, No. 9018 touched 61m.p.h. on the falling gradient to Welshpool, with a final late arrival of half a minute. This was a very creditable performance considering the circumstances, especially with a stopping train; not the easiest of situations in which to recover lost time. She had steamed freely and ran like a little race-horse. These were fascinating little engines with small diameter wheels which really gave one the impression of speed, especially so when covering the mile a minute. I was very loath to climb down from No. 9018 as she was detached to perform shunting duties, whilst our four coaches were worked forward to Shrewsbury by an ex-LMS 0-6-0 locomotive.

Our return trip to Aberystwyth was made on yet another of the 'Manor' class engines, this time on No. 7811 *Dunley Manor*, a Shrewsbury-based locomotive, at the head of the 'down' 'Cambrian Coast Express'. From my point of view it was most interesting, because it was to prove an old bone of contention.

During our wait at Welshpool, Douglas Sinclair had found out from Control that the 'down' express was running very late, so we were both naturally surprised to see her run into Welshpool only six minutes late. A quick look at the fire and boiler pressure gave me the impression that the Shrewsbury crew had either hit the engine very hard, or had paid little or no attention to the fire on their relatively short and easy run from Shrewsbury. No. 7811 was a good engine, but poor Tysul Davies had to put in some really hard work as far as Newtown, raking and dressing that fire until everything was finally back to normal. In spite of the crew's obvious verbal silence, Bill Baker nursed the locomotive, knowing full well that his mate would put matters right.

From this station back to Aberystwyth there were no problems. The locomotive, now coaxed back to her true form, flew up the rising gradients from Moat Lane Junction to Talerddig Summit, just prior to which Fireman Davies had spotted a leading coach door not properly closed. That stupid delay cost us three favourable minutes. However, Driver Baker made amends by giving the locomotive her head, and she flew down Talerddig Bank and continued her good performance from Cemmaes Road to Machynlleth, eventually coming to a halt at Aberystwyth on time. All credit where it was due, but never on my many runs to Shrewsbury have I ever seen the fire in such a state. Those problems vanished when, eventually, Aberystwyth men won the job right through and back with the same engine; obviously this was the only depot that could work both the 'up' and 'down' trains.

On the double road between Moat Lane Junction and Newtown the 'up' 'Cambrian Coast Express' is headed by No. 7818 *Granville Manor*.

P. Dalton

Much later I was fortunate to make the same runs on two further occasions, but on both 'up' runs alas not on a little 'Dukedog'. The few that remained were out of action so I was once again treated to the versatile 2-6-0s Nos. 4377 and 6371 and, on the 'down' runs, on the footplates of 'Manor' class Nos. 7822 *Foxcote Manor* and 7828 *Odney Manor*, the latter then being an Aberystwyth-based engine. Unfortunately, I never had the opportunity to ride the original 9300 class (renumbered as 7300 2-6-0s) except for one very short ride from the Carmarthen Bay platform at Aberystwyth, tender first, around the triangle and back on shed; the locomotive was Carmarthen-based No. 7340, this particular locomotive having a side window cab.

The BR Standard Class 4 (75000 series) 4-6-0 locomotives, by no means strangers to Cambrian metals in the post World War II period, presented a marked contrast although, admittedly, they were Class 4 engines compared with the Class 5 of the 'Manors'. Personally, and without bias, in appearance they did not even present a comparison. They kept time on express trains and could not be faulted on that aspect, yet they appeared to lack that extra bit of punch. They were very noisy and surprisingly draughty, yet on the other hand they ran very well, and were much freer overall than the 'Manor' class. Once again I was extremely fortunate to have ridden quite a few of the class on the main and coast lines. My notes quote Nos. 75004-6, 75015, 75020, 75023, 75026, 75027 and 75029, the first and last both with double chimneys. Some of those mentioned made some very fast descents of the Borth Bank from Llandre and indeed, one was reported to have touched 80m.p.h. between Glandyfi and Ynyslas on level running.

One particular run comes to mind on the footplate of No. 75015. She was not a regular engine, and was working a 'down' freight from Carmarthen to Aberystwyth. Very few BR Standard engines ever penetrated this branch. However, on that occasion, I joined her at Llanrhystyd Road. On the first falling gradient west of that station, the regulator was closed and, believe it or not, she ran like a greyhound the entire two miles to the stop board at Aberystwyth. Later, some of the class acquired double chimneys. This modification must have been justified, but regarding performance and steaming, the ones I rode showed little or no difference to the original prototypes. Again, personally, it improved their appearance especially in Brunswick Green livery. The double-chimneyed engines had a very distinctive bark; one that could be described as harsh and metallic.

The BR 80000 series 2-6-4 tank engines were without doubt the best of the BR Standard locomotives to have worked the district. In sharp contrast to the 75000 types, the former were very lively performers, a joy to ride upon, together with a nice roomy and comfortable footplate, and were universally popular with enginemen. On one occasion I rode one of this class from Welshpool to Whitchurch in both directions, just prior to the line being closed. The 'up' journey was made bunker first on No. 80097. Appearancewise she was decidedly shabby, yet performancewise, she could well have been ex-factory. To sum up my own personal experiences on the Cambrian main line, I remain convinced the secret of timekeeping lay with the local drivers' intimate knowledge of the road, their unsurpassable technique in tablet exchanging and the all-important manner in which they allowed their locomotives to run down the banks. Glaring examples were often seen during the fever heat traffic of summer months, when Tyseley men had to work holiday trains through to the coastline. Time and again when the heat was really on, delays were often due to these trains running late, simply because the 'foreign' drivers' knowledge of the road and tablet exchange techniques were way behind the local boys, which of course was understandable. Hitherto, I had always prided myself that I knew the Cambrian highway by heart, but this was not so. Even very familiar stretches presented a very different picture from the footplate, which only goes to show what knowing the road really means.

Riding the coast road from Dovey Junction to Pwllheli presents a very different picture from that of the Cambrian main line from Aberystwyth to Whitchurch. Railways that run along the sea-shore have a very distinctive fascination, and possibly the 54 miles to Pwllheli are unrivalled in the British Isles. Throughout its length it is a single line system, characterised by short passing loops, the tightest of reverse curves, together with short but severe gradients set in a background of extreme beauty. The line not only clings to cliff walls, bathed in salt, but crosses high sand dunes and rocks, continually hugging the shores of Cardigan Bay, turning inland only to make an easier crossing of the many wide estuaries which continually intersect its path northwards to Pwllheli. Naturally a road of this nature, with its many intermediate stops, does not call for spectacular running. No speed records were smashed here; it was more of a case of watch and admire how enginemen coped with their environment.

During the post-war steam era, I rode the coast road in both directions many times on a variety of locomotives, but none were greater favourites than the versatile ex-GWR Churchward 2-6-2 tank engines of the 4500 class. Those little engines could well have been constructed especially for the line. They had wonderful acceleration, the required strength, and rode the curves like a Rolls-Royce. Later, their successors, the BR Standard 82000 series, were admirable substitutes. The coast road can also claim the distinction of having seen, at some time or other, every class of locomotive to have worked the ex-Cambrian main lines, together with the occasional invasion of 'foreigners'. Possibly the 'Manor' class were wasted on this route; when extra power was required the established GWR Moguls were surely the answer. Not surprisingly, logs of footplate journeys along the coast road indicate little or no difference, even to the extent of riding passenger trains. Certain passenger trains with limited stops covered the section quicker, and on paper looked more spectacular. For this reason, I have selected an 'up' and 'down' run from Machynlleth to Pwllheli and back which involved riding three engines, all with separate crews.

My 'up' journey was made on the 6.40a.m. mail train from Machynlleth in June 1959. At that period, the mail train was diagrammed for a 'blue' category engine, as from Barmouth northwards its normal complement of five coaches was increased to nine as it carried some heavy school traffic between Barmouth and Harlech. Normally a Machynlleth GWR Mogul or Machynlleth's sole 'Manor' class locomotive would head this train northwards. However, an interesting summer innovation was in operation; that of the 'North Wales Cruise'. The latter train was highly popular and very well patronised. It started at Pwllheli and covered a large circular route of North Wales, down the Cambrian coast to Barmouth, then up the branch as far as Corwen. At this point it branched off over ex-LNWR metals via Denbigh to Rhyl, returning down the North Wales coast main line as far as Caenarvon.

The last section back to Pwllheli was again over ex-LNWR metals over the single line branch (now withdrawn) between Caenarvon and Afonwen Junction. Western Region engines with outside cylinders were not permitted over the Corwen to Rhyl section, so that during the summer months Machynlleth Shed had forfeited one of the 'blue' engines to Oswestry and were loaned two Class 4 Standard 4-6-0 locomotives. It was with no surprise that Machynlleth handed over No. 7806 *Cockington Manor* to Oswestry. She had put up such a miserable

The approach to the summit of Talerddig with No. 7819 *Hinton Manor* at the head of the 'down' 'Cambrian Coast Express'.

P. Dalton

performance on the main line from Aberstwyth that she finally was relegated to the coast road.

On the occasion of my footplate trip on the 'up' morning mail, once again it was to be the case of a good engine, BR Standard 4-6-0 No. 75020, very recently having passed through Derby Works. This was apparent from some of the footplate fittings, such as blower injector valve handles and of course, its fully lined out black livery.

Inspector Douglas Sinclair had again made an early start from Oswestry to accompany me, with two more old friends, Driver Llew Roberts and Fireman Gareth Jones of Machynlleth Shed; so I was in good company. Llew Roberts was the complete master and handled No. 75020 beautifully, right through to Pwllheli. These engines were very prone to violent spasms of slipping, and on occasions would excel a 'Duke' or 'Dukedog' who were also very light on their feet. In spite of overnight rain, however, never once did she show the slightest tendency to that form of misbehaviour. Gareth equally excelled on his part and fired most intelligently. These BR Class 4 engines, when fired with soft South Wales coal, were soon in trouble if the box was filled up, but Gareth kept a nice clean fire, and in return she rode and steamed equally well throughout the run.

We were four minutes late leaving Machynlleth, but had quite easily regained a minute at Aberdovey with no intermediate stops. The odd six miles from Dovey Junction to Aberdovey are possibly the most picturesque of the entire run; indeed the scenery throughout the journey north could fill a book and my pen could never do it true justice. From the first quaint little halt of Gogarth, the railway runs along a sea wall, winding and twisting through short tunnels and rock cuttings clothed in heather and wild plants; a fantastic spectacle at any time of the year.

Our stay at Aberdovey was very brief and we had gained another half minute over the gentle rise of 1 in 98 to Towyn. North of this station, the home of the Tal-y-Llyn Railway, the line climbs steadily past several halts to Llwyngwril, the next crossing station. We were held for several minutes here to cross a 'down' passenger train headed by a BR Standard 2-6-0 Class 2 locomotive. The line now drops over the famous Friog to Fairbourne, the site of another narrow gauge railway, to Morfa Mawddach, formerly Barmouth Junction.

The Friog is one of the most exposed sections of railway line within the British Isles. The track runs along a shelf, literally carved out of the rock overhanging the sea 200ft. below. Twice it has been the scene of railway disasters; the first was in Cambrian days — the train ran into a landslide. Fifty years later a GWR train (in fact the same mail train which I was riding) suffered an identical fate and once again her crew perished as in the previous accident. In both cases the locomotives were hurled on to rocks far below at sea level. When ex-Cambrian GWR locomotive No. 874 made her last run, Driver Humphreys from Machynlleth did not have his regular mate with him. At the last moment his normal fireman changed shifts with Fireman Kenny from Pwllheli who wished to pick up a ferret somewhere along the line. I knew his brother, Driver E. G. Kenny, very well, and rode many miles in his company. That change of duty was the former's death warrant.

The critical ledge of the Friog, a masterpiece of railway engineering, has since been protected against falling rock by a massive shelter, but vigil is still constant at this point, and look-out men are invariably present. On a clear day the view from this point, especially from the footplate, is breath-taking. Far below, stretches the wide expanse of the Mawddach Estuary with its framed railway bridge, whilst to the north one sees the Cambrian coastline to the head of the Lleyn Peninsular backed by the mountains of Snowdonia. It is not surprising that this section of road eventually brought ruin to Thomas Savin, late constructor to the Cambrian Railways. Riding across the Barmouth railway bridge on the footplate is an experience in itself, especially when a south-westerly wind is blowing.

Our late arrival at Barmouth, due to the Llwyngwril check, was easily rectified as the normal booked wait was 18 minutes. We were away on time now with an increased load, and in spite of calling at every little halt and crossing station to pick up school traffic, we had no problems in keeping time, and No. 75020 was never worked hard.

There is a rising gradient from Barmouth at 1 in 75 right through Llanaber, Dyffryn Ardudwy, Llanbedr and Pensarn to Harlech, where its famed castle stands guard high above its little crossing station. From this point the line runs inland for 4½ miles of dead straight road beside yet another estuary, that of the River Dwyryd, before tackling an abrupt rise of 1 in 50 and a similar falling gradient at Minffordd, the exchange point for yet another little steam line, the Ffestiniog Railway. The line, true to character, now traverses yet another estuary, that of the River Glaslyn, well protected on the seaward side by the Treath Mawr embankment. The latter carries the Ffestiniog narrow gauge line from Boston Lodge to the seaside terminus at Portmadoc. This latter estuary holds the most vivid memories for myself; here one is treated to the richest of scenery backed by famous peaks which include Moel Hebog, Snowdon, Cnicht and the Meolwyns with their ever changing colours — the dream of a landscape painter.

The Wern Bank out of Portmadoc winds up a picturesque valley once again at 1 in 50, which No. 75020 tackled with ease and then the line suddenly drops again on a similar gradient, via Black Rock, to Criccieth, the home of Lloyd George. Even today one is made conscious of his dynamic influence; his late residence holds a commanding view of what must be one of the best kept stations, especially from an architectural point of view. The final eight miles to the northern terminus at Pwllheli are on a gentle falling gradient via the windswept changing point of Afonwen. In its heyday, the latter junction (today no more) in spite of its sparse amenities, oozed with character. Happily, the main station building still stands, a living memorial to the LNWR days who connected with the Cambrian Railways at this point from the main line to Holyhead.

Another mile of easy running brought us to the vast man-made holiday camp at Penychain. This 'smile darn you, smile' arena somehow does not blend into the natural beauty of North Wales, but one must never forget that it has been a vital factor in keeping the coast road alive. Our arrival at Pwllheli was two minutes ahead of the booked time, with a beautiful clean fire. The last firing, a mere few shovelfuls, having taken place between Black Rock and Criccieth; all credit to Gareth Jones.

My stay in Pwllheli was very brief and I only had to cross over to the opposite side of the platform to board ex-GWR 2-6-2T No. 5541, heading the 'up' 'Cambrian Coast Express' as far as Dovey Junction. Driver Roberts and Fireman J. W. Jones of Pwllheli were in charge, neither of whom had I previously met. With a very reasonable load of five coaches for 155 tons tare, we had an exhilarating run back to Dovey Junction on time. Once again, it was brought home to me what ideal little locomotives these Churchward engines were, especially for this type of road. The riding qualities of the latter class brings to mind an amusing tale concerning a late Machynlleth driver, who obviously knew the coast road by heart.

It would appear that once he had his train moving, he would insert a wooden wedge behind the regulator; almost an automatic pilot. One day his train was moving a little too smartly for his liking as it approached a reverse curve, and he failed to remove his wedge. However, the locomotive rode the curve to perfection. My own recollections of the gentleman concerned were those of rather untidy overalls and a battered GWR cap. Another distinguishing characteristic was that he only did up the top button of his jacket. One dark evening he was working a coast train back to Machynlleth with one of the 4500 class tanks. As usual, he was seated on his flap-seat, the customary wedge behind the regulator, whilst his jacket, with one solitary button secured, billowed open like a spinnaker in a gale. Glancing at the fire, he drew the attention of his mate. The latter drew some coal forward and, with his pick, swung at one very large lump of good South Wales coal which had tumbled forward from the bunker. Suddenly, to the fireman's horror, he saw his mate lying prostrate in front of the firebox doors. Apparently as the former had swung his pick, he had accidently caught the driver's jacket, inflated by the wind, and promptly hooked him off his flap-seat. Eventually I gathered they booked off still the best of friends.

Returning to my 'down' footplate voyage at Dovey Junction, the three leading coaches were attached to

Aberystwyth Shed and carriage sidings can be seen from the footplate of No. 7819 *Hinton Manor* as she approaches the terminus station with the 'down' 'Cambrian Coast Express'.

P. Dalton

the rear portion of the 'up' 'Cambrian Coast Express' from Aberystwyth, headed by an old acquaintance, No. 7803 *Barcote Manor*, looking immaculate. At that time, No. 7802 *Bradley Manor* was the regular performer for this task, but was undergoing a boiler wash-out, and the former had been assigned to the task. No. 7803 had approximately 60,000 miles under her belt, and in spite of outward appearances, those few odd miles to Machynlleth proved that for a two cylinder engine she was riding a bit rough — true to form, especially so on the fireman's side. As I climbed down at Machynlleth I heard her driver, D. B. James, shout to his mate (with Talerddig Bank ahead) 'Don't forget, this is 03 not 02.' Those boys really knew their horses.

My footplate rides took me but once, over the Mid-Wales line from Moat Lane Junction to Brecon, just prior to the line being closed. It was on the footplate of Ivatt 2-6-0 No. 46518, which was in excellent condition. This was a fascinating run with an extremely light load of two coaches through the most beautiful countryside — especially down the Wye Valley from Rhayader, all the way to Three Cocks Junction in close company with the river, highlighted by trees, which were already turning that unpaintable Autumn Gold. The landscape changed abruptly from Talgarth up into the Black Mountains via Talyllyn Junction and on to Brecon. Both 'up' and 'down' journeys were made at a jog-trot, on time every-

where, but the impression I got on this run, was that personally I much preferred the Ivatt 2-6-0 locomotives to their counterparts, the BR Class 2, 78000 series, stationed at Machynlleth, with which I was far more familiar. The sound of a Stanier or Caledonian hooter through the Welsh Valleys certainly presented a strange and unfamiliar contrast. Those runs unfortunately were marred by the fact that my camera misbehaved itself — a nice roll of 36 shots was wasted, under perfect conditions, alas, never to be repeated.

Last, and by no means least, from the footplate, I come to those 56 miles of single line, that wound and twisted through fertile valleys, over fast flowing rivers, amidst mountain grandeur of great beauty, the Aberystwyth to Carmarthen branch line. This ex-Manchester & Milford line was nicknamed, not without surprise, by local drivers, the 'Burma Road'.

This branch line was raised from 'yellow' to 'blue' classification in May 1939 and, in August 1950, clearance tests took place between Carmarthen and Aberystwyth with an ex-GWR 2-8-0, 2800 class locomotive. Possibly the Western Region were already thinking in terms of potential oil traffic from Milford Haven. It was proved that this class of locomotive could work over the route, provided platform clearances at Pencader and Conwil were improved. However, in view of the availability of other permitted engines in the 'blue' group, the expense of such modifications was not considered justified. Conwil was a bit of a black spot. I recall an ex-Aberystwyth driver telling me how the cylinder casing of No. 7803 scraped the platform at this station, as he was running through on a football special to Swansea. Some of the passing loops on this branch were very short, and interesting rules operated at certain stations. For example, two passenger trains were not permitted to cross at Bryn Teify, Derry Ormond, Pont Llanio or Trawscoed, but a passenger and freight train could do so, provided the latter was admitted into the loop, so that the passenger train could run over the main line. Trains crossing or passing each other at Trawscoed were not allowed to leave Llanilar or Strata Florida, the next stations north and south, until the train to be crossed or passed was safely in the siding. At Llanrhystyd Road (2⅝ miles south of Aberystwyth) an intermediate train token key magazine was in use, to enable a goods train to be shunted on the loop for a goods or passenger train to pass.

The Carmarthen branch set out from Aberystwyth on a vicious note, and climbing started almost immediately on a very tight curve to a maximum gradient 1 in 42, which entailed crossing the Vale of Rheidol line and the river itself by two under bridges, followed by a similar bridge over the main motor road to the south.

At the present time, the Vale of Rheidol line uses the old Carmarthen bay platform at Aberystwyth, its new exit now passing south of the locomotive shed, joining the original route just prior to the exchange sidings, near Plas-Crug crossing. The normal gauge line followed the course of the River Ystwyth inland through extremely picturesque scenery to Llanilar via Llanrhystyd Road. From this point the road rose abruptly for four miles over some of the toughest climbs on the Western Region — steepening at its worst to 1 in 41, with intermediate stops at Trawscoed, and Caradoc Falls Halt, well up the bank. From this point on the footplate one really felt airborne, with the winding course of the River Ystwyth far below.

The top of this formidable climb was heralded by a short tunnel, before the line suddenly dropped on a similar gradient to Strata Florida, with its historic remains of a Roman abbey. From this station, the line set off on what was really the only reasonable stretch of straight road; approximately 5 miles of level running across the famous Tregaron bog. It has been stated that within the British Isles there exist only two floating bogs, Borth and Tregaron. The latter is now preserved as a bird sanctuary, the home of wild geese in the winter — surely the coldest of places in an east wind. Tregaron, a crossing station, lies to the east of this wide expanse of marsh land. The next 23 miles to Pencader ran through varied scenery as the line wound along the banks of the ever-growing River Teify, rising and falling via the oddest of halts to Aberayron Junction, whose signals and points were controlled electrically from Lampeter box, 1¼ miles south of the junction.

From Lampeter the line continued its zigzag course, still hugging the banks of the River Teify via Llanbyther to Maesycrugiau. It is many years since I visited this latter minute hamlet, with its beautiful little church perched high on a hill overlooking the river. The station was typical of this line, with its passing loop, yet it holds nostalgic memories.

During the 1930s, I used to visit Maesycrugiau at very regular intervals, not to watch trains, not that they passed unnoticed, but the real mission was the River Teify and the famed salmon that lay within her deep pools. It was a notorious salmon run, for which, over many years, my father had a rod. He would fish these waters for salmon, whilst I fished ahead with my fly rod for trout. My father had a theory that this was a good practice. It certainly paid dividends. There was one particular pool below the station which contained a natural hazard — the remains of a Manchester & Milford Railway engine which apparently blew up and ended its days on the river bed. I would hate to count the number of casts and flies I lost on that unknown locomotive, and appropriately it was always known as the 'Boiler Pool'.

My memories of Maesycrugiau do not end here. A man by the name of Taylor, now no longer with us, was the signalman at that time, who naturally, in spite of his devotion to duty, thought more of the swift running waters than of his lonely signal cabin. Often I have seen him grass a fine fish for my father, even to the expense of a train whistling at the home signal.

Last, but not least, alongside the railway line stood an isolated building, 'The Railway Inn', operated by the late Dai Davies, the best natural comedian I have ever met. His house was open all day, regardless of the hour. If the fish were not moving, we would retire to his stone-floored bar and consume vast quantites of local ale — I think it was 'Buckleys'; anyway, it was excellent.

The nearest policeman was stationed at Pencader, three miles to the south. His sole form of transport was a bicycle and it was a hard old ride to Maesycrugiau. Being of a portly nature, his weekly visits to Maesycrugiau were made by train, and naturally the signalman at Pencader would inform his mate to the north that the hand of the law was on the on the next 'down' train. This would give Signalman Taylor ample time to set the road, and slip down to the 'Railway Inn' to inform Dai and his out-of-hour customers of their impending visitor. Not surprisingly, on the sergeant's arrival all was above-board. He would duly indulge in a couple of pints on 'mine host', and then return on the next 'up' train to Pencader. Now Dai was a Jack-of-all-trades, and alongside the pub had a slaughter house where we would hang up our catches, and also harbour out-of-hour customers. During World War II, poor Dai was caught red-handed, slaughtering a pig, and duly appeared before the magistrates in Carmarthen. When asked in the witness box why he killed the pig, Dai came out with the incredible statement that he was sorry for it, as it was having fits. His Worship asked Dai how he knew the pig was

The approach to Coleham Shed at Shrewsbury, as seen from the footplate of the 'down' 'Cambrian Coast Express' hauled by, on this occasion, No. 7818 *Granville Manor*.

P. Dalton

subject to fits. Dai then gave a classic demonstration, together with the appropriate squeals of an afflicted pig. The Court was in an uproar, and happily Dai was exonerated.

Returning to the railway line, which, having traversed the 100 yards of Bryn Teify Tunnel, came to the end of the late Oswestry District at Pencader Junction, from this latter point, with its remote little branch line to Newcastle Emlyn, was the start of the most fascinating part of the entire run. The line now fell rapidly at a gradient of 1 in 80 and finally at 1 in 55 through very rugged scenery, down the valley of the River Gwili. The prevailing speed limit was 35m.p.h. which was understandable, as the line snaked its way down the gorge, surrounded by high wooded hills and overhanging rocks. This tortuous course, with check rails on every curve, continued down through Conwil and Bronwydd Arms to Abergwili Junction, then in sharp contrast, the remaining two miles to Carmarthen were in the 'red' classification, with certain exceptions.

Although the branch line was very familiar to me since childhood days, my footplate experiences over this line were very limited compared with the ex-Cambrian main line — in fact I was only once privileged to ride over its entire length in both directions.

The train I chose to ride was the 'up' 7.15a.m. stopping passenger from Aberystwyth, returning on the 'down' 10.45a.m. from Carmarthen. This afforded the chance of riding two classes of ex-GWR engines. From Aberystwyth we had Collett 0-6-0, No. 2271, with light load of three coaches (93 tons). Once again, my old friend Douglas Sinclair accompanied me, whilst Driver Danny Rowlands, prior to becoming supervisor at Aberystwyth was at the regulator and yet another Davies was fireman (Peter Davies). I must point out that every fireman at this depot was not blessed with this name.

We were delayed seven minutes at Aberystwyth as we had to wait for the 'down' Whitchurch mail train which was running late, and also for Inspector Sinclair who travelled down on the same train. He must have secretly cursed me many times on these early runs; if he did, he certainly never betrayed his feelings.

Danny Rowlands did extremely well, in spite of our light load, to reach Tregaron only three minutes late, as we had encountered a very severe slack at Abermad Bridge (undergoing repairs), together with an unexpected halt at Caradoc Falls half-way up the great Trawscoed Bank. Recovery over this sort of route was not easy, especially with a '2251' class locomotive; not the ideal passenger engine. However, in spite of several delays at further halts, our final late arrival of two minutes at Carmarthen reflected the greatest credit on the crew. Peter Davies fired and manipulated his injectors with great intelligence on both runs; boiler pressures were very constant and my log indicates the only instance of 'blowing off' occurred at Lampeter for a very short period on the return run. No. 2271 appeared to ride well, even as she squealed and ground her way down the Gwili Valley to Carmarthen. Our return journey to Aberystwyth was on a Carmarthen engine — ex-GWR 2-6-0 No. 6355, green liveried and ex-works — yet another good one. She was riding very smoothly and with her pony wheels rode the Conwil curves to perfection, so that Danny Rowlands had no problems in keeping time. Our load on this run had been increased to 177 tons for nine vehicles, the extra weight being made up at the rear of the three coaches by a string of empty milk wagons which we disposed of at the Milk Marketing Board Depot at Pond Llanis, between Lampeter and Tregaron. A good Mogul is indeed an excellent engine to ride upon, especially on this sort of road where they did sterling work, possibly like the coast road, far more adaptable than the 'Manor' class locomotives.

This run concludes my rides in the Oswestry District, as unfortunately I never rode any of the short branches on the footplate. I made one interesting ride with Inspector Bill Parcell from Shrewsbury to Swansea and back, down the Central Wales line which touched Cambrian territory at Builth Road. It was on the first BR Standard Class 5, 4-6-0 to work that line, No. 73094. Again, wonderful scenery and some excellent running, especially from the Sugar Loaf down to Llandovery, and along the seashore at Swansea Bay, over tracks that were covered with golden sand. I had little experience on the versatile 0-6-0 pannier tanks, and in the case of the 7400 class working the yard at Aberystwyth, it was just a case of climbing up for a chat, or in and out of a siding. Occasionally, when in the Midlands, I would join a very old friend of mine on the footplate of the more powerful 5700 class pannier tanks, during station pilot duties at Wolverhampton (Low Level). Here again, the actual running was very limited; it was more a case of reminiscing of runs on the larger main line engines, outside the Oswestry District.

No. 7818 *Granville Manor* approaches Rock Cutting above Commins Coch (Talerddig Bank) with the 'down' 'Cambrian Coast Express'.
P. Dalton

Chapter 10
Strangers on the Cambrian

Before steam on our railways finally came to an end, it had been widely prophesied that the Cambrian system could well become a graveyard for that form of motive power. However, time proved that certain other sections of British Railways retained steam long after such forms of traction had become a thing of the past on Cambrian metals — yet there could well have been interesting possibilities, especially when the late Oswestry District came under London Midland Region rule.

It would have appeared that the latter region was not as specific as the Western Region in operating unclassified locomotives. For example, in 1966 a Standard Class 5 4-6-0 (73000 series) once worked the 'up' 6.20p.m. goods out of Aberystwyth. Another occasion which I recall was on a Sunday in 1965, when I was returning from the Midlands by road, and noted an ex-LMS 8F 2-8-0 in charge of a demolition train at Moat Lane Junction. To the best of my knowledge, neither locomotive had undergone clearance tests. In fact, I mentioned the incidents to a locomotive inspector a few days later and he was more than surprised, and assured me that Class 8 locomotives from the London Midland Region had undergone clearance tests as far as Welshpool and no further. As an enthusiast, I had hoped that under Western Region administration those restrictions would possibly have been eased to permit those most versatile of ex-GWR engines, 'Grange' class, to operate. Their increased tractive effort would certainly have 'paid off' on Talerddig Bank — however, it was not to be. Yet under London Midland Region rule, the hopes of regular workings by Stanier Class 5, and 8F freight engines became a reality, but again, as events have proved, this probability was not to take place. It was by no means a flung dream. Away across the border from Cambrian territory, on the Central Wales line, very similar in character, the latter locomotives had worked that line with great success for a considerable period, whilst an ex-GWR 'Hall' class locomotive worked through to Builth Road, but got no further, ripping her cylinder casing off on the platform.

In spite of high expectations, the Cambrian finally returned to BR Standard engines which I have already covered in a previous chapter. However, strangers did penetrate her lines on rare occasions. Southern locomotives heading narrow gauge specials appeared. These included a Wainwright 4-4-0 and an ex-LSWR Class T9. The last and oddest invader was an ex-Lancashire & Yorkshire Railway 2-4-2 tank, which finally failed at Machynlleth with a piston packing gland, and spent three days at that shed before returning light to her home territory. She presented an unfamiliar sight at Machynlleth, and her failure gave me the opportunity of really exploring her one Sunday morning.

Under Western Region regulations, certain London Midland Region engines were permitted, with restric-

tions — for example Class 4 ex-LMS 2-6-0 and 4-4-0 tender engines were permitted between Oswestry and Whitchurch, together with 2-6-4T Class 4 locomotives, with a maximum speed of 40m.p.h. This ruling also applied to the Class 4 2-6-4T engines between Oswestry and Welshpool, but the restrictions were much more severe between Pool Quay and Buttington Junction. London Midland Region 0-6-0 engines were permitted between Pwllheli and Dovey Junction — not that I ever noted such — but had the same restrictions as those attached to Western Region engines in the 'blue' category with outside cylinders.

Royal Train workings, which were no unfamiliar sight on the Cambrian, were always a source of great interest. There was always the uncertainty of what form of power would be employed; one in particular, during Western Region days, provided great speculation and finally dismayed the enthusiastic locomotive punters. In August 1955, HM The Queen and HRH The Duke of Edinburgh visited Aberystwyth to open a new wing of the National Library of Wales. Their journey by rail from South Wales included the difficult section from Carmarthen to Aberystwyth, which entailed the stiff climb up the valley of the Gwilli to Conwil on the 'down' run, and the ascent to Trawscoed Bank from Crosswood to Strata Florida on the return 'up' run. The actual Royal Train was made up of eleven vehicles, a total of 497 tons; a considerable load. Speculation as to the form of motive power was rife — indeed every class of Western Region engine was mentioned, with the exception of a couple of 'Kings'. However, the motive power department soon put an end to enthusiasts' unrest when a trial run over the route was made earlier in the year. Two London Midland Region 2-8-0 8F locomotives, with an equivalent load of sixteen coaches, made a mock run from Pembroke to Aberystwyth and back. It was highly successful and the Stanier engines coped with the severe banks and reverse curves with ease.

On 7th August 1955, the Royal Train which comprised a brake first, dining saloon, sleeping car, saloon, sleeping car, saloon, saloon, dining saloon, HM The Queen's saloon, saloon and brake first, departed from Neyland at 10.30p.m., arriving at the stabling point just east of Llanilar, a distance of approximately 93 miles, at 2.43a.m. on 8th August. The train was hauled by two immaculate London Midland Region locomotives, Nos. 48309 and 48707 which, on arrival at Llanilar, proceeded light to Aberystwyth Shed, whilst that depot's best 2-6-0 Mogul, No. 6371, was attached to the rear of the train to provide overnight steam heating. Promptly, at 8.45a.m., the two Staniers returned to draw the Royal Train forward, over the last four miles and 23½ chains of its 'down' journey to Aberystwyth. Stanier engines were always extremely

No. 48309, an ex-LMS 8F locomotive stands outside the shed at Aberystwyth beside 'Dukedog' No. 9025 and an ex-GWR Mogul. The view is taken from the footplate of No. 7802 *Bradley Manor*, on 8th August 1955, whilst hauling the 'up' 'Cambrian Coast Express'.

P. Dalton

handsome, but that morning they were a sight for sore eyes, with highly polished black livery, as they drew the Royal Train into No. 1 bay platform at Aberystwyth, without a visible feather of steam. Aberystwyth's senior drivers, the late Eddie Richards and Albert Humphries, were on the respective footplates. Those two black horses certainly made locomotive history at Aberystwyth and later, on shed, presented an unfamiliar sight, especially alongside some of the little 'Dukedogs'.

The return 'up' journey was made at 2.30p.m., this time with Carmarthen men on the footplate. I have often thought about that memorable day and regret that I was unable to photograph those locomotives ascending Trawscoed Bank on their return journey.

That August morning also marked the final appearance of a standard 'Dean Goods', one of the last of her class at Oswestry, No. 2516, (now preserved), which stood by in attendance with the Shrewsbury steam crane.

The 'Manor' class engines worked subsequent Royal Trains while steam still reigned supreme on the

Cambrian. These involved workings to Welshpool and lastly Aberdovey when HM The Queen and HRH The Duke of Edinburgh visited the Outward Bound School. This working involved six 'Manor' class engines, Nos. 7827/28, which worked the train from Aberdovey to Morfa Mawddach. At the latter station, Nos. 7819 and 7822 headed the train up the Ruabon branch as far as Chester. No. 7821 was the standby engine. The operation created a touch of local rivalry. Three of the Aberystwyth's 'Manor' contribution, Nos. 7819, 7821 and 7828 were sent to Oswestry to be cleaned. I was fortunate to be able to view Nos. 7819, 7822 and 7828 at Machynlleth prior to the Royal working and, in all fairness, they were not comparable with Danny Rowland's Cambrian Coast engines; rough justice.

For a brief period, Carmarthen Shed developed the practice of working some of the large ex-GWR prairie tanks of the 5100, 6100 and 8100 classes on the branch passenger trains, and on one occasion I noted an 8100 class locomotive working an empty stock working out of Aberystwyth to Aberdovey.

Carrying a 27C shed plate (Southport), ex-L&YR 2-4-2T No. 50781 stands outside the shed building at Machynlleth, having failed with a piston packing gland problem.

P. Dalton

Ex-L&YR 2-4-2T No. 50781 pilots 'Dukedog' No.9021 on the approach to Aberdovey, as the locomotives head a Tal-y-llyn Railway special.

P. Dalton

Finally, the largest steam locomotive I have ever seen on Cambrian metals was in the early spring of 1975. It was almost the rebirth of a new age. I had wandered on to the platform at Machynlleth and met a very old friend, the late Driver Evan Hughes from Aberystwyth. He was in charge of a diesel locomotive and told me she was to haul ex-LMS Pacific No. 46203 *Princess Margaret Rose*, the following day from Butlin's Camp at Penychain, back to Derby. Luckily, I was staying at Dolgellau, and naturally the following morning found myself, with no persuasion, at Barmouth railway bridge.

It was a very exciting moment as that massive locomotive emerged from the Barmouth rocks, and moved slowly out at 5m.p.h. on to the bridge. I was able to photograph her at Fairbourne, and again at Friog, near Llwyngwril. She looked beautiful in her highly polished maroon livery, the entire motion was intact, and even with the absence of steam, one could hear her cylinder exhaust working. Almost as if in appreciation, the sun shone from a cloudless sky, set in a background of sea and mountains; this was real nostalgia. As I watched her finally disappear, my thoughts went back to the late 1950s when I made a footplate trip on one of her sister class locomotives, No. 46209 *Princess Beatrice*, from Crewe to Carlisle, again through countryside of grandeur; that of the Lune Valley and the rolling hills of Cumberland.

After nearly two hours of greedily climbing up and down embankments and hanging over high rocks, I finally returned to my car. My patient little wife greeted me, but with obvious excitement. 'That was a very sad sight, that beautiful engine looked almost human,' she said.

Having reassured her that the engine was not to be slain, her face lit up. My wife could never be classed as a dedicated steam lover.

No. 6203 *Princess Margaret Rose*, an ex-LMS 'Princess Royal' class Pacific, approaches Friog Rocks whilst en-route to Derby Works from Butlin's Holiday Camp at Pwllheli.

P. Dalton

Chapter 11
Storm and Tempest

Mishaps on the Cambrian were fairly numerous, invariably in the form of landslides or washouts. However, history also records that unfortunately the Cambrian was also tarnished with accidents — two of which were very serious — that of Welshampton, and the tragic climax to the Cambrian's reign, at Abermule. In sharp contrast, her successor, the GWR, was almost accident free, with the exception of the Friog Rocks. This latter misfortune was, surely, more an Act of God. The blast of the locomotives' exhausts excited a rockfall, which was already imminent. However, the GWR, like her predecessor, equally suffered mishaps, ninety per cent of which were the result of storm and tempest destroying large sections of the railway line. History has a nasty way of repeating itself, invariably at the same places. It was at these points that the Oswestry District was faced with its greatest problems, in the form of swollen rivers that burst their banks, and the endless waves that hurled themselves, year in and year out, against certain sections of the line which ran in close proximity to Cardigan Bay.

Very soon after the absorption by the GWR of the Cambrian Railways, very severe flooding took place at Aberystwyth, in September 1922, to such an extent that all rail traffic was suspended. The original Vale of Rheidol station was completely under water to a depth of nearly 3ft. The whole of the main line station was flooded, whilst in the locomotive shed, water actually rose up to the firebox levels. This disaster was caused by the River Rheidol, but high winds were absent on this occasion.

The next major disruption took place in November 1927. On this occasion, sea water, backed by a ferocious gale, brought havoc to the railway system in South Cambria. Often I have heard sailors at Aberystwyth, and the older inhabitants of Borth, state that every ten years or so in comes the sea, right through the houses. This certainly is remarkably true, in spite of the constructing of various forms of sea defences and breakwaters, and it nearly always follows the same pattern. Nine times out of ten it is a 17ft. tide that does the damage, and not the 22ft. tides, as one would imagine. The former has far more run, backed by a high wind. The usual picture is a dead south wind for days, building up a very heavy swell, and then, at the critical hour, the wind veers south-west, and in comes the sea, hurling everything before it like matchwood — a terrifying sight. The great storm of 1927 made the most fearful inroads into Aberystwyth; away went the end of the pier, houses on the sea front were smashed to pulp, and rowing boats floated about in sea water right outside the station. Ten years later it all happened again, and very few Cambrian Coast resorts escaped the wrath of those gigantic waves. It is not surprising that long sections of railway line, exposed to the coast, vanished, with the result that train services were very seriously disrupted.

The height of the 1927 storm hit the Cambrian Coast line approximately between 7 and 8p.m., by which time mammoth waves were rolling up the normally peaceful Dyfi Estuary, hurling themselves against the meagre Cambrian embankments. Away to the east, 'Duke' class locomotive No. 3270 *Earl of Devon*, heading the last 'down' passenger, was battling her way through the fiercest of gales. On arrival at Machynlleth her crew looked anxiously to the west, as sparks flew from her tall narrow chimney. Eventually, they negotiated the deep flood water at Dovey Junction, and proceeded cautiously south to Glandyfi. Here, they met the signalman waving a red lamp. All communications with Ynyslas box and the south were dead. *Earl of Devon* drew her five coaches forward, then set back into the goods siding. She was on safe ground, well above the river, and in spite of flying spray, her fireman threw out the fire, whilst the unfortunate passengers took refuge in the small station house.

In the early hours of dawn, a GWR bus (Guy), having negotiated fallen trees and debris, finally rescued the passengers and conveyed them to Aberystwyth. It had been a terrible night, possibly one of the worst in living memory, and daylight revealed the appalling havoc that had been caused by the cruel sea up and down the coastline. The main road from Borth to Ynyslas had vanished overnight, being replaced by a deep bed of shingle. Vast stretches of the bogland east of the railway resembled another ocean, sea water had poured through the culverts on the embankments, whilst nearly three miles of railway line between Ynyslas and Glandyfi had vanished. Huge gaps existed, and ex-Cambrian metals hung with no support, resembling Christmas streamers. The sea front at Aberystwyth and Borth appeared as if they had been subjected to a heavy naval bombardment; windows were smashed and basements were full of sea water and sand.

This scene of destruction was not only confined to the Cardiganshire coastline, large sections of line between Dovey Junction and Aberdovey had gone, whilst to the north, it was the same picture — torn up track between Harlech and Penrhyndeudraeth, and even as far inland as Penmaenpool on the Ruabon branch. It was a case of washouts everywhere; a heart-breaking sight. Two days later, my father drove us in an open Sunbeam car as far as Glandyfi to view the damage. I can still see No. 3270 *Earl of Devon* dead in the goods siding, her boiler splashed with salt spray, and rusty streaks standing out on her cold smokebox door.

In spite of the fearful havoc of that storm, the GWR were not long in getting operational again. The sole Guy bus at Aberystwyth ran a feeder service to Glandyfi, whilst rail repairs went on day and night, and within two weeks trains were running again, but under severe restrictions. Naturally, the vulnerable points were very heavily

Complete with snowploughs, a 2251 class 0-6-0 carries out steam heating duties at Aberystwyth during the winter.

P. Dalton

reinforced, and vast lumps of rock were deposited from the quarries at Llanbedrog and Llyndys, with the hope and belief that the sea would never make such inroads again.

Nearly ten years later, January 1936, there was another fearful gale. This time it reached its height at about 6a.m., but again, as in the previous storm, it was a 17ft. tide. Aberystwyth took a similar battering, with the loss of a large proportion of the Marine Promenade, and once again, another slice of her already denuded pier. Railway damage, in spite of washouts, especially on the coast road was, however, not as severe, and with not such serious disruptions of services; but that year was to leave some deep scars in the Oswestry District.

One Sunday night, in June, there was one of the most fearful thunder storms, again with serious destruction. For days preceding the storm there was a very heavy atmosphere with overcasts skies. Throughout the Saturday, prior to the storm, there were odd claps of thunder — this continued throughout the night and all day on the Sunday as the air seemed to get heavier and heavier, and the barometer slipped back. Something had to happen, and surely enough at about 7p.m. all hell broke loose. I have witnessed electric storms in Italy during the war, but they were nothing in comparison with that particular night. For four hours it never let up, with torrential rain and the most alarming display of lightning which appeared to be everywhere. It was during this fearful storm that the Dulas railway bridge, near Scafell, was washed away, and only the presence of mind of a railwayman and his daughter averted what could have been a major railway disaster. Together they ran back down the track and stopped the 'up' Sunday mail train from Aberystwyth which had already left Moat Lane Junction.

It was over a week before a temporary bridge was erected, and single line working began. Meanwhile, a series of Crosville buses conveyed passengers between Moat Lane and Newtown. The new bridge was not completed with double roads until the following November. Here again was the case of history repeating itself, as the same bridge had been previously damaged by flood water in May 1931, leaving one track suspended.

In November 1952, another ferocious gale hit the shores of the Cambrian coast, and yet again there was a 17ft. tide. On that occasion, I left Aberystwyth by car to return home to Ynyslas. A passer by told me about the very heavy sea that was running, so I decided to take the main road to Machynlleth and approach Ynyslas across the marsh in order to avoid Borth and the suspected sea spray. I had not realised the force of the wind until I diverted on to the lonely stretch of road across the bog. Suddenly I became aware of white streaks crossing my path, and realised the wind was stripping the bulrushes which eventually matted up the nearside windows of my car. I arrived at Ynyslas Crossing at approximately 6.30p.m. and noted all signals in the 'on' position. The crossing gate was closed, obviously for the 'up' mail, but as nothing happened, I then noticed that the seaside gate was open. I contemplated going up to the box, but having seen the sparks flying from her chimney stack, decided to sit tight in the car which was already swaying about in the wind. Away to the north something was approaching slowly on the 'down' loop. Eventually No. 7803 *Barcote Manor* drew in with the starter still on. Suddenly I realised Jack Caffrey the crossing keeper, and Bill Evans, the signalman, were unable to push the east gate open against the force of the wind. In the end, it took six of us to move that gate, whilst No. 7803 took well over twelve minutes to cover the two miles to Borth. She was getting virtually no adhesion on the salt-coated rails. She was subsequently held at Borth for several hours due to an obstruction on the line near Llandre. Later that night, for mere seconds as the moon came out behind the racing clouds, I was treated to the most amazing sight. From a bedroom window I got a fleeting glimpse of the boiling waters beyond the sand dunes; it was one of the biggest and most spectacular sights I have ever seen — those south-westers were something to remember.

The railway between Aberystwyth and Dovey Junction had a let off on this occasion, but the motor road and adjacent golf course to Borth was once again a shingle bed, and impassable for days. The coast road was not so fortunate, and sustained several bad washouts. Vast sea defence work has now been carried out north of Towyn and Barmouth, where trains are continually bathed in salt spray during gales. On one footplate trip on this line, a driver pointed out to me the remains of scattered Cambrian ballast well inland near Talsarnau Halt, a reminder of the strength of these tidal waters when backed by a strong wind.

Salt water was not the only enemy of the Cambrian; swollen rivers also attacked her system from time to time. We have already seen how the River Rheidol spitefully washed away Aberystwyth's rosy chances of a permanent

A begrimed No. 7806 *Cockington Manor* approaches Aberystwyth with a 'down' goods train during a spell of arctic weather.

P. Dalton

No. 7822 *Foxcote Manor* passes Ynyslas on a wintry Sunday morning with a 'down' mail train.

P. Dalton

Storm damage on the Cambrian, between Dovey Junction and Glandyfi, in December 1976.

John Roberts

site for the Royal Welsh Show. During BR days, the rivers Dovey and Severn equally staked their destructive claims, with serious washouts at Caersws and Derwenlas, between Machynlleth and Dovey Junction. Both were the result of 48 hours of torrential rain in December 1964, and could now be looked upon as the beginning of the end. Already the Aberystwyth to Carmarthen line, and the Ruabon branch, were listed for closure. However, on both lines, bridges were washed away, which merely accelerated their already impending doom. No further trains ran, except those for the purpose of track lifting, but on the Carmarthen line, there remained goods traffic only from Lampeter to the south. This too was short lived, before the whole line's fate was sealed.

Normally the warm prevailing south-westerly winds counteracted serious snow hazards, especially in South Cambria; however, this section did not always escape entirely. There was a very heavy fall of snow in February 1937, when a train was buried in a deep drift at Carno, but in the famous winter of 1947, the great blizzard that swept the entire country brought the Oswestry District to a standstill. I had just been demobbed and remember my father pointing out a frozen spring on the north side of Pendinas. The latter is a hill at Aberystwyth which separated the Carmarthen branch from the main Cambrian line to the north. It is a familiar landmark with its tall chimney, the remains of an uncompleted monument to the Duke of Wellington. The ice had apparently been there for weeks and my father assured me mischief was afoot. How right he was. The great blizzard struck soon afterwards, and engulfed the entire British Isles. By early light the snow was falling fast, fine and powdery, which seemed to swirl back up into the sky and blew off the roofs in great white gusts. The 'down' Oswestry to Aberystwyth mail train had a terrible struggle, finally reaching Machynlleth, where she became

completely snowbound. The 7.35a.m. ex-Aberystwyth train got as far as Ynyslas and ran into similar trouble. However, her locomotive managed to get on to the 'down' loop and eventually propelled the coaches back to Aberystwyth, bunker first, before the line became totally blocked. Snow ploughs tried desperately to open up the section between Machynlleth and Aberystwyth, but no sooner was one drift cleared, than another built up behind them. It was the same story everywhere — fighting a losing battle. The snow continued to fall well into the late afternoon. Crosville Motor Services had been most enterprising and kept a local service running as far as Llanbadarn, a mile and a half out of Aberystwyth, but as conditions grew worse, they too threw in the towel, at midday. It was now total disruption, and nothing moved; roads and hedgerows had vanished and the landscape became a great silent white blanket of snow. If one could disregard the disruption, it was a strange and beautiful sight, with the incredible light, especially after dark, and the uncanny silence, together with that unmistakable sterile smell of newly fallen snow. Once the snow eased, the railway snow ploughs set to work again, and the early morning mail train eventually struggled into Aberystwyth, approximately at the time when she normally set out for Oswestry and Whitchurch in the evening.

To the South, the Carmarthen branch line fared far worse. One of the last remaining 'Duke' class locomotives, heading a 'down' passenger train, ran into a mammoth drift at Lampeter, and her passengers and locomotive crew were marooned for three days. A rescuing engine set out from Aberystwyth but met the same fate at Strata Florida, on the edge of the wind-swept Tregaron bog. She was followed by a second, and yet a third locomotive. Finally, this trio of steam charged the snow drift but impact was so severe that all the panes of glass in the signal cabin were shattered. It was many days, even weeks, before rail and road services got back to normal; in fact for two days the only reliable transport was by sea. Fishing boats plied up and down the coast, delivering the bare essentials to remote villages and hamlets.

Snowfalls in the west, especially on the Cambrian coast, are but short-lived. The warm westerlies would soon thaw out these intruders. However, in 1947, this was not so. A cruel east wind persisted, and blew the dry snow from the open spaces, resembling a second blizzard. At the top of Talerddig Bank, the snow was piled up to the tops of the telegraph poles, but the thaw eventually had to come, and with it the swollen rivers, carrying thousands of dead sheep who had perished on the bleak mountain sides — a pathetic sight.

The winters of 1962-4 were possibly even more severe. The snow at sea-level was by no means so deep, but this time it was frost which penetrated everything and everywhere. The BR Standard locomotives were sitting ducks with all their external pipes, whilst Collett 0-6-0 locomotives stood by constantly in steam with snow ploughs attached. On many occasions when I crossed the fields from my home to Ynyslas Station, the surrounding flats were covered with weak hungry wild geese — too weak to move, whilst day in and day out for weeks, a cruel east wind blew from a cloudless sky. The 'down' loop at Ynyslas was frozen solid; it was unthawed time and again, but immediately froze up. So deep had the frost penetrated, that even the sand dunes were rock hard. The main water supply froze at Aberystwyth and it was with the greatest credit that railwaymen managed to keep the wheels turning under such conditions.

Finally, I must mention an incident during this bleak period, which today is amusing, but was not so at the time. Owing to frozen water mains, the Machynlleth Fire Brigade were unable to cope with a serious cinema fire on their home ground. A make-shift fire appliance was quickly assembled at Aberystwyth and, in great haste, was dispatched by rail. A 7400 class pannier tank was assigned to the task, and her driver was the late Jack James, a real Aberystwyth character, who I shall enlarge on in a subsequent chapter. Briefly, he was a notorious flyer, together with the element of devil. This mission was right up his street. He had guaranteed signals on the 'up' main, no loops, and no checks. That pannier tank certainly had the run of her lifetime, and all Cambrian records were smashed, never to be repeated! It is stated that Jack never closed the regulator between Aberystwyth and Machynlleth, and covered the odd eighteen miles in even time. I believe the descent of Borth Bank and his passage through that station would have more than risen the eyebrows of Sir Nigel Gresley himself.

If one visits the Cambrian coast resorts in summer, it is difficult to realise that such diverse climatic conditions can exist, yet I recall many years ago in the company of my father, climbing rocks of Aran Fawddwy, the birthplace of the River Dyfi. Half-way up that stiff scramble, we paused for breath and gazed back at the soft velvet blue mountains that surrounded us. It was the high noon of summer, in a cloudless sky, with not even the faintest puff of wind. I remarked on the beautiful and peaceful picture and, after a pause, obviously equally captivated, my father turned and said, 'Yes, it is, but never underestimate the mountains or the force of water, as they can change like the wind.' Wise words which I have never forgotten.

Two 'Manor' class locomotives stand beside the water tower outside the shed building at Aberystwyth. They are Nos. 7811 *Dunley Manor* and 7802 *Bradley Manor*. Note the turnout of these locomotives; a characteristic of Aberystwyth Shed and Danny Rowlands' 'spit and polish'.

P. Dalton

No. 7822 *Foxcote Manor* is pictured at Machynlleth with a 'down' stopping train from Oswestry.

P. Dalton

Chapter 12
Summer Saturdays and Photography

No. 7814 *Fringford Manor* pilots 2251 class Collett No. 2217 on the 'up' 'Cambrian Coast Express' over the last lap of Talerddig Bank on 15th August 1959.

P. Dalton

From my home at Ynyslas there was a commanding view of the main Cambrian Line, as it stretched from Borth to Ynyslas, and across the marsh to Glan Dyfi and distant Dovey Junction. Whilst across the Dyfi Estuary, on a reasonably clear day, it was a simple matter to follow the progress of trains from Aberdyfi right along that coast section to Dovey Junction.

Summer Saturdays in the 1950s were days of extreme activity — in fact from dawn until dusk, the long sections between Borth—Dovey Junction and Aberdyfi were never without steam of some sort, either in the form of a booked train, or light engine. Naturally, the picture would change with climatic conditions. There were days when the wooden platforms at Ynyslas sweltered under the burning rays of a midday sun, whilst the surrounding Cambrian mountains would recede into a white haze of shimmering heat, not a feather of steam would then be visible from locomotives; such was the degree of humidity. Once, on a full tide, I actually witnessed a mir-

age — a Mogul (63 series) locomotive and six coaches way above the trees at Glandyfi. Yet too often it was the reverse, days when soft rain blew in from the sea, not only obliterating those magic mountains, but also my home station Ynyslas, a mere quarter of a mile inland.

Way back in the thirties, I possessed a Brownie box camera. Many shots were taken of the family, some of the aircraft of Sir Alan Cobham's Air Circus, and very occasionally, a stationary 'Duke' locomotive — alas, those wasted years, but far worse was the fact that I did not appreciate the importance of retaining and looking after negatives. Little did I realise then what valuable material was being cast to the four winds, and it was not until our railways were nationalised that my fearful blunder dawned upon me. From then on, I took up railway photography in earnest, hours and hours of intense satisfaction. Now armed with a second-hand Zeiss Icinta, I set about trying to photograph as many of the locomotives of the ex-Cambrian railways as was possible. It took a long time, and some of the early efforts were terrible, and at great expense too, but gradually I began to get the hang of it, never, however, to perfection.

Summer Saturdays gave me a great deal of scope, especially on a single line, packed with holiday traffic, and hauled by a variety of locomotives. My lineside passes were, of course, invaluable, and gave me access to all railway departments with the exception of tunnels; the Cambrian happily, was blessed with few, and always very short. Fortunately, for me, set up in such a background assisted invariably by an excellent light, my railway photography days really commenced on a 'bed of roses'. The 'ups' and 'downs' between Borth and Aberystwyth afforded great possibilities, whilst in contrast, the long open stretches between Ynyslas and Dovey Junction, barren of human activity, were ideal spots. Throughout my life, the tendency has been isolation, which was certainly true on this latter section. Indeed it was literally a case of 'me and my camera', apart from the wildfowl on the marshes who worked endlessly in the saltings of the Dovey Estuary alongside the track. These creatures never seemed the slightest bit disturbed by passing trains, but would even appear to show some

strange form of fascination.

Dovey Junction in the height of summer afforded endless shots; trains of all types and sizes, set in a background of salt water and mountains — while the coast road to Aberdyfi, with its exquisite scenery, was possibly the railway photographer's dream. Finally, for really hard working locomotives, mostly handling ten or twelve bogies, invariably double-headed, no better site could be found than Talerddig Bank. With such a wealth of sites right on my doorstep, it is with no surprise that 99.9 per cent of my negative album contains South Cambrian steam.

Throughout the 1950s and 1960s my expeditions were very lone affairs — not once can I recall meeting another photographer with the same objective in view. However, on one particular Saturday I spent probably the happiest of all days in the company of the old master himself, H. Gordon Tidey. He had previously contacted me with an eye to a day's photography together, paying me the enormous compliment of being the 'uncrowned King of the Cambrian'. Although very much my senior in years, he missed nothing, and scrambled up and down those embankments like a mountain goat, taking endless

BR 2-6-4 tank No. 80096 storms away from Dovey Junction with a 'down' 'Butlin's Express'.

P. Dalton

No. 75015 is seen in trouble as she approaches Commins Coch Halt with an 'up' express *(see Chapter 12)*.

P. Dalton

A 2251 class 0-6-0 Collett No. 2264 and a BR Standard 4MT, No. 75006, double-head an 'up' Manchester express between Machynlleth and Cemmaes Road in September 1957.

Ex-GWR 2-6-2T No. 5570 pilots No. 7801 *Anthony Manor* on the 'up' Pwllheli to Paddington train at Machynlleth in August 1962.

P. Dalton

shots over a very wide area of railway territory. Needless to say, in such company I subsequently learnt a lot on the subject of railway reproduction. However, inevitably towards the end of steam every bridge and embankment became almost a camera shop, especially Talerddig Bank; it was never quite the same.

The Saturday prior to the original August bank holiday, weather permittting, was certainly the day to choose, not only for watching trains, but also for photographing them, as many of the normal services were duplicated, together with specials running in two parts; days of great steam activity. It was on one such Saturday during the mid-1950s that I set out for Talerddig Bank to watch and attempt to record the traffic with my camera. I arrived early on the little station platform of Talerddig at the top of the bank, and made my way to the cabin to inform the signalman of my proposed whereabouts for the day. This practice I always adhered to, especially when on railway property. It was a warm morning with just the right amount of sun and cloud to highlight my shots. I waited for the first train to arrive, the 'down' 8.20a.m. from Oswestry — the key train of the day. It had become an established fact over the past few years that if this train ran to time, there was

an excellent chance that the rest of the day's programme would fit together like a jigsaw puzzle; however, if she got behind the clock, it was a very different story.The 7.55a.m. and 8.05a.m. Birmingham expresses, close on her heels, would be held back. They, in turn would affect the 11a.m. 'up' Aberystwyth—Manchester, and the 9.25a.m. Pwllheli—Paddington ('Cambrian Coast Express'), through failing to meet at a scheduled crossing station.

On that particular Saturday, both 'up' and 'down' trains ran well to time, possibly due to the 'down' 8.20 passenger from Oswestry really doing her stuff, headed by Oswestry's best BR Standard Class 4, No. 75020. Having seen her on her way I wandered back down the bank to select a likely spot to get shots of the 'up' and 'down' expresses. Railway embankments are the most fascinating places, the complete absence of the public and grazing animals often resulted in the discovery of all kinds of wild plants. Nearly all the 'up' trains had assistance from Machynlleth which varied from the 0-6-0 2251 classes, BR Standard Class 2, 2-6-0, 4500 class tanks, and 'Dukedogs'. It was always a thrilling sight watching locomotives approaching the deep rock cutting at the top of the bank. They certainly raised the echoes

A double-headed 'down' Birmingham to Aberystwyth express approaches Commins Coch cutting on a summer Saturday.

P. Dalton

Double-heading on Talerddig Incline between Llanbrynmair and Chapel Crossing in August 1957. Ex-GWR 2-6-2T No. 4599 and BR Standard 4MT No. 75024 head an 'up' North of England express.

P. Dalton

here with wide open regulators.

A few Saturdays previously, I had been treated to the reverse sight, everything late. The 'down' 8.20 passenger from Oswestry was in trouble all the way. Her BR Standard Class 4 was losing time through dirty tubes; she certainly dropped a spanner in operations that morning. The 'up' Pwllheli—Paddington was now really running late and had been held at Llanbrynmair to cross an equally late 'down' Birmingham express.

From my vantage point I was able to follow the former's slow progress from Llanbrynmair up the valley; the latter was already dark with smoke and as the train came in to view it was obvious that both No. 75026 and her 'Dukedog' pilot were making very heavy weather of the final 1 in 52 climb. She was a heavy train, eleven bogies packed with a considerable number of heads hanging out of the windows. By the time they drew level with me, the speed was down to about 5m.p.h., whilst the exhaust blasts echoed round and round the high rocks. The fireman of the train engine, a Machynlleth man, shouted down to me, 'We're not doing very well are we?' and as a gesture of despair, offered me the shovel. Anyway, they eventually made it, but worse was to follow; the 9.25a.m. Pwllheli—Paddington relief was in dire straights. No. 75015 would not steam and had no assistance with a lighter load, and she sat for a good 25 minutes at Llanbrynmair with the blower on, before she eventually got away, but the damage had now been well and truly done and everything was subsequently very late that Saturday. It was a very still morning, and just before these two unfortunate ascents, I had been down at Llanbrynmair leaning over the road bridge. I clearly heard the 9.55a.m. Aberystwyth—Shrewsbury stopper get away from Cemmaes Road, and restart from Commins Coch Halt. The roar of her exhaust clearly told me a 'Manor' class locomotive was in charge, and what is more, by her bark I would have put my shirt on it as to whom it belonged. It was with no surprise when the roar eased for Llanbrynmair, that No. 7803 *Barcote Manor* appeared in great style.

It took me back to my own footplate experience on her when the gentlemen of Coleham Shed mocked us getting away from Shrewsbury. That particular morning Driver Billy (Windy) Evans was in charge. Now, I had always presumed that he had earned this nickname by the way he handled an engine — he was a real flyer. However, he always wore a cloth cap which I had never seen off his head. Unknown to me, he was virtually bald, and this sensitivity resulted in the cap always being in place; hence his nickname. Billy got No. 7803 away from Llanbrynmair in a flash and made very short work of the last few miles to the summit.

The entire length of Talerddig Bank back to Cemmaes Road was packed with possible photographic positions, and there were always the numerous assisting engines running back light, who, virtually without coming to a standstill, would pick me up and drop me off at the next likely spot.

Almost at sea-level, west of Machynlleth, Dovey Junction equally provided an excellent place for steam photography. Her activites were not confined to summer Saturdays, but day in and day out during the summer months, and apart from normal trains, there were light engines, troop trains to Tonfanau camps, and empty stock workings.

To readers who may not be familiar with Dovey Junction, apart from steam trains, here was, and indeed at the time of writing still is, surely the most fascinating of railway junctions. Set in the midst of marsh land, with no approach other than the solitary footpath alongside the line from Glandyfi, the next station to the south on the main line, her boundaries have the distinction of being in three counties — formerly Cardiganshire, Merioneth and Montgomery — today known as Dyfed, Gwynedd and Powys. The windswept junction has little protection from the elements, bounded on the north by the tidal waters of the River Dyfi, and to the south by bogland, clothed with bulrushes, right up to the foothills of the surrounding Cambrian mountains. Being within the bounds of tidal waters, severe flooding can take place, and it is not surprising the the GWR had plans to eliminate the junction entirely, and double the road to Machynlleth. Undoubtedly, this would have eased the traffic problems, but lack of space at Machynlleth, together with World War II put paid to that project.

Dovey Junction has been rebuilt during BR days and has lost much of its original character, but its atmosphere still lives on today in spite of the lack of steam. Sometimes I would spend the whole day at the junction photographing 'up' or 'down' expresses — the latter always dominated the afternoon performances, with the added advantage that the signalman on duty could always keep me in touch with their whereabouts. Summer Saturdays provided two interesting workings, that of the 'up' and 'down' Butlin specials, through workings from Swansea to Penychain. This operation involved the reversal of trains at Dovey Junction, together with a change in motive power. Naturally, Saturdays of such activity put the greatest stress on all motive power departments. Everything was in steam, including foreign engines from Shrewsbury and Tysley, whilst when the heat was really on, it was no unusual sight to note locomotives operating from as far afield as Chester and Carmarthen sheds. Some of these strangers would spend a week by the sea before returning to their home depots, whilst Aberystwyth engines in turn would work the Black Country lines. This was how I became acquainted with No. 7805 *Broome Manor*.

Days of uncertain weather were often spent at my home station, Ynyslas. The 'up' main was a very long loop, so that lowly Ynyslas was worth her weight in gold on such days of heavy traffic, in fact it was surprising how often when looking across to the station, throughout the day, something would be sitting in either the 'up' main or 'down' loop.

Finally, I come to one of my favourite spots, the 5½

In August 1957, No. 7803 *Barcote Manor* is pictured heading the 'up' 9.55 Aberystwyth to Shrewsbury train as it approaches Llanbrynmair, unassisted.

P. Dalton

miles of railway line which crossed the bog from Ynyslas to Glandyfi, in close contact with the Dyfi Estuary. Half-way across that strip of barren land, the line rose and fell at Trer-ddol Bridge, a wooden construction at the mouth of the River Clettwr.

However, in spite of the lure of the railway line and its associates, ever since the days of extreme childhood the great expanse of hard sands at Ynyslas claimed an equal fascination. Like a piece of steel to a magnet, I was constantly drawn to those wide open stretches. Man and his progress have failed to alter the image. Twice daily, year in and year out, the endless waves sweep clean the sands, obliterating all signs of human trespass. At intervals the man-made breakwaters and sea defences are wounded or destroyed by her force, possibly a reminder as to who stands supreme. I would spend countless hours walking the high water marks, collecting driftwood, the spoils of the aftermath of great storms, but more often wading into the silvery surf and casting my tackle out into the breakers for Bass. There were days of great catches and equally those when my fish sack was brought home empty, but it was always the same; the peace and hours of rumination, just sea, sand, and wind and the endless darting to and fro of the sandpipers. Yet from that beach it was possible to see, and if the wind was

in the right direction, hear trains starting from Aberdyfi before finally plunging into Penhelig tunnel.

Now somewhere, sometime, I read an article on the subject of catching Bass and Sewin on a flood tide in tidal waters. Trer-ddol Bridge, way out on the bog, fitted the pattern to a tee. Ultimately one August evening I set out for this lonely spot to try my luck. Having walked along the man-made embankment which protects the surrounding marsh from the river, I eventually reached the railway bridge and started fishing from the saltings on the seaward side. It was a beautiful evening with a strong north-westerly blowing. Aberdyfi stood out sharply across the estuary and I felt I could almost touch the houses. I was quite alone except for the Dunlins or Oyster Catchers chattering away, as they fed on the saltings, but the tide was making fast, and not wanting to be cut off I retraced my steps to the railway bridge.

Up to this point I was well within my rights, with a lineside pass in my pocket, but alas, I now ceased to be what I had previously considered myself, a good railway-man, and certainly violated my pass. A glance at my watch showed it was approximately 8p.m. Having ensured that the track was clear, the 'down' 3.55p.m. Shrewsbury had crossed the 'up' 6.20p.m. goods at Ynyslas, there were no specials, I had confirmed that in Ynyslas box that morning, so that only left the last 'down' passenger 8.45p.m. from Machynlleth. Picking up my rod I cast up stream with confidence and started trolling as the flood tide rushed under the bridge. Little did I realise as I watched my fly bobbing about in the rough water, that I was about to repeat a second G. J. Churchward act.

Normally, one can hear a train approach, its movement is transmitted through the rails; but standing on that wooden bridge with a strong gale in my back, all was silent. To this day I do not know what made me turn my head at the vital moment. There to my horror, running bunker first on to the bridge, was none other than one of Mr Churchward's engines. In sheer panic I dropped my rod and took a flying dive over the end of the handrails of the bridge. Luckily my fall was cushioned by the soft sand alongside the water. I think I heard a whistle, but away went an ex-GWR 2-6-0 Mogul travelling at great speed. It was sometime before I finally dragged myself out of the soft sand, unharmed but shaking from head to foot. My rod was hanging from the pillars of the bridge. I tried to recover it, but was too shaken, and decided to return at day break, I was very attached to that rod, and did not want it to fall into the hands of a dawn poacher. The following day it was a simple matter, but that incident had taught me a very good lesson.

A few months previously, I had walked from No. 1 Platform at Paddington to Ranelagh Bridge yard alongside the track, in the company of Inspector Bill Parcell. He gave me a lot of good advice, especially on what not to do when walking railway lines. It must have all gone in through one ear and out through the other. Many months later I was chatting to my old friend Jackie Jones, an Aberystwyth driver, on the subject of fishing tidal waters. He asked me if I had tried Trer-ddol Bridge. Whereupon I said, 'Once, and once only', and related my experience. 'Oh God, it was you! I saw someone drop on the bank, but knew they were all right. We were running fast and the coal dust was flying all over the place. I had a Machynlleth loco boy on the footplate, and he wanted to catch the last bus to Aberayron.'

Ever since that night, light engines spelled out a lot more to me than they had in previous years, and not surprisingly, I became the most cautious railway photographer, especially within the bounds of railway property.

Chapter 13
Swansong

1965 was a forlorn year on the Cambrian, it marked the closing down of the locomotive sheds at Oswestry and Aberystwyth and the transfer of the entire remaining Manor class locomotives to Shrewsbury. For a brief period they continued to work over Cambrian metals from the latter depot, until finally the surviving stud were condemned and awaited their fate. Locomotivemen, with the exception of some Shrewsbury drivers, were one hundred per cent Western bred, and naturally mourned the passing of the most favoured locomotives ever to have worked the system. There were the odd one or two men who preferred the replacement Standard 4-6-0 Class 4 75XXX series. Driver Bill (Merthyr) Jones, of Machynlleth Shed was such a one.

At that time my impending departure from Cardiganshire was close at hand, and the tide of time was running out fast. The tiresome business of winding up my practice had resulted in my working irregular hours which culminated in my using a car and forsaking my normal railway travel. However, one summer evening, fate sent me back to my past and a more pleasant form of transport. Clad in the palest of grey suits I darted on to No 2 Platform at Aberystwyth to board the 'up' 6p.m. mail train, (then known as the Aberystwyth—York mail) with about two minutes to spare. Spotting an empty compartment I was about to jump in when suddenly I heard my christian name being called out way up the platform. Normally my usual routine would allow at least ten minutes before departure to inspect the locomotive and have a chat with my chums up in front. That evening I recognised Driver Evan Hughes standing alongside an unidentified Manor class locomotive, furiously beckoning to me. In a flash his message was read and without a moment's hesitation I took to my heels and sped up the platform.

—Evan said, 'Take it easy, we won't go without you,' then from the opposite side of the footplate one of my old Inspector friends appeared, clad in his customary blue dust coat and brown trilby hat.
—'Come on up and come for a ride, he said. They're trying to get rid of us all, I'm on the way out and what better way to go.'

Such an invitaion did not require the slightest hesitation and within a split second I was up and over the fireman's side of the cab. Just as we got away Evan shouted across to me. 'You won't see this one again. She's being given the chop.'
The locomotive was an old favourite, No. 7802 *Bradley Manor*, very begrimed, minus both her official name and number plates, but her number had been crudely scrawled in chalk across the cab side. Yet she lived up to her past reputation, as strong as ever. In spite

of my unsuitable attire it was wonderful to be back up in front again, especially in the company of old friends, though intuition told me this was the end of the road and my 'swansong' on the Cambrian.

Over the years the odd few miles to Borth had become engraved in my mind, so much so that I could have told, blindfolded, exactly where we were by the feel of the road, the working of the locomotive and the click of the rail joints, but that evening I drank in every inch of that 'up' run to Borth. I remember looking down at the wooden fencing as we passed Plas-Crug crossings — that was where it had all begun. They were not as white as they used to be, but had outlived Lewis Rees, the Cambrian and the GWR. *Bradley Manor* must have been near to the 75,000 mileage mark, probably even over, but ran like a hare down Borth bank, even to the extent of putting a 75 Standard 4-6-0 Class 4 series to shame.

All too soon my short run had ended. Ynyslas, my station of the past, had already fallen; the buildings still stood but only the 'up' main was operative. The signal box was boarded up, and the only form of human activity was the solitary crossing keeper; alas not even a passing loop. Down on the platform at Borth, I bade farewell and gave grateful thanks to my companions. My Inspector friend I have not seen since, but I understand he is happy in retirement, whilst for Evan it was not goodbye locomotivewise. Later, in exile, I was enjoying his company on yet another trip to Devil's Bridge aboard locomotive No. 7, one of the last reminders of steam on Cambrian metals.

Evan was ample in structure but of a gentle nature, distinguished latterly by his beard. He was the son-in-law of the late Richard Putt, a well-known character in Aberystwyth, who from the age of eleven years remained faithful throughout his life to our family dental practice, almost a blood relative; thus, there was something very special about Evan. Tragically he died recently, and is sadly missed by his comrades at Aberystwyth.

Unfortunately, I was never to see No. 7802 again; her death sentence fell but a few days later. Over the years some of the younger and possibly brazen enthusiasts informed me that she still stood silent and rotting in the Barry cemetery. Today, possibly, I have become a sentimentalist to the extreme, yet no pilgrimage to that graveyard was ever one of my ambitions. My visualisation was indeed somewhat parallel to hoisting a skeleton above a grave stone in a churchyard. (N.B. Locomotive No. 7802 *Bradley Manor* has been rescued from the breaker's yard and is in the process of being restored at the Severn Valley Railway's headquarters).

That evening, as my wife drove me home to Ynyslas by car, it was still possible to follow the passage northwards of that 'up' mail train as she threaded her way alongside the endless saltings of the Dyfi Estuary. Silently, I thought to myself what a perfect way to end a chapter in one's life. Much later that same evening as the sun sank in the west, alone I wandered, with no real purpose, on to the sand dunes, and finally the fairways of the seaside golf links. Meditation lay undeniably with my apparent last steam run and, in spite of a crushed outlook, I took heart that my last run had been on the Cambrian.

There had been many exciting footplate runs on the main lines on some of the most powerful express locomotives, yet none were sweeter than aboard the smaller-wheeled engines working the Cambrian lines. I cannot deny that the men of Aberystwyth and Machynlleth, on occasions, gave me some buckshee rides — today it is water under the bridge; the majority of my companions have retired and some have passed on; they were a wonderful breed and trusted me. In return, I never tried to take advantage of their generosity and kept my ex-

ploits silent. Way back in my youth Uncle Lewis, and later the men of the banking engines at Bromsgrove, had taught me the rules of the footplate. Rightly or wrongly, I was not the first to be treated to a free ride, but possibly one of the last in the Cambrian steam era. It is therefore in a form of tribute to those men that I now break my silence.

Retracing my steps across the deserted golf links, my idle wanderings ended on the seventh hole; a par three. One could always get into a vast amount of trouble before reaching this particular hole. The tee was cut out of a hill side, possibly the only rising gradient in Ynyslas, namely Moel-Ynys (The hill of Ynys). Many years previously an old and faithful member had presented the club with a beautiful teak rectangular seat, which for years rested at the back of the tee with the appropriate inscription: 'Rest and be Thankful'. That night, those simple words could well have been chosen specially for myself.

Chapter 14
Exiled

Invariably, the saddest part of a really good party is the end. Such was my case on the Cambrian way back in May 1966. Steam that remained was already sparse, only the 'up' and 'down' 'Cambrian Coast Express' trains and goods workings were the sole survivors of that form of traction. All other services had the new look in the form of diesel multiple units; the end of a long tradition was drawing to a close.

After long and considerable thought I finally decided to leave the shores of Cardigan Bay and repitch my tent on the unfamiliar plains of Hampshire, in the Southern Region. At that time, the Weymouth—Bournemouth—Waterloo lines had been designated as steam-hauled until July 1968. Both the Aberystwyth and Machynlleth enginemen openly stated that my trek south was entirely due to my ultimate thirst for steam to the bitter end. It was a nice thought from old friends — but not true. Far greater issues were at stake; yet undeniably another two years of steam was a slight consolation for all the upheavals of moving.

The Southern was, however, no stranger. Guy's Hospital sits virtually beneath London Bridge Station, so that I was familiar with many of their locomotives, either working to Charing Cross and Cannon Street stations, or to the south-east. Again, towards the end of the war, I returned to my brethren — this time as a patient at one of her sector hospitals at Orpington. After considerable surgery and a stay of nearly seven months in her tender care, I was able to renew my acquaintance with the 'King Arthurs', those classical 4-4-0 'Schools' class engines and a variety of locomotives, as they pounded their way up the bank from Orpington to Knockholt — alongside the hospital. On my final return to the south, the rebuilt 'Merchant Navy' and 'West Country' class locomotives were newcomers to me. Sadly, by this time they had seen better days and were now very run down and uncared for. Occasions arose when I watched them slip violently in an attempt to get away from Brockenhurst up Sway Bank to the west, on the Bournemouth to Waterloo line. A few abortive attempts were made to photograph them, but my past background was missing and the adrenalin would not flow.

One evening, an obvious Southern enthusiast remarked that the stiffer climb was from Christchurch to Hinton Admiral in the opposite direction. Being a relative newcomer to the south and not wanting to cross swords, I held my peace, but silently wondered what Cambrian men would have thought of that bank — merely downhill running to them — and inwardly I gloated when I thought of the tortuous Talerddig and Trawscoed climbs, especially with eleven or twelve on. However, in all fairness to the Southern Region, it was, already in spite of a long reprieve, the same dismal picture on their pitch. I had seen it all before on the

Cambrian when steam was doomed. How some of the main line locomotives carried on was a miracle; the shabbiest return for years of gallant service. David Shepherd with the skill of his brush, depicted the true state of affairs in his classic work, 'Nine Elms'.

Although miles away from my native heath, two little incidents took place — reminders of the past, and as if the Cambrian was restaking her claim. When I finally decided to reorganise my life, the prospects were exciting, but I did feel that I was somewhat of a 'Judas', especially so, deserting the system in its dying hours of steam. Now safely installed in the south, one evening over a glass of ale, my fellow companion casually mentioned that a new stationmaster or, more correctly speaking — Area Manager, had arrived at Brockenhurst, and apparently his previous station had been Barmouth. The following morning, poste haste, my first port of call was Brockenhurst, hurriedly inquiring from the ticket collector the name of his new boss.

'Mr Trodgen, he's a Western man. He's in his office, second door on the right'.

Almost brushing aside my helpful informer, I burst into the Area Manager's office. Mr Trodgen, whom I had not met before, rose from his desk, obviously taken aback by my unheralded entry.

Before he could utter a word, I blurted out: 'You won't know me, but I gather you were on the Cambrian at Barmouth'.

Immediately he relaxed and with a knowing smile said, 'You must be . . .,' quoting both my christian and surname.

Completely dumbfounded, I replied: 'How did you know that?'

'Ah,' he responded, 'we have a mutal friend; Oliver Veltom. He's already rung me up and told me all about you, and if we had not already met he said it would not be very long!'

Here was a Cambrian man. Within seconds we were talking about Tom, Dick and Harry. 'How was Barmouth Bridge?' 'Did the school train still call at Dyffryn Ardudwy', and so on. Unfortunately, my new-found Cambrian companion's stay was very short and he moved on to a higher appointment at Waterloo.

The Cambrian was not going to release her strangle hold on me that easily. A few months later I was waiting on the platform at Brockenhurst for the Lymington Harbour branch train, and it drew into the platform headed by a BR Class 4, 2-6-4 tank engine, almost unbelievably, it was none other than No. 80096, still with Machynlleth shed plates on her smokebox door. I rushed up to her ageing driver, who must have been coming up to retirement, and excitedly inquired what she was like.

'She's a stranger; not had her before,' was the reply, but in spite of her very shabby outward appearance, she ran beautifully, bunker first, to Lymington Town. It was the first time I have ever patted the cabside of a locomotive on climbing down from her footplate.

Back on the Cambrian, March 1967 saw the last steam working. It fell to Leslie Milverton, an Aberystwyth driver, to work the last steam engine out of the southern terminus. BR Standard Class 4 No. 75033 was the locomotive. Thus, the curtain was brought down on Cambrian steam, — one of the saddest of days in her history. Although miles away from that scene of remorse, I lived every dying moment of Les Milverton's final steam run, almost as if I was up in front with him again. That evening, the rest of my family had gone out, and as I pottered around the house my thoughts were constantly with the progress of that 'up' last steam mail train, and as each minute passed, I was there. I could smell the aroma of the footplate, her characteristic rattle was in my ears as she ran down Borth Bank; again that old familiar rumble of the past as she crossed Afon-Leri at Ynyslas. Again and again, the bark of her exhaust rang out through a silent house as she topped Talerddig Bank. I rode with her down the winding road to what was once Moat Lane Junction, and along the banks of the River Severn to Welshpool. Finally, the last climb up Breiddon Bank to Westbury before handing over to Shrewsbury men. What were Leslie Milverton's thoughts as he finally climbed down for the last time from that almost human iron horse? Did he quietly mutter to himself, 'Cheerio, old girl', or 'well done'? Knowing Leslie, the answer is definitely, 'Yes'.

Later that evening, my watch told me No. 75033 had completed her run. What future lay ahead for her? Already the hangman's rope was near her neck. Would she be permitted a few more hours of reprieve at some last stronghold of steam, or would it be sudden death? I never knew or even tried to find out; this was the end — well and truly nightfall on steam.

Sitting back and filling my pipe, I thought, 'Well, that is that — there must always be an end', but automatically, my thoughts drifted back to that final day. Given the opportunity would I, or would I not have liked to have been with Leslie Milverton on his last run? No, I was glad I was not there at the kill. Intuition told me that all through that sad day, a battery of cameras would have fired away from every bridge and embankment, as No. 75033 made her last 'up' and 'down' runs between Shrewsbury and Aberystwyth. No, I wanted to recall the Cambrian in my memories as I knew her; that of peace, isolation, superb scenery and railway freedom beyond the realms of possibility.

A year or so later, in the autumn, I returned to Wales and Cambrian territory for a short spell, fully prepared to find many changes. Railway periodicals and the press had kept me reasonably abreast of what was going on. Aberystwyth was my first port of call, and aware that alterations must be expected, I wandered on to her platforms. It is one thing to live with changes, as day after day once accepts and even becomes acclimatised to them to such a degree that often the original picture becomes obliterated, but what I saw that day was far more than I had anticipated. It was a complete transformation from what I had recollected of the past; a deserted station with not a sign of life. There were empty platforms and barren tracks, and the carriage and goods sidings were lifeless and devoid of rolling stock. Completely stunned, I wandered down No. 2 Platform; of course steam was a thing of the past, but that awful silence — was it the fact that sounds of a past pannier tank, with those short sharp beats of her exhaust, were now absent, or the squeal of bogies as coaching stock were stabled into their berths, or perhaps it was the lack of the sound of trucks being marshalled? No, it was something far deeper. Ironically, as a reminder of the past, a good old 'south-wester' was blowing, but that wind now rang a different tune; it was mournful, like the wind through an empty cell. The transformation was way beyond my anticipation. Hurriedly, I sought my car and drove north. Bow Street, as a station, was no more, just a coal depot, whilst the station building at Llandre still stood — but that was all. Shocks were coming too quickly; so much so that I dared not look at Borth Station and continued northwards. Running alongside the golf links, I suddenly spotted a two coach d.m.u. heading south. It appeared to be empty as it coasted past Box 87 and Borth distant signal — but it was something alive.

Within minutes, greater shocks were in store. Ynyslas itself, had become commercialised beyond recognition. Even my station had been bulldozed flat; nothing remained but a few remnants of the 'up' platform, whilst the 'up' main line had been slewed over as a single track to afford a better run through. Those massive level crossing gates that I used to put a shoulder to, had long since departed. The media had told me that twice, early goods trains had ploughed through them — possibly poetic justice — but their memorial was now an unmarred crossing with unfamiliar flashing lights. It was difficult to digest this complete and utter slaughter.

Later that day, I decided to go to Machynlleth; it was the same story, no sign of life except for a solitary d.m.u., belching out black fumes, sitting in what I used to call the 'coast loop'. However, by this time I had become accustomed and prepared for these sweeping changes which I had encountered all the way north from Aberystwyth, and began to ask myself the whys and wherefores. Signals — where had all the previous ex-GWR and the few remaining long-armed Cambrian lower quadrants gone? There were now upper quadrants everywhere. Was partisanship still rife or had the previous signals rotted overnight? Possibly the cutting out of stations and loops had resulted in a surplus of unwanted lower quadrant types.

Finally, I decided to have a fleeting glance at the coast road and pressed on to Aberdovey. The gale had blown itself out, and the seafront was already bathed in brilliant sunshine. Aberdovey is a fascinating little place, unspoilt and always blessed with the best of weather with a southern aspect, yet the powers that be have been very long-sighted — no squallor here. Its fascinating features have wisely been retained, but alas the station is battered and boarded up, with broken windows and no paint; in fact something resembling the 'Wild West'. Enough is enough, I thought, it was obviously the same everywhere. Disappointed, even down-hearted, I retraced my steps to an enchanted cottage tucked away on the foothills of Plynlimon near to Taliesin's grave — that famed Welsh poet of the past.

That night, as I lay in my bed with windows open, inhaling the soft pure air, my thoughts momentarily drifted back to the railway and the slaughter I had discovered; her future was a dismal image. As I turned one thing after another over in my mind, the sound of a tumbling waterfall lulled me off into oblivion and another world — way beyond that of the Cambrian.

For the next week I climbed the mountains, and only got glimpses of the railway from far away heights. Time and man had not changed the latter. The last day of my stay in that haven of peace was one of those typically damp Welsh Sundays, a day that neither kept one indoors or out. Heavy grey clouds hung low over the Cambrian Mountains yet, as I have so often recalled in the past, the wind would freshen by evening and veer to the north-west. That evening, almost as if on request, the heavy clouds rolled away and once again the surrounding mountains stood out an inky blue; I felt I could almost reach out and touch them. Momentarily, the Dyfi Estuary became a blaze of fire as the sun sank in the west. Here was an invitation not to be turned aside, so I

decided to have a last look at one of my favourite past haunts and set out to walk the banks of the Afon Clettwr to Trer-ddol Railway Bridge, way out on the marshes. A vast amount of water had passed under that wooden structure since I last visited that lonely spot, yet time had not changed her. Nostalgic voices drifted across that incredulous space of the marshes; very noticeable was the haunting cry of the curlew, while the dunlins and oyster-catchers, as if in appreciation, appeared to accelerate their endless chatter. Amongst this clamour, across the waters of an ebb tide, the bells of Aberdovey rang out clearly. There is the fascinating Welsh word of 'Hireath', which means longing. Intoxicated with the surroundings, and with my lungs full of sea air, surely this was it to its cup full. Climbing the stile, I walked beside the thinly rust-coated track, and gazed down at the tidal waters as they swirled under the bridge. There were no Sunday trains now, but that evening, alone on that bridge, it was as if the clock had been turned back so much so that once again I heard the bark of a 'Manor' class engine; again I saw a little 'Duke' class engine running fast, and finally I smelt that unmistakable smell of Cambrian smoke. I read and re-read the old notice-board 'Trespassers will be prosecuted — by order'. It had stood there for many years and, in spite of many coats of obliterating black paint, the words at the top 'Cambrian Railways', stood out foremost. I took heart, and suddenly my recent apprehension melted into the surroundings — surely, while rails remain, so will the Cambrian spirit live on.

When treading my steps homeward in the twilight, I became doubly aware how very green was my Cambrian territory and that possibly I was back where I belonged; 'Mae hen wlad fynhadau', which means 'Land of my Fathers'. The following day I set out on the long trek back to the south, and momentarily, when crossing the border and looking back at the distant blue hills, I thought, 'Ah yes, they would be there when I next returned; but the Cambrian, who knows. Only time will tell'.

BR 2-6-2 Standard tank No. 82034 is pictured in steam on the 'back road' at Machynlleth Shed.

P. Dalton

No. 75003, a BR Standard 4-6-0, takes the coast loop at Dovey Junction.

P. Dalton

Chapter 15
Some Incidents on the Footplate

Recently, an old friend said to me, 'You have done a lot of running on the ex-Cambrian lines — surely you must have had many amusing or exciting moments on the footplate.' He was correct in the first instance, when referring to the mileage runs, but strangely enough there were very few out of the ordinary incidents, except for the odd case of a fractured water glass or, on the rarest of occasions, the missing or dropping of the token. Of course, on a line such as the Cambrian, there was always the thrill of descending some of the steep banks at speed.

One evening, just after the Standard Class 4 (75000 series) locomotives first appeared at Oswestry, the late Driver Llew Jones took me by the arm, on the platform at Aberystwyth, and said, 'Look what we have got here' when escorting me up to BR Standard Class 4 No. 75023. She looked a picture, in her fully lined out black livery; in fact almost brand-new. Llew continued, 'Come on up'. Needless to say, I refrained from mentioning that I had already ridden her the previous night. A set of Aberystwyth men always worked the mail train for a week, except a Wednesday night when they enjoyed a rest or 'spiv' day; hence Llew's presence on that particular evening. I am certain that his regular mate, Mike Evans, no longer in railway service, was present. Llew was a first class engineman, but a bit of a flyer, and was obviously fascinated with his new machine, wandering around the footplate inquisitively like a person with a new motor car. We got away, albeit with one short spasm of slipping, and all went well up to Llandre.

Llew, without doubt, was now full of confidence with his new steed, and away we went at breakneck speed on the sudden drop to Borth. These locomotives were fitted with speedometers, although they were never reliable, and as I stood behind Llew, Borth appeared to race to meet us. I watched him make the brake application, but we kept going, and I experienced quite the fastest descent I had ever made. Borth platform raced past us and we eventually came to a grinding halt, with the tail lamp of the last van just short of the north end of the 'up' platform. It was the one and only occasion I can recall where we had to set back at that station. Undaunted, Llew set off in great style for the next few miles to Ynyslas, finally putting me down on the platform at the latter station almost in true taxi style.

I also recall that on one evening, when aboard No. 75005, I witnessed a partial blow back; unfortunately, the fireman was attending to the fire, and had the hair on his hands and arms badly singed.

Turning to the comical side, the late Jack James, then in the 'top link' at Aberystwyth, could suitably be described as upredictable. One morning, when aboard Vale of Rheidol locomotive No. 8 *Llywelyn*, as she duly rounded the original river curve south of the Aberystwyth football ground on an 'up' train to Devil's Bridge, Jack shouted to his mate 'Keep her going', and jumped down from the footplate and grabbed an old motor tyre lying on one of the allotments alongside the track. As quickly as he had jumped off, he was back up on the footplate, having slung the tyre on top of the locomotive's side tank, and took up his position behind the regulator. It was presumed that he had collected the tyre for one of his boatmen friends, and the 'up' journey towards Devil's Bridge proceeded without anything out of the ordinary happening. However, strange things were about to happen. Just above the old Rheidol lead mine, Jack brought his train to a halt, climbed down, grabbed his motor tyre and wandered off to a sharp ledge of rock overhanging the gorge which was hundreds of feet below. Not a word was said as we silently watched with our mouths open in dismay. The guard, Jack Holland, was already down on the track, while a handful of bewildered passengers had their heads stuck out of carriage windows. Unconcerned, Jack poised himself on the piece of rock and, after taking careful aim, set his tyre in motion. Away it went, gathering speed with terrific leaps as it hit each piece of rock on its downward path, finally jumping over trees before it vanished out of sight down the ravine far below. Jack then returned to his locomotive, with delight and amusement written all over his face. He never said a word but just climbed aboard and sounded the whistle. He gently opened the regulator and got his train moving without a trace of a slip and, what is more, arrived at Devil's Bridge dead on time. That was Jack, a man with whom one never knew what would happen next.

From the point of drama in my personal experiences those were but mild, so I must leave the Cambrian and move away to another region. The London Midland Region had very kindly granted me footplate facilities on the three cylinder 'Jubilee' class locomotives; these being the graceful locomotives that worked the Birmingham (New Street) to Euston trains, a journey timed at two hours. Believe me, for that class of locomotive, it was a very tight margin, although the first of these runs was made from Wolverhampton (High Level) to Euston. Eventually, the train drew into the 'up' platform headed by No. 45733 *Novelty*, with the locomotive coming to a standstill way off the platform. A hurried glance up and down the platform showed no sign of the presumed inspector to accompany me, and as the hour of departure drew dangerously near, I made my way down the track shouting up to her crew, 'I'm coming with you' and, at the same time, waving my locomotive pass. Driver Radford, from Bescot, had a look at my pass. 'Where is the Inspector?' I enquired. 'Don't know,' was his reply, 'but you're on the right train.' In the nick of time his mate, who was watching the platform, shouted out, 'Here he is, it's Jack Allan.' A hurried exchange of handshakes took place and we were away; I glanced at the fire and thought to myself, 'we won't go far on that'. However, I had forgotten I was on an LMR locomotive to which thin fires, little and often and hard coal, were the norm, this being the reverse procedure from a Western Region engine.

We called at Dudley Port for a few minutes, where Jack Allan came across to my side of the cab saying 'I'm sorry I was a bit late. Hell of a train, this one — something always happens.' He carried on 'I've been off sick for six weeks. The last time I rode this one, a piece of coal from a passing train, near Rugby, hit me on the head'. I thought to myself, what a start, and the first bit of drama was not many minutes away.

We drifted quietly out of Monument Lane Tunnel on to one of the many platform roads at Birmingham (New Street). Suddenly, to my horror, there was the tail end of a 'Black Five' standing at the top end of our road. I grabbed Jack Allan's arm, saying, 'Look!' He turned to me, totally unconcerned, and said, 'Yes, we are being doubleheaded to Rugby.'

It was a very slick operation as we drew up behind her, coupled up and were away in no time. Now, the LMR permitted some workings which would have been unheard of in my more familiar Western Region world. Indeed, I recall a few weeks earlier being granted passes for a day on the banking engines at Bromsgrove. Here again, unfamiliar workings were in operation although possibly, they were long-standing manoeuvres which I had forgotten since my school-days. For example, engines were assisting trains up the bank without being coupled up and again, it was no unusual sight to see several banking engines sitting in the Blackwell sidings waiting to get the road back to Bromsgrove South.

On my latter visit to Bromsgrove, having ridden up the bank on the great engine herself (now renumbered 58100), we found four 'Jinties' sitting in the sidings. The 'down' road was clear and 'Big Bertha' crossed over on to the 'down' road, followed by the four little 'Jinties' which were not coupled up. Therefore five of us ran gracefully back, presumably on the steam brake of the great old lady. Such manoeuvres on the Western Region would call for the severest of reprimands, or possibly the sack.

After my hair-raising experience at Birmingham (New Street), we ran beautifully, and kept well within the schedule. However, it was not to be the end, drama-wise. Just as we plunged into Weedon Tunnel I saw a flock of sheep cross the tunnel mouth. The next moment we were in the dark, then we emerged faultlessly into daylight. The final run into Euston was most spectacular on the falling gradients all the way from Tring. It was most interesting passing Harrow & Wealdstone, on the 'up' fast, as it was not long after that ghastly pile up, and I was given an excellent view of her signals from the fireman's side of the cab, when travelling at close on 60m.p.h. I had formed two possible causes of that disaster which, oddly enough, coincided with those of Jack Allan. However, no further comments on that issue.

On arrival at Euston, Jack Allan asked me if I had seen the sheep at Weedon to which I replied 'Yes', how many were there?' An inspection of the front end of the locomotive showed no signs or remains of slaughter. Jack said quietly, 'I didn't say anything to the driver, I did not want to upset him. Anyway they must have been moving fast.'

Having a considerable time to hang around Euston before returning to the Midlands on a 'down' express, Jack and I retired to the refreshment room where he told me his life history. His early driving days were spent on LNWR engines of which he said, 'They were sparse and crude on the footplate, but how you could hammer them. They thrived on a good thrashing'. One of his tales was highly amusing. Apparently he had worked a special up to Euston on a particular locomotive, named either *Llandudno* or *Colwyn Bay*; anyway, on arrival at Euston, his mate was taken sick and was unfit for duty on the return run. Being a Bank Holiday, it was difficult to find a replacement but eventually a young lad, more or less a passed cleaner, was assigned to the task. Jack told him not to panic but to fill up the box, and all would be well. It was, I gather, a tight margin back to the Midlands due to the locomotive riding a bit rough. All went well at first, but half-way up the climb to Tring, they began to lose time. Jack was impelled to open her up, resulting in the unfortunate kid losing his nerve and wanting to jump for it. Jack described, most realistically, his impossible task of getting the best out of his bucking locomotive, keeping an eye open for signals and attending to the fire all the way back to Birmingham, whilst his other hand was hanging on to the shirt tails of his horror-stricken new mate. Apparently the latter, very soon after that outing, threw in the towel and terminated his railway career.

Our return run to Wolverhampton was made on the footplate of 'Jubilee' class No. 45676 *Codrington* which was manned by a Camden crew. Just before we climbed aboard, almost as if to restore my confidence, Jack remarked, 'I remember riding this same train, and as we approached Bushey a bloke ran out of the bushes and laid his head on the line as cool as a cucumber. There was nothing we could do running fast . . . off it went!' 'Here we go again', I thought to myself. However, our 'down' run as far as Birmingham was above reproach, although the riding of No. 45676 was not as good as that of No. 45733 on the 'up' run. We had a very reasonable wait of at least ten minutes at Birmingham (New Street), so Jack and I got down on the platform to stretch our legs and watched what appeared to be coloured members of the railway staff sweeping down the upper surfaces of the platform verandas. Clouds of black soot, empty beer cans, and what have you, came crashing down on to the deserted platforms. Jack suddenly remarked, 'It's not safe around here, we should all wear tin hats'. That was the prelude for the last spot of drama.

It was a very hot midsummer's day as we approached Dudley Port with the locomotive working hard. Suddenly, half a brick came through the open vent in the cab roof and shattered on the footplate floor. Fortunately,

Jack was standing behind the driver, while I was in the other corner with the fireman. It was a very good aim by, I presume, some evil-minded youth, as we were about to pass under an overbridge.

'What did I tell you?' Please shut up for the last few miles'. I knew him well enough by now. This he did, and so ended my baptism with the 'Jubilee' class. However, subsequent runs in Jack Allan's company were faultless — obviously these were not any of his particular 'bogey trains'.

This irresponsible action by young people undoubtedly still goes on, not only involving brick throwing but even attempts to sabotage the track. It is a very alarming state of affairs. Indirectly, there was a similar occasion when riding 'King' class locomotive No. 6005 *King George II* from Wolverhampton (Low Level) to Paddington. My old friend, Driver Bob Plant (with a typical Staffordshire surname) was in charge and yet another old companion, Inspector Bill Parcell, was my guardian. It was a good run, being uneventful except for picking up water. We dropped the scoop at Hatton Troughs and took little on, repeating the process south of Bicester and finally at Denham.

Later, at Ranelagh Bridge Yard, it was discovered that the scoop had obviously hit something, presumably at Hatton Troughs, and had become buckled. It was hammered out, as a temporary measure, but when working the ex-2.10p.m. service out of Paddington, the same thing happened when the scoop was lowered at Denham. We subsequently stopped for water alongside the water-column at Banbury, and again at Leamington Spa.

Later, when we were back at Wolverhampton, Bill and I were wandering down the platform when we spotted Chief Inspector George Holland sitting on a seat looking as if he had the cares of the world on his shoulders. 'What are you doing here, George?' asked Bill. 'Having a rest,' replied George drily. 'Anyway, where have you both been?' 'Padd.,' said Bill. 'What did you have, and what train?' '8.33 and 'down' 2.10, with No. 6005'. 'What about you?' 'The one before you; bloody *North Star*, buckled her scoop up on Hatton Troughs after some kid threw a brick near the Hawthorns and smashed the cabside window, cutting the driver's face. Anyway, the police got the little bugger.' George seemed, however, to take heart when he learned we had suffered a similar fate, albeit to a lesser degree. As it turned out, I never knew the end of the water trough hazard.

Tunnels, I must admit, were never my favourite places, being long dirty black holes containing a foul stench which I always seemed to think we hit with a bang, especially when running at speed. However, in spite of my firm dislike, there could also be the element of thrill. I remember riding a 'Hall' class engine which, strangely enough, carried my surname. It was *Dalton Hall*. Once again, I was with my old friend Bill Parcell. For a spell, at that time, I seemed to ride everywhere in his company. Anyway we had, on that occasion, worked a very round-about trip on a variety of locomotives and, in this particular instance, were about to enter the 'Big Hole' or Severn Tunnel from the English side. There is quite a drop in this tunnel, with a nasty well before coming up again on the Welsh side, and it was here that Bill apparently said to the driver, 'Give him a bit of a run down through the tunnel'. The driver certainly granted that request and I was thankful to emerge on the Welsh side, having already passed an 'up' South Wales coal train working hard and banking in the pit of the tunnel. Later, as we coasted along to Newport, Bill told me what he had said to the driver, but admitted he had put the wind up himself too!

Inspector Harry Smith, from Worcester, made the same request for my benefit on the footplate of 'Castle' class locomotive No. 7007, which bore the proud name *Great Western* and was possibly the pride of Worcester Shed. It was working the 'down' 'Cathedrals Express', with which Driver Widdowson made a fantastic start from Chipping Campden. Away we went into the tunnel which we were through in no time, although it was not always quite as quick and healthy in the reverse direction. However, with her nose to her stable, No. 7007 really flew down Honeybourne Bank with her speed well into the nineties; a 'Castle', once in her stride, could really move, due to those 6ft. 9in. driving wheels. That thrilling dash quickly wiped out my tunnel dislikes and, what is more, we bagged a brace of pheasant before coming to a halt at Evesham.

Throughout my many hours on the footplate I have never found two drivers alike, as each would differ in some small way. There were the 'wide open regulator' boys, whilst others had a 'Peter Pan' touch. Stances would vary, even when sitting or standing, as did the manner in which they would acknowledge signals. Some would chat away throughout a run or, conversely, others would not utter a single word. An example comes to mind concerning a trip on 'King' class locomotive No. 6001, *King Edward VII*, again in the company of my old friend Inspector Bill Parcell. The train was the 'up' 8.33a.m. Wolverhampton to Paddington working and, on that occasion, I stood behind the driver for the entire journey. It was an excellent run all the way up to Old Oak Common but then we suffered a series of checks which resulted in an eventual three minutes late arrival. The driver had not said one word throughout the journey, but as we came to a halt and he wound the reversing gear to neutral position, he took out his watch and quietly said to me, 'The passengers won't be very pleased with us today.' Originally, we had decided to return to Wolverhampton with the same crew and engine working the 'down' 2.10p.m., but with a few minutes to spare we caught the 'down' 'Cambrian Coast Express', headed by 'Castle' class No. 4094 *Dynevor Castle*. Once again I took up my position behind the driver who also stood, and in sharp contrast to my previous host, he never stopped talking. We suffered quite a few checks, but he bawled and shouted at everyone up and down the line almost to a degree of embarrassment. Some crews adopted or inherited little rituals which I have often heard spoken of and must now be legend. An example comes to mind on one of my footplate trips on the London Midland Region on the West Coast route.

I had been granted facilities to ride those beautiful Stanier Pacifics, designed by Sir William F. Stanier. On this occasion, my actual run was from Birmingham (New Street) to Carlisle, once again in the pleasant company of Inspector Jack Allan from Bescot. We had an excellent run as far as Crewe, on rebuilt 'Royal Scot' class No. 46120 *Royal Inniskilling Fusilier*, but from Crewe our train was worked forward by 'Coronation' class No. 46243 *City of Lancaster*. As we waited on the platform for the locomotive, one of the largest of LMR engines, to back on to her train of seventeen coaches, Jack Allan told me, 'We shall have Glasgow boys on her; they are all right, but probably you won't understand a word they say'.

We duly climbed aboard and the usual introductions took place; I received the merest dry nod from the driver. We hung about with no sign of a start, possibly this being the reason for his seemingly unfriendly attitude, but there was quite a tense atmosphere on the footplate. Later, at Carlisle, I gathered that the driver was not too pleased because the 'down' 'Royal Scot' had been given the road with only fifteen on. I muttered something to the driver as we approached Runcorn, but either I was completely ignored or possibly he did not hear, or perhaps could not interpret my dialect. However, all went well as we progressed north, in spite of a series of pitfall slacks. We were checked a couple of times at Lancaster, this being the start of the great climb to Shap Summit. Incidentally, up to this stage, neither driver nor fireman had exchanged a word. No. 46243 *City of Lancaster* made an excellent climb considering everything, and we eventually approached Tebay. Now the driver was perfectly entitled to a banker here, for the last few miles to Shap Summit, but naturally I did not dare ask him, at this stage, if he was going to call for assistance. However, my curiosity was to be short-lived, for he thundered round the curve of Tebay Station with no easing. Obviously the same thoughts had been running through Jack Allan's mind and, unobserved, he gave me a little nod from the other side of the footplate.

Speed dropped as we pounded our way up the last lap and past the tall signal of Scot Green, finally labouring over Shap Summit at 21m.p.h. In theatrical style, the driver turned to his mate and bowed; this act apparently stems way back to LNWR days, yet it was really something to witness. However, the most amazing thing was the immediate change of atmosphere on the footplate. As we drifted down the falling gradients through Penrith to Carlisle, the wee Scots driver turned round, filled his pipe, and chatted away to me non-stop. Anyone would have thought we were lifelong pals.

Down on the platform in Carlisle, I said to Jack Allan, 'Well, that's the best yet.' He smiled and said, 'I told

you, they are a rum lot, but good enginemen. I've seen that act many times, but he went through Preston a bit sharp — platform road too.'

In the case of enginemen getting upset, happily, in my experience, these instances were few and far between. However, one little example took place on the Cambrian. One morning, while sitting in the box at Ynyslas waiting for the 'down' 8.10a.m. passenger train which daily conveyed me to work in Aberystwyth, an empty stock train of eight bogies drew to a halt on the 'up' main. Signalman Bill Evans went down to pick up the token, and it was apparent from the box that a somewhat heated argument followed between him and the driver. The particular driver has since passed on, so shall be nameless, but I knew him well, having ridden many a mile with him, and he was always extremely kind to me. Eventually Bill returned to the box.

'What's up, Bill?' I enquired. 'Something has upset him', Bill replied, 'and he's one of the nicest chaps. He wants the road, but I've told him the 'down' passenger has got priority. He says he's short of water, but I've pointed out he's already passed a column at Borth. Anyway, it will all pass — I've seen him like this before.'

Apparently the empty stock was going to be stabled at Aberdovey, but another interesting feature of that little episode was the locomotive; it was the one and only occasion on which I had noted one of the larger 8100 class 2-6-2 tanks working north or Aberystwyth. Towards the end of steam they became regular performers on the Carmarthen branch to the south of Aberystwyth.

The enginemen were a wonderful breed, who always made me welcome on the footplate. Many still remain the greatest of friends and still communicate with me, even in retirement, and I sincerely hope the younger generation are the same. Of course, my enthusiasm died with the death of steam, and although diesel traction is more practical and, until recently, more economical, to my mind, the romance and human touch has gone, and this view is shared by many of the senior steam drivers.

After the very recent wash-out in the Dyfi Valley, one Sunday morning, I walked from Trer-ddol Bridge to Glandyfi to survey the destruction, and quite near to the latter station came upon a stationary ballast train headed by a diesel locomotive; its class or type conveyed nothing to me. Its driver was one of many of my Machynlleth pals, who shouted down to me, 'Come on up, Pat.'

Subsequently, we spent nearly three-quarters of an hour chatting away about the old days and previous wash-outs. Finally I asked, 'How do you like these things, Len?', referring to his diesel locomotive. 'Well, you come home clean, the missus is better-tempered about the washing, and going up Talerddig you are not always watching the needle; but they are not the same. I miss the old steamers, brought up on them, get a failure on one of these, you've had it, but nine times out of ten you could coax the steamer home. Not often they let you down.' Another old friend, Jackie Jones, met me and said, 'No. 7819 has been saved from the scrap-yard

No. 7819 *Hinton Manor* heads the 'up' 'Cambrian Coast Express' out of Dovey Junction.

P. Dalton

and is back on the Severn Valley line. I would love to have her regulator again.' To those of us who were brought up on and loved the steam age, such remarks ring very true. However, mention must be made of a not so pleasant incident which gives food for thought.

Quite recently, I had travelled up 'on the cushions' from Brockenhurst to Waterloo aboard one of the semi-fast electric sets. There was some excellent running, with a prompt arrival at Waterloo. As I got down on to the platform I noticed, on the adjacent track, what I presumed to be one of the largest diesel locomotives. Time was on my side so, out of sheer curiosity, I made a closer inspection. Finding myself vaguely interested, I inquired of the driver what her class was. He was young and extremely fat and, to accentuate matters, was devouring one of the largest and thickest sandwiches I have ever seen. He looked down at me with a mouthful and an air of complete amazement, then turned to his mate saying nothing; but if looks could speak he was saying, 'We've got a right Charlie here.'

He then climbed down out of the cab and replied to my question saying 'It's my tea break', and wandered off through the barrier gates. Not quite the reception I was accustomed to in my student days, when I used to wander on to the 'green' at Paddington and chat to unknown drivers for hours. Has the code and breed changed? One always has to meet the odd 'nigger in the woodpile'; perhaps he was the one and only case or maybe some little thing had upset him like my past friend on the empty stock train at Ynyslas. I hope so, especially for the younger enthusiasts brought up in the age of diesel traction.

In conclusion, mention must be made of one incident on the footplate when emergency working came into force. On a typically damp and windless November evening, during the dying hours of the GWR, I was about to board the 'up' 6p.m. mail train at Aberystwyth, when my presence was requested up front. Normally, one of Oswestry's three 'Manor' class engines would be designated to work the train. However, on that particular evening, which turned out to be one of misfortune, a 'Duke' class engine was attached, this possibly being the reason for my invitation. It was not unusual at that period to find a 'Dukedog' assigned but it was a surprise to come across one of the former class, although the odd one or two were still around. The locomotive was No.

3254 *Cornubia*, and she was just within her load of six coaches. In spite of her age she looked, at a glance, to be in good trim. She had a nice clean fire, and her boiler pressure stood at just under the 180lb. mark. Possibly the crew (alas, no longer with us) had anticipated bad weather, because the storm canopy was erected which stretched from the cab roof to brackets on the tender.

We got away promptly on time, and not uncustomarily indulged in a slight spasm of slipping as we entered the 'up' main. There was another slight slip at Plas-Crug crossings, but all went well up to Llanbadarn crossings where the token for the single line was picked up. Alas, from that point, disaster fell upon disaster; the engine began to slip from one slip into another, whilst the curve of the line, on to what is known as Factory Bridge, did not help. We were now down to walking pace, and ahead lay the long climb of Fronfraith Bank at 1 in 75. The little engine struggled on, but it was now almost a case of continuous slipping until we eventually passed under the first overbridge, and then came to a standstill — she was beaten. Three or four abortive attempts were made to get her moving but to no avail, in spite of the coaxing chatter from her driver. The fireman eventually climbed down, only to find the rails were thick with wet Beech leaves, so he made his way back to consult the guard who, I am certain, was my old friend Jack Holland. It was decided to operate emergency working and split the train. I presumed the guard had carried out the necessary precaution to protect the remainder of his train, and eventually we got away with the three leading coaches, struggled up the bank, and ran down the other side of the incline to Bow Street, halting at the home signal which was in the 'on' position. In short, a lot of vital procedure had to be undertaken which I was not to witness.

At that stage of my life, I was only very recently married, residing in our temporary home in the village of Borth, and that particular night my wife had promised to cook something special for my supper. Anticipating a considerable delay, I quickly bade farewell to my companions and made haste to the station yard gates, with the hope of catching the bus or possibly hitch-hiking a lift. Earlier on, as I entered the station at Aberystwyth, the 6p.m. bus to Borth was standing in the bus bay. I took particular notice, because Crosville had recently changed their past familiar livery of LMS Crimson Lake to a rather drab green, but that night, the vehicle on duty was one of the old original Leyland Lions that were still adorned in the Company's old colour. Her journey to Borth was something of a devious route, so I set off up to the village in the direction of my home. Never can I recall so many cars and buses passing me, all in the wrong direction until eventually a passer-by told me that the bus had long since passed, and there would not be another for at least an hour. For some unknown reason, the

'local' was not open, and the solitary telephone box was out of order. Down-hearted, I decided to retrace my steps to the station, but was greeted by the familiar sound of a 'Swindon' whistle. No. 3254 had rescued the rest of her load and, in fact, I was extremely fortunate in being able to dive, in the nick of time, into an empty compartment before we were away; as I suspected, there was no assisting engine. The subsequent climb to Llandre was a bit of a struggle but she made it, and we crossed the 'down' 3.45p.m. ex-Shrewsbury passenger train which should normally have been crossed at Dovey Junction. Fortunately we got the road, and galloped down the next incline to Borth.

Almost before the train had drawn to a halt I was out, and dived into the waiting-room to collar my bicycle. Low and behold it had a flat tyre. There was nothing for it but to footslog almost the entire length of the village and, as if enough was not enough, it had started to rain. Half running and half walking I splashed my way down that endless deserted village, and had almost reached our front door when, as if adding insult to injury, the wretched bus came along, now on its return trip to Aberystwyth. Her driver, one Harold (Bach) Jones, spotted me, pulled up, and with hoots of amusement, shouted down from his cab, 'I've just passed the mail by the Golf Club, and I've been out to Trer-ddol and back. Better come with us next time, we'll drop you at the door.' Words were beyond me at that stage; in silence I lifted my head in a gesture of despair and opened the front door, making certain it was banged shut with the appropriate force the situation called for. My poor little wife greeted me with a somewhat worried expression saying, 'You are late. I do hope our supper is not ruined.' Normally she would estimate my arrival home to a split second by watching the mail run down the bank from the kitchen window. Alas, that night, the dice were contra-loaded. Possibly my reply was something rude concerning No. 3254.

However, should the powers that be ever have found out what transpired that unfortunate evening, I'm certain their verdict would have been 'Serve him right, he's had his punishment.' Ironically, the very next night, my faithful watch played tricks and I arrived at the station at Aberystwyth to see the mail already drawing out. Much to the amusement of the bus crew I was forced to join them, but a more sophisticated Leyland Tiger vehicle got me home for supper in record time.

Finally, on the topic of food, one frosty morning many years later, I joined my friends on the footplate of 'Manor' class No. 7819 *Hinton Manor* working the 'up' pick-up goods to Machynlleth. We had a lengthy wait at Ynyslas to cross a 'down' passenger train, and were treated to one of the best fried egg sandwiches cooked on the shovel in front of the firebox doors. Something good always came out of that particular locomotive.

Chapter 16
Some Cambrian Characters

The Cambrian network was a sprawling affair with numerous short branches which ended abruptly, yet in spite of her spread-eagle nature, she was very much a family affair, a characteristic which still lives on. Indeed, what remains has not changed that endearing nature. Enginemen, guards and, to a lesser degree, signalmen, were responsible for conveying gossip and practical jokes from one station to another. Being predominantly Welsh, it is not surprising that no end of good-hearted humour existed up and down the line, and each station had its particular characters, together with the most appropriate nicknames that were so typical of the people. To really get to grips with a cross-section of the railwaymen, from the top to the bottom of the ladder, no better place could be selected than a first aid or ambulance meeting.

It was via these important and entertaining occasions that I first met Oliver Veltom, the late District Traffic Manager of the Oswestry Division of the Western Region of BR. 'O.V.', as Cambrian railwaymen often spoke of him, was a dynamic figure who, during his reign, undoubtedly created more for that district than anyone. Apart from his vast railway knowledge in all departments, he possessed all the qualities of a great leader, being firm, very fair and never sarcastic. One of his many outstanding qualities lay in his incredible knack of always being present at railway functions, irrespective of their importance. He not only knew the men in his division, but invariably also knew their christian names.

During times of distress and, not often, discontent, Cambrian railwaymen were never afraid to approach the 'Guv', knowing full well they would get a fair hearing. Those who had failed in their duties knew they would be on the mat, and risked being torn off a strip — but there it ended. It is not surprising that Oliver Veltom very quickly made his mark in the Oswestry Division, and was held in the highest esteem by all who served under his

A 'couple of old rogues'; Bill Evans (signalman) and Jack Caffrey (crossing keeper) seen on the 'down' platform at Ynyslas.

P. Dalton

command. It was cruel justice that one who had completed so much for a district eventually had the painful task, towards the end of his term of office, of having to witness the closure of lines he had fought so hard to keep open. The final injustice came prior to his retirement.

Regional changes, and the transfer of headquarters from Oswestry to Shrewsbury, resulted in his relegation to Assistant Traffic Manager for his final railway hours. This tragic and unwarranted move was the shabbiest of railway rewards. It not only shocked, but was deeply felt by his entire Cambrian flock. Happily it never changed Oliver, and to all concerned he was still the boss.

One of many typical and amusing incidents concerning him was related to me by Bill Evans, then senior signalman at Ynyslas. Bill and Jack Caffrey, the crossing keeper, were sitting beside the stove in Ynyslas signal box one afternoon when Borth, the next station on the line to the south, asked if Ynyslas would accept an 'up' light engine. It was duly acknowledged, and Bill went through the normal procedure. Picking up the 'Ynyslas Glandyfi' token, this being the next station to the north, Bill told Jack he would close the level crossing gates because he wanted to go to the booking office. Jack was already quite familiar with the layout of the box, and told Bill he would 'pull off'. Away went Bill, down the wooden platform with the token under his arm. As Bill approached the gates a familiar car drew up, and out stepped Oliver Veltom. Now Bill was no mug, and was well aware of the wisdom of his boss — he was certainly in a tight corner. Oliver walked up to Bill, shook hands with him, and in a flash sized up the situation.

'Well, young man, what are you going to do?' asked Oliver, as the light engine had come to a standstill at the home signal and had whistled.

Bill looked anxiously back at the signal box and, in sheer desperation, said he had come to close the gates.

'Together with the token?' replied Oliver.

Bill quietly closed the gates with his heart in his mouth. Oliver then inquired who was in the box, and Bill replied that it was the crossing keeper. Bill's silent prayers had been answered; Jack, like an old cormorant, missed nothing; he had already spotted the car and, as cute as a monkey, said to himself, 'Damn! who is Bill talking to? I don't think I'll pull off.' Bill duly made his way back to the box, accompanied by the 'Guv'. He went through his normal duties, pulled off, and set the light engine away on her course northwards — a close shave!

Oliver introduced himself to Jack, whom he had not met before. 'You are an ex-goods guard? You live in the station house? Is that your wood stacked outside?'

'Yes Sir,' replied Jack. 'You know all the rules and tricks?' Oliver continued. Again, after a pause, 'Yes sir.' 'So do I,' replied Oliver.

A deathly silence followed, then Oliver drew out a packet of cigarettes and offered one to each of the railwaymen and, knowingly, together with a twinkle in his eye, said, 'Good afternoon, gentlemen — you couple of old rogues.' and went on his way.

A few weeks later, after that recorded event, I was travelling home to Ynyslas, on the 'up' 6p.m. mail train from Aberystwyth, when four men got into the compartment, brought out a pack of cards and started to play. They were all unknown to me but, by their conversation, were obviously railwaymen. When the mail train reached Ynyslas, Bill Evans, the signalman on duty, was standing alongside our compartment door on the 'up' platform, and one of my fellow companions showed his cards to Bill. Bill had a few words with him, then closed the door and said to me, 'The Governor has got a good hand.' It was then that I asked Bill if the gentleman to whom he had spoken was Oliver Veltom. 'Yes, why didn't you introduce yourself, he's a lovely chap.'

I explained to Bill that I had never seen or met him, whereupon Bill suggested I send him a rather amusing photograph of the Vale of Rheidol that I had taken a few weeks earlier. Later that night, a print was duly despatched and, by return, I received a grateful letter with a suggested meeting in Aberystwyth in the not too distant future.

Now, by coincidence, Wynfford Vaughan Thomas was running a daily radio programme advertised as *Over the Rails*, a day to day cross-country railway journey from South Wales to Holyhead. Previously I had been approached and asked if I would discuss the Aberystwyth to Carmarthen branch, live, for five minutes. Unknown to myself, Oliver Veltom had also been asked to do a recording on the Oswestry District.

On that particular night, I arrived at the Cambrian Hotel, which was situated opposite the railway station at Aberystwyth, from where the programme was being broadcast, and here I was ushered up to a small bedroom which was alive with BBC officials. Hurriedly, I showed Wynfford my rough script.

'Excellent,' was his reply, 'but that's what I am going to say.' 'The part I want to discuss with you is from Llanidloes to Strata Florida.' With a horrified expression I feebly stammered, 'But there never was a railway, apart from a few miles of track which ended abruptly at the small village of Llangurig.'

My humble protest was waved aside with an air of confidence, and eventually five terrible, almost lifelong, minutes followed as my imagination was stretched to its limits.

Later, several Aberystwyth listeners, who obviously had no knowledge of this mythical railway, congratulated me on my performance and well-informed history on the subject. My impossible task had not been made any easier by the obvious expression of amusement on Oliver Veltom's face as the volume of questions fired at me increased and I continued to flounder hopelessly. How-

The last of Aberystwyth's Dukedogs', No. 9015, leaves Aberystwyth for Swindon and the graveyard in May 1960. Driver Tim Abrahams and Fireman G. Hughes are in charge of this final journey.

P. Dalton

ever, his turn was to follow, and my slight consolation was apparently obvious when his recording was mysteriously cut short at a vital point.

Later on we left the Cambrian Hotel together and agreed that the show was a classical mess-up, especially so, since neither of us had received the customary remuneration for our paltry efforts. Later, however, I discovered that they had gone to a good cause, the Railway Benevolent Fund.

There is a very true saying, 'Something good comes out of everything', because Oliver then suggested that I should accompany him to a railway ambulance meeting taking place at another hotel in Aberystwyth. My car was outside the Cambrian Hotel and, low and behold, on the back seat lay an old working timetable snatched from Ynyslas signal box, clearly marked 'private and not for public use'. Oliver's hawk-like eyes spotted it in a flash and, turning to me, he said 'You cheeky . . . . . ; where did you get that?'

From that very moment we became the closest of friends, and subsequently I attended every ambulance

and railway meeting. He introduced me to influential members of all departments, and through his influence I obtained a most generous supply of locomotive passes over the Oswestry District. Indeed, I look upon Oliver, apart from being a very dear friend, as my golden hour, and owe him an immense debt.

Tragically, Oliver died recently after a short illness, and it was his wish that his ashes should lie alongside his beloved Vale of Rheidol Railway. Thus, one evening, after the last 'down' train from Devil's Bridge had arrived at Aberystwyth, a party of past and present railwaymen made the sad journey to a point above the Rheidol Falls, where a short service of thanksgiving for his life was conducted.

Sometime in the future, his many friends intend to provide a memorial tablet to be set in the rock above where his ashes were scattered, to commemorate the life of the most beloved chief the Cambrian has ever known. One of his former staff was heard to say, 'We have never had his like before, and we shall never see his like again.'

The late Lewis Hamer, stationmaster at Aberystwyth,

Mr Lewis Hamer, late stationmaster at Aberystwyth, photographed in August 1957, complete with the usual rose on his lapel.

P. Dalton

has already been mentioned in a previous chapter concerning the Vale of Rheidol line. He was undoubtedly one of the best railway officers ever to hold the position, being a remarkable man who commanded the highest respect from his staff. Aberystwyth was probably unfortunate in the fact that his term of office there was so short before his retirement, yet his brief reign was to have far-reaching effects. Not only did the station take on a completely new look, but his co-operation with Oliver Veltom installed new life into the little Vale of Rheidol line. One of his strongest attributes was his eye for business. He would sally forth into the town and bargain with local traders for railway traffic, and will be well-remembered for arranging innumerable excursions, always insisting that a buffet car was attached. If higher authorities declined, he would threaten to cancel the arrangements but, needless to say, invariably he won the day. One of his classic remarks, well-known to railwaymen at Aberystwyth, has now become legend. He once stated to a railway official that he was running the station as if it was his own business.

Many years previously, I had won a tussle with the Management at Oswestry regarding the 'up' 6p.m. mail calling at Ynyslas to set down. Possibly success had gone to my head because now, many years later, with Lewis Hamer in command, I chanced my arm once more. My previous request was really most reasonable under the existing workings although, however, the next was more than doubtful, especially so since it concerned a well-established express train. The ex-12.35p.m. Aberystwyth to Whitchurch train, in its passage to Machynlleth, called at Borth and Dovey junctions only. During the summer service, a 12 noon stopper (Saturday only) left Aberystwyth, calling at all stations to Shrewsbury. Too often I found it impossible to catch the latter train, which resulted in my riding the express and terminating my journey home at Borth. My wife would meet me with the car, but at less fortunate times, her domestic duties with young children would result in a my having a two mile trek along the shoreline. Spotting Lewis in the station I really stuck my neck out, and asked him what the possibilities were for the 12.35p.m. express, calling at Ynyslas on Saturdays only throughout the year to set down. It was a bit of a tall order but the interesting point was Lewis's reaction, bearing in mind that he had served at Control throughout World War II. If my request was not on, he would have been first to say so.

'Why not,' was his reply. 'No time like the present', as I accompanied him into his office. Picking up the telephone he got straight through to Control. After a short pause I gathered the abrupt reply was a precise 'No', whereupon, with an air of confidence, he boomed back, 'Put me to the top of the fountain.' A few words were exchanged, and he put the telephone down with a broad smile. 'I'm looking for revenue, not trying to lose it. The 12.35p.m. will call at Ynyslas from Saturday next.' Lewis Hamer was certainly a 'true railwayman', who faithfully served the Cambrian, the GWR and British Railways (WR).

That little request paid off because, in spite of the working to 'set down only', the station staff at Ynyslas booked passengers on to the train, similar to the 'up' 6p.m. mail. At first, the Oswestry drivers who worked the express were not too pleased, but their mild resentment was short-lived and subsequent research on my part revealed that my personal request caused no delay or late running of the express over the following years. Lewis Hamer certainly knew what he was doing, and the so-called hierarchy at Control were not going to cross swords with him.

I met two locomotive inspectors on the Cambrian, these being Messrs Douglas Sinclair and Glyn Taylor, who accompanied me over hundreds of miles. Another old friend, Bill Parcell of Wolverhampton (Stafford Road) Depot, also became a Cambrian companion on brief occasions when he was temporarily loaned to the Cambrian at Shrewsbury. Chief Inspector George Holland often penetrated the district, in spite of his

Inspector Glyn Taylor leans out of the cab of No.7822 *Foxcote Manor* and poses for a photograph with a visitor.

P. Dalton

headquarters being at Wolverhampton. The latter was no stranger, as I often met him in the Midlands with Bill Parcell and Harry Curiton (Shedmaster at Worcester). This was a trio who really let their hair down when they were together.

George who, unfortunately, is no longer with us, was a great character and really enjoyed a night out with the boys — and why not? Way back in the 1950s, on one occasion when he had a few days leave, he had been invited to attend either a dinner or a meeting tied up with the Tal-y-llyn Railway Society at Towyn. He travelled down on the 'Cambrian Coast Express' to Aberystwyth, the entire journey being spent in the restaurant car where he consumed a great deal of 'refreshment'. Having visited a few of his chums in Aberystwyth he then joined Bill Neal, then shedmaster at Machynlleth, to board the 'up' 6p.m. mail train to complete his journey to Towyn. At this stage George was a little the worse for wear Having joined them in an empty compartment, he spluttered out to me:,

'Hello, are you still going up and down to Shrewsbury on the 'Cambrian Coast Express?' I replied, 'Yes, whenever

I can get a pass.' George continued, 'You want to do the entire run from Paddington, I've got to do it soon, you had better come with me.'

Bill Neal said, quietly, 'You want to take him up on that'.

However, under the circumstances, I was quite certain that George would soon forget that invitation. Not so. He kept his word, to which I have made a brief reference in a previous chapter. In spite of the relatively short distance from Aberystwyth to Ynyslas, I'll swear Bill Neal reminded George at least half a dozen times that he would have to change trains at Dovey Junction. It would only mean crossing the platform and boarding the first train to arrive. George appeared disinterested; he just sat opposite me, with a perpetual smile on his face, and kept winking at me, rather implying that Bill was talking a load of codswallop. I bade farewell to both at Ynyslas and, apparently, Bill put George out at Dovey Junction, indicating the platform where his train would arrive. Those who know this junction will appreciate how wind-swept it can be, and the sparseness of platform staff. The fresh air must have hit George and, within a few minutes, the 'down' 3.55p.m. Shrewsbury to Aberystwyth pass-enger train ran in. George got straight into an empty compartment, on the same platform at which he had just dismounted from the mail, and promptly fell asleep, eventually waking up back at Aberystwyth at 7.25p.m. with no hope of reaching Towyn. His short slumber must have revived him because he sought out his chums, which included Lewis Hamer, and some session took place that night.

George returned to Wolverhampton the following morning on the 'up' 'Cambrian Coast Express', once again in the restaurant car, but this time just sipping plain tonic water. That was George Holland enjoying recreation. He started his railway life like most engine-men as a cleaner, and steadily climbed the ladder of promotion until he finally became a Chief Inspector. George Holland was the opposite type of person on duty to that described in this latter paragraph.

The majority of enginemen with which I rode on the Cambrian were those of Aberystwyth and Machynlleth sheds; in fact, the number of occasions that Oswestry and Pwllheli men were involved could be counted on one hand. Many of my old comrades have long since retired and even passed on. It would be impossible to mention them all in one chapter, although several have already been mentioned in preceding chapters.

One of the first drivers I rode with in post-war days was the late Jack James, known at Aberystwyth Shed as 'Jack Jarms'. Local inhabitants will no doubt recall him, especially when cycling an old ladies' tall bicycle, clad in an open-necked shirt and, invariably, with a string of mackerel hanging from the handlebars. Jack was un-doubtedly the unofficial Cambrian 'record breaker' and was a good engineman, but he had his distinctive method and had little or no time for officialdom. When he first realised my fascination for steam locomotives, he must have got it firmly implanted in his mind that there was only one place for me; riding with him. He would walk down the platform peering into coaches and, even on bank holidays, regardless of who was present, would haul me out demanding my presence up in front, the usual excuse being that it was far too crowded. Poor old Jack died before retirement, way back in the 1950s, and Aberystwyth Shed certainly lost a character.

One morning, during a spell of almost arctic con-ditions at Ynyslas, the 'down' loop was frozen solid so that 'down' trains had to be flagged on to the 'up' main. Normally the 'down' mail passed Ynyslas at approxi-mately 6.35a.m. but, on this particular morning, con-ditions had been so bad along the line that this train had reached Machynlleth two hours late, and was eventually classed as a stopping train from the latter station to Aberystwyth. My normal train, the 'down' 8.10a.m. service, followed as empty stock. Under normal con-ditions, Oswestry men worked the mail train into Aberystwyth, returning home on the 'up' 7.35a.m. passenger working. However, that particular frozen day, Jack James and his mate had worked the latter train as far as Machynlleth, returning to Aberystwyth on the late running mail train. I had been keeping myself warm in

the signal box before crossing over the 'up' platform and diving into the first compartment to hand. There I sat until signalman Bill Evans eventually opened the carriage door, letting in a blast of cold air. 'Come on, quick. You're wanted up front.'

'Nothing doing, Bill,' I replied. 'I'm staying here.' 'For Heaven's sake,' said Bill, 'otherwise we shall be here all day.'

Jack and his mate had spotted me, and Jack was standing on the 'up' platform with an open-necked shirt, in the teeth of the gale, beckoning me to join him. I ran like a hare up that platform, and clambered up the frozen steps on to the footplate.

'It's warmer up here,' said Jack, 'and we've time to make up.'

We did too, by really hitting that Standard Class 4 all the way to Aberystwyth.

Over the years, Jack has made some classic descents of the tortuous Talerddig Bank to Cemmaes Road. On one occasion, while working the 'down' 'Cambrian Coast Express', he climbed down on to the platform at Machynlleth and was quickly confronted with an ex-tremely irate dining car conductor concerning his smashed crockery. Jack, with an element of mischief in his eyes, retorted, 'What the hell do you think I'm pushing; a . . . . . wheelbarrow?'

Dickie Lewis was another character. He was reputed to be as deaf as a post, and I'm certain he got by by lip reading, yet on the footplate he could hear a pin drop. He was the master running warm fisherman, always the acme of politeness, and would never leave the riverside, even in the dark, without wandering up and down the banks to bid goodnight to fellow fishermen.

Albert Humpheys was a 'Royal' driver and, prior to his retirement, carried out a lot of supervisory duties in the shed at Aberystwyth. I used to spend many of my lunch hours in the locomotive office reading through the 'trains book' and reminiscing.

Tim Abrahams was gifted with the most beautiful copper-plate style of writing, and one of his idiosyncrasies was the habit of repeating himself. Every time I rode with him he would have his hand on the regulator, say-ing 'You get the feel of her; see.' He steamed the last 'Dukedog', No. 9015, out of Aberystwyth en route for Swindon and her ultimate graveyard. I went to Llanbadarn box to photograph them. Tim and his mate knew I was going to be there, and really posed for my shot, as the locomotive virtually crawled past my vant-age point and entered the single line minus the vital token. The signalman at Llanbadarn Crossing, uncon-cerned, had casually witnessed their tokenless passage. 'Dull . . . . . . ; they won't go very far.' was his dry comment. Sure enough No. 9015, within 100 yards, came to a halt and gracefully retraced her steps. Tim

At Carmarthen Shed three Cambrian men pose for a picture. Left to right are Inspector Sinclair, Fireman P. Davies and Driver D. Rowlands.

P. Dalton

leaned out of his cab and shouted down to me, 'We thought you would like to take another snap; it's the last you will get of her. Anyway off they went again up the bank; this time above reproach.

History has often proved that on railways, mishaps, and even disasters, can occur twice at the same place. Sometimes enginemen can be cursed with a run of bad luck, while a minor mishap, with no fault on their part, can often continue. Such was the case of Tim, when he was working a goods train on the branch line to Carmarthen. Near Tregaron a farmer, at the last moment, decided to dart across an unmanned crossing on his tractor. The farmer's time judgement was way out, and Tim's locomotive hit the unfortunate person. The accident was fatal.

A few weeks later, Tim was involved in a pile up after dark at the east end of Aberystwyth Locomotive Shed. He was bringing a 'Dukedog' off the shed when his locomotive collided with a 2251 class engine backing on. The impact took place on some manually-operated points and caused total disruption, to the extent that no other locomotives could get in or out of the shed. Both locomotives were derailed and the tender of the 'Dukedog'

reared up on its end, which prevented the locomotive falling over on its side. Considerable track damage resulted, and it was a good 24 hours before everything was rectified. I never discovered who was at fault but, as if this was not enough, Tim unfortunately ran through some stop blocks a few weeks later. However, that was his lot, and the rest of his railway days were above reproach. Undoubtedly some enginemen, like a good motorist, can suddenly see a long standing record ruined by an event which, although they were involved, was due to no fault on their own part.

David Roach, another old faithful friend, for some unknown reason passed a 'stop' signal at Port Llanio on the Carmarthen branch. He was coming up to retirement, but that mishap resulted in his last railway hours being reduced to station pilot duties. He was the great politician who mysteriously moved his allegiance from extreme left to intense right, and made no attempt to disguise the fact.

Johnny (Bach) Davies was the smallest of locomotive drivers that I had ever met, but in spite of his minute stature, he could make the sparks fly when the occasion arose. One November evening, during the mid-1950s, the 'up' 6p.m. mail train had been held at Aberystwyth, with a final late start of approximately seven minutes. Cambrian men never liked late running, and always made all possible efforts to recover lost time. On this particular night Johnny set off with Standard Class 4

No. 75006 in a spectacular fashion; indeed, it was one of the fastest approaches I have ever experienced to Llanbadarn crossing. Standard engines were never the quietest to ride upon, and that night No. 75006 put on a real rattle. Llanbadarn crossing signal showed a 'clear' green, so Johnny, attired in his familiar bib and brace, with a muffler round his neck and a cloth cap upon his head, kept his right hand on the regulator. There was no easing as his little short legs appeared to dangle from his seat, while his deep set eyes peered ahead as we approached the acutual crossing. Johnny's mate, unconcerned, moved across to the left-hand side of the cab to sweep up the Llanbadarn to Bow Street token. At the critical moment as he leaned out there was a sudden bang with steam everywhere — a waterglass had blown. I heard the regulator close with a slam and, even louder, ... hell!' from Johnny. We were well past the crossing gates before we came to a standstill, and the token was eventually found down the embankment in a clump of broom; poor old Johnny and his mate had obviously juggled with it before finally putting it down. Because of this incident, their eventual arrival at Machynlleth was somewhat late. No. 75006 came off there, and the Oswestry men who took over had to content themselves with a Class 2 'Mickey Mouse' engine, but were assisted to the top of the bank by 2-6-2 tank No. 5510.

A few days later, I met Johnny in the street; he said, 'Pity too, she was going well. We would have been on time at Ynyslas.' I often thought about that night as in fact, but for that not unfamiliar mishap, we would have been well ahead of time. In passing, I must mention a few drivers who I have been privileged to ride with, namely O. B. Jenkins, Gwylim Davies (Well, Well), Chick Evans, Bob Davies (Bob John) and, finally, Jim Everson. The latter got the cab of No. 7803 *Barcote Manor* caught on an obstruction on the coaling stage at Aberystwyth, and despite routine visits to Swindon, the slight buckle was never straightened out, and Jim always regarded the defect with a touch of personal satisfaction.

Before leaving the locomotive side of things, I must mention a very old friend, the late Tom Dummer, a well-remembered supervisor at Aberystwyth Shed in the post-World War II era. There was something very distinctive about him, in that he was very quiet and never became ruffled. He was, in fact, one of nature's gentlemen. He originally moved from South Wales and, possibly, during his early railway life, saw service with the old Brecon & Merthyr Railway or the famous Taff Vale Railway. Significantly, enginemen never spoke of or addressed him by his christian name — it was always Mr Dummer.

Portraying his character briefly, it is suitably illustrated by recording a small incident I witnessed one lunch hour in the locomotive office. I had been fingering through the pages of the massive 'trains book', and had come across a reference to locomotive No. 9016. The latter had stood dead for well over a year, at the end of what was known as the 'back road'. I asked Tom Dummer the reason.

Leaning back on the desk, clad in his familiar blue dust coat and blue-black trilby hat, he started to record a list of defects relating to the locomotive. Suddenly, he was cut short when a certain Locomotive Inspector, who shall be nameless, burst in to the office like a red dog. One of the boys had really upset him, and what he was going to do was nobody's business. Tom never altered his stance but listened and just nodded. After a moment's silence, Tom quietly said to the irate Inspector, 'Mr . . . . , why don't you just walk round the yard and slowly count to ten?' Whereupon the Inspector glared at him, turned on his heels and departed, banging the door behind him.

That almost volcanic eruption had no effect on Tom and neither did he refer to it, but quietly continued to relate to me the problems of the dead 'Dukedog' locomotive as if nothing had happened. However, within minutes, the Locomotive Inspector returned and now, in sharp contrast, was as peaceful as a lily on a pond on a summer's day. He just smiled at Tom and said, 'You're quite right, Mr Dummer', whereupon the three of us spent the most amicable half hour chatting away about this and that. Such was Tom Dummer.

Somewhat naturally, the men of the Cambrian who were the most familiar to me were those on the locomotive side, but in my home territory of South Cambria other departments were not excluded, such as signal and permanent way inspectors, local signalmen, and station staff. On the signal side, my thoughts reach back to Inspector D. Jones of Aberystwyth. He was a very precise little man, who took his duties very seriously and would regularly visit signal boxes under his wing. Quite rightly he would question the signalmen on the rules and regulations and, in the true Welsh style, earned himself an appropriate nickname; that of 'Twenty Questions.'

Already, in past chapters, I have mentioned the signalmen that I really knew well, but I must return once again to Marshall Phillips, Bill Evans' mate at Ynyslas. Marshall had many distinctive characteristics, one of these being his ability to mimic, and one afternoon, when activities in the box were slack, he decided to ring his mate in the next box to the north, this being Glandyfi. Putting on one of his best acts, he informed his chum that he was Inspector Jones, and that he would be calling on the next train. A hurried clean-up of Glandyfi box took place, together with some revision of the rule book. The 2.35p.m. ex-Aberystwyth passenger train eventually drew into Glandyfi Station, but with no Inspector Jones. Marshall's unfortunate victim realised at once that he had fallen hook, line and sinker for this practical joke and, what is more, guessed its source. Now, by coincidence, the unfortunate man also 'took off' Inspector Jones remarkably well, a fact well-known by Marshall who naturally awaited the reprisal. About two weeks elapsed, then the expected voice came through to Marshall on the telephone at Ynyslas box. 'Inspector Jones will be calling on the 9.55a.m. train from Aberystwyth.' Marshall replied, 'Right you old . . . . . . , I'll be waiting for you' and hung up with the broadest of grins. However, his smile vanished like quicksilver when an extremely white-faced and naturally irate Inspector Jones stepped down from the next train. Knowing Marshall, I would have given a lot to have heard his explanation.

Owen (Bach) Jones was a faithful member of the Carriage & Wagon Department, and was one of the prime characters at Aberystwyth. He was a small man, as round as a ball, and quite unpredictable and he was full of his own theories; in fact, he could well have been labelled as the 'Archimedes of the Cambrian'. One of his many peculiar traits was his assumption that you were always aware of what was going on in his thoughts. Often he would walk up to me on the platform and say, 'I've told them they are wrong, what's the use, they won't listen', then wander off. Needless to say, nine times out of ten, I had not the vaguest notion as to whom or what he was referring.

This character was a regular member at ambulance meetings and, regardless of what was taking place or who was present, he would jump to his feet to voice some grievance. Olive Veltom would sit and listen to his outbursts with great sincerity and, on one occasion, whispered to me, 'I love that little man, he's one of the best characters in the Division.' Naturally, he was a target for leg-pulling, especially from the Locomotive Department which appeared to be his arch-enemy. On one occasion a member of this department approached him, with tongue in cheek, and asked him if he could see his way possible to give the boys a lecture on the working of the vacuum-brake. Owen agreed, and I understand it was a hilarious event, especially the questions and answers. However, I am certain it was a case of 'he who laughs last . . .' and that the little man secretly set out to be a clown at the expense of the enginemen.

The late Owen Humphreys was a familiar passenger guard on the Cambrian, especially during the GWR era, and was typical of that period. He was an extremely good-looking man and a very keen gardener and one of his own roses invariably adorned his buttonhole. Although he worked all over the Oswestry District, he will be best remembered for his long stints of duty on the Carmarthen branch. Indeed, he had the distinction of working the last Manchester & Milford train into Aberystwyth from the south; many years later he performed the same duty on the final GWR train from the south.

It would be impossible, in such a short space, to mention all the railway guards operating the District that I can recall. However John Roberts, the passenger guard at Machynlleth, must not pass unmentioned. John and I have been lifelong friends, a friendship that began way back in our schooldays. During holidays, and later through university vacations, we used to play rugby football together for Machynlleth; his native heath. John was a born gentleman and was blessed with a great sense of humour. He will best be remembered on the coast road between Machynlleth and Pwllheli, not only for his courtesy and concern for his passengers, but also for his

stirling efforts to encourage railway revenue when, latterly, the number of passengers on the line began to dwindle. Unfortunately, John had to retire prematurely owing to ill health, but in the past I have often heard enginemen state that it was a pleasure to work a train with John. Such remarks speak for themselves.

On the comedy side, undoubtedly the late Bill Humphreys of Welshpool could be classed as 'Top of the Pops!' He started his railway life way back in Cambrian days, and is reported to have been present on the stopping train involved in the Abermule disaster. In fact, he had been on the railway for such a long time that he was appropriately nicknamed 'Rocket'. Possibly he had the wrong calling in life and should have taken to the stage, as some of his antics displayed at railway ambulance competitions had to be seen to be believed.

'Rocket' possessed other abilities as well as those of acting; he was as sharp as a needle and invariably, by the end of a run, knew the destination of all his passengers together with their status in life. There was method in his inquisitive nature. He would make a careful selection of his passengers, allowing for the allotted waiting time at Welshpool, and would calculate how many cups of tea he could carry back to his chosen few within station waiting time. No doubt here was co-operation with the refreshment room staff, as he was never kept waiting. On several occasions I have watched him make at least two trips to the refreshment room with trays loaded with cups of tea, in spite of the brisk trade within.

During World War II, two railway comedians from Machynlleth decided to use their free passes to spend a couple of days in London and to bolster their stay, they took a large parcel with them which contained either some pork or a Dovey salmon. Such goodies at that time could well be disposed of in the blitzed city, on what one would call the 'darkened' market. When the train drew into Machynlleth 'Rocket', who was the guard at the time, spotted them and, very quickly, sized up the situ-

Inspector W. G. Parcell is pictured at Wolverhampton (Stafford Road) Shed, in January 1958, beside ex-GWR 'Castle' No. 4083 *Abbotsbury Castle*.

P. Dalton

ation. The two unsuspecting railwaymen, together with their vital package, settled down in an empty compartment very close to that of 'Rocket'. By the time the train had reached Moat Lane Junction, panic had set in — what if they were caught? Perhaps it would result in a very heavy fine or even imprisonment or worse still, even the sack. Anyway, they agreed their parcel was too hot to hold, and decided to get rid of it by throwing it out of the carriage window. Unobserved, 'Rocket' knew what was taking place. Luck was on his side because the outer home signal at Newtown, the next station north, was 'on', so the train drew to a halt. As expected, the package went flying out through the window, and landed alongside 'Rocket's' compartment. In a flash he was down on the track and, within seconds, it was safely transferred to his brake van. The train then got the road, with the occupants unaware of what had taken place. It is presumed that the two clear-conscienced railwaymen enjoyed a brief stay in London, whilst 'Rocket' disposed of his treasure at Welshpool at a handsome profit.

While on the subject of something extra for the pot, enginemen and guards working the coast road were all sportsmen, with skills which included shooting, fishing and ferreting. It is stated that many footplate crews carried binoculars and even shotguns to poach something, if the occasion arose. Such activities are often carried out by the best of sportsmen, of which my father was one. He was one of the best fly fishermen that I have ever known; he would always fish into the teeth of a gale, casting a beautiful straight line, but had no qualms about swelling his bag with a few illegal hand lines. On one particular occasion, a gang of painters from Shrewsbury were redecorating Afonwen Junction Station, and were fully aware of the poaching activities of the coast men. They had erected a corrugated galley a few yards up the lineside, to the north of the station, where they would retire and have 'breakfast bach' as it is referred to in Wales. In those happy days the menu was rashers of bacon swelled with fried eggs. One morning they knew the goods would be passing, and were already familiar with the locomotive crew and guard — all arch-poachers. An excellent meal was had by all, but the egg shells, carefully split in halves, were preserved. Just before the goods was due they were carefully placed in a field adjacent to the track, resembling mushrooms. Having artfully laid the decoy, they took cover behind the corrugated sheets to watch the ensuing pantomime. Slowly, as the goods came labouring up the rising gradient from Afonwen to Criccieth, her crew spotted the white objects and, in a flash, brought the train to a halt with shouts of 'mushrooms'! There was a mad scramble over the boundary fences, together with the guard — whilst the painters enjoyed the curses of the goods crew as they returned to their stationary train, unrewarded and fooled.

That tale was related to me by an old friend, Albert Caffrey who, during his railway days, carried out a lot of billposting duties, especially on the coast road. Naturally, he moved from station to station by passenger train and would, whenever possible, carry out the necessary posting, then board the same train to the next station and repeat the performance. Waiting time at some stations was extremely brief so he had to be very sharp, often being encouraged by shouts and whistles from the cab of the locomotive, and 'Come on Albert', resulted in some bills appearing upside-down. However, whenever possible, they never left Albert behind. Albert appeared to have been a bit of a 'jack of all trades' on the railway. He started as a cleaner in the Locomotive Department at Machynlleth, and his early responsibility was the cleaning of Cambrian locomotive No. 54 (later GWR No. 874) which was destroyed on the Friog Rocks.

It would be impossible to mention all the Cambrian characters in one chapter, but I have endeavoured to describe a cross-section of them, and briefly, the unglamorised station platform staff must not go unmentioned.

Alfe Lee at Aberystwyth was a dry humourist. One morning at the latter station, the platform was unduly crowded when Alfe, in his porter's uniform, approached me as he was carrying a bag of golf clubs over his shoulder. Without a flicker of a smile, and with all the dignity of a local laird, he inquired, 'Which is the train for Borth my man? (Borth being renowned for its golf links). That was a typical example of his humour. Unfortunately he suffered from a thrombotic leg, and was compelled to retire from his platform duties. His mates stated that he had been promoted to General Manager of the Gentlemen's Toilets, but Alfe never lost his sense of humour; in fact, his dry wit was enriched in that department.

One other member of the platform staff will be well-remembered, especially by local inhabitants. His name has eluded me, but he was the very essence of courtesy. He held himself erect, his uniform was always above reproach, and when he spotted a would-be traveller he would dart forward to assist with any baggage and find them a seat. In view of his refined nature, he earned himself the nickname of 'Swanky Porter'.

In conclusion, to sample the true Cambrian atmosphere in more senses than one, no better place could be chosen than the lengthy winding promenade at Aberystwyth; possibly the longest of its type in the British Isles. For generations, it has been the custom to walk its length and 'kick the bar'. This ritual was not only shared by local inhabitants but also by university students and naval and military personnel, the latter when on courtesy visits. My recollections stretch back to those golden pre-war evenings, with the sun sinking in the west. Here, one could meet one's friends, or escort one's true love with pride for all the world to see. It was a happy and peaceful environment; violence and vandalism were still a long way away. Those colourful parades of all walks of life so often included railwaymen, especially members of the Locomotive Department, if they had an hour to spare. Engine crews, not only from Aberystwyth, but sets of men from Machynlleth and Oswestry, would form part of the picture, clad in beautifully laundered denim blue overalls and distinctive GWR caps. In spite of the re-cession in the 1930s, most people took a pride in their turnout. Does that happy atmosphere still exist? I hope so.

The Aberystwyth to Carmarthen train approaches Strata Florida and prepares to cross the 'down' 12.05 passenger working, which is standing in the station and is headed by ex-GWR Mogul No. 6355.

P. Dalton

A view of Conwil Station, its water-tower and the dense vegetation beyond, is seen from the footplate of No. 2271 on an 'up' run.

P. Dalton

Sister locomotives Nos. 7820 *Dinmore Manor* and 7821 *Ditcheat Manor* are pictured at Aberystwyth. No. 7820 heads the 'up' 6.20 goods out of the yard whilst No. 7821 waits to back on to the ash road, having worked in with the 'down' 'Cambrian Coast Express'.

P. Dalton

Bearing the 6C shed code, BR Standard 4-6-0 No. 75071, with its high-sided tender, is pictured in the 'down' loop at Borth on a summer Saturday.

P. Dalton

Chapter 17
The Decline of the Cambrian

Understandably, from a personal point of view, the Cambrian system was, in my eyes, akin to some rare exotic plant raised on the poorest of soils. In its high noon, it ran through the most pleasant yet the thinnest of railway territory. Thus, like a delicate plant exposed to extreme elements, it managed to survive and, indeed, even produced branches with buds which, for brief periods, blossomed into flower. In spite of established roots, alas the branches have since been lopped, and the main trunk pruned to such an extent that its survival must now call for considerable doubt.

Today, the remaining Cambrian metals are but a mere shadow of the former Oswestry District. All that remains is the single track from Shrewsbury to Aberystwyth and a similar system from Dovey Junction to Pwllheli, while both sections have lost previously served stations. How long these solitary tracks will continue to carry traffic calls for much speculation, especially so if one recalls a quite recent proposal to lift all rail systems north of Glasgow and Edinburgh. Under such drastic measures, survival in Mid-Wales would hold the bleakest of prospects. However, the Cambrian has not been alone in this gradual strangulation — many other lines of equal status have suffered the same fate, as have some that the Cambrian, even in its heyday, would never have dared equal.

Having lived alongside the Cambrian for the greater part of my life, several factors would appear to have played a vital part in its ultimate decline. However, it is essential at this stage to stress that they are entirely my personal views and, all-important, that there are always two sides to a story.

Casting my mind back to childhood, in spite of the Cambrian's thinly-populated territory, traffic throughout the 1920-30 period certainly justified the railway's existence. Fares were reasonably cheap, while the dreaded road motor services, although already growing quickly, made little or no impression at that stage. Rail passenger services were well patronised, especially during summer months, whilst a very considerable amount of freight and goods traffic was carried. During World War II, in spite of the absence of heavy coal trains which were a feature of World War I, Cambrian metals were never idle and indeed, my own recollections were those of extreme activity. Passenger and troop trains were packed to overloading, whilst freight and munition trains provided a similar picture. The immediate aftermath of six years of war obviously did not produce dramatic changes, but slowly a new form of recreation began to take place. Railway camp coaches became less popular as industry began to reorganise itself to peacetime, with more and more motor cars becoming available to the war-weary public, together with a new image, the birth of the caravan age on a massive scale. Hotels and the past system of boarding houses gradually began to

disappear — for decades they had been the lifeline of the Cambrian Coast resorts. Many hotels were taken over by public authorities, whilst holiday camps sprang up overnight like mushrooms. Planning authorities would have appeared to cast all principles to the four winds, granting planning permission to camp and caravan sites on open stretches of beautiful coastline, which was once farm land. Local traders, hotels and boarding houses lost out, whilst rail passenger traffic dropped dramatically. Yet the petrol pumps worked overtime selling relatively cheap fuel; the inevitable breakthrough of the internal combustion engine had taken place on a large scale, even to the degree that manufacturers were exporting cars, buses and trucks all over the world. They were the bread-winners and, naturally, were entitled to holidays by the sea, and wisely took their food and homes on wheels with them. This change in life became very apparent in the mid-1950s; daily I witnessed the transformation as I made my routine rail journeys between Ynyslas and Aberystwyth.

Many past passengers had taken to road passenger transport as it was a much cheaper proposition, virtually a door-to-door service on double-decker buses which operated along some of the narrowest of roads. British Railways was already in debt and the hideous upward spiral of fares had commenced, together with the fact that they had become very choosy as to what sort of freight they would carry. Road haulage, be it nationalised, denationalised, renationalised or whatever, grabbed at the handout, whilst express bus services became more and more evident. Cattle traffic, an excellent past revenue-earner on the Cambrian, was meekly handed over to road transport. At that time, the all-important Transport Commission would appear to be floundering like a ship without its rudder; their only answer was to push up fares on a very restricted service, which ultimately drove revenue away from the railways. Anyone who was railway-minded, especially those employed on a minor line like the Cambrian, naturally became very despondent. Many of the younger firemen and cleaners left the service, and set out for the Midland's motor industry which offered better prospects — and who could blame them? I am also certain that, at this stage, BR's ever-changing policies and Government interference was a vital factor. Changes in Government and ministers, all with divergent promises and unnecessary regional changes, together with their different forms of administration, all poured oil on the fire. No wonder true railwaymen who had descended from railway families became frustrated, especially as the debt grew alarmingly. Such a state of affairs did not call for confidence, and many such men on the Cambrian openly admitted this to me.

Just prior to the Board's decision to discontinue

livestock traffic, an interesting little episode, which was personal, took place. One of my daughters had a beautiful little Welsh pony which was kept at Glandyfi, away across the marshland from Ynyslas. Unfortunately, it developed a brain infection, and the decision was made to return the unfortunate creature to its previous owner at Pembroke Dock. Unknown to me, my family were making arrangements to have the horse conveyed south by road. Naturally, I was horrified, and asked 'what about rail travel?' No, the poor little thing could not be bumped and banged around in some dirty old train, it was cruel. However, I took the law into my own hands and set off to see an old friend, Ernie Roberts, then stationmaster at Aberystwyth, and told him my story. He got straight through to Oswestry who were non co-operative — either they had no horse-box, or the only one there was was in a bad state of repair. Finally, it was decided to contact Crewe who, in turn, dispatched an immaculate horse-box to Oswestry. On the appointed day of transporting the pony, the horse-box was attached to the 'down' morning mail train and duly shunted into the small cattle bay at Glandyfi.

Later that morning, the little invalid was quietly coaxed into the horse-box and made comfortable. Slight problems arose, as the horse-box would have to be attached to the 'down' 10.20a.m. passenger working from Oswestry and, due to traffic arrangements, this operation had to be carried out at Dovey Junction to the north. Ernie Roberts contacted my friends at Machynlleth Locomotive Department, who responded by sending BR Standard Class 4 No. 75002 light to Glandyfi. She picked up the horse-box, propelled it back to Dovey Junction and, eventually, attached it to the 'down' passenger train. On arrival at Aberystwyth, the station pilot transferred the box with great care and attached it to the coaching stock of the 'up' 5.15p.m. passenger train, which was already stabled in the Carmarthen bay platform. The station staff then gave the little creature fresh straw and water, prior to its last lap of the journey to the south. At 8p.m. the same evening, we received a telephone call, stating that the pony had arrived at its destination without any form of distress. Naturally I was delighted, and paid my sincere thanks to Ernie Roberts and all concerned. The interesting point was Ernie Roberts's assurance that this had not been a special favour but good railway revenue which, incidentally, was cheaper than the estimate for road haulage. I quoted the entire operation far and wide, but the only comments were 'Of course you were a special case, you've got friends on the railway.' I wonder if they had ever bothered to find out under similar circumstances.

Returning to the gathering clouds on the Cambrian, the next vicious blow to her system came from the railwaymen themselves. Industrial action by the men of the footplate who were often, in the past, referred to as the aristocrats of our railways, brought everything virtually to a standstill for approximately seventeen days. No one relishes industrial action and, undoubtedly, it could not

have come at a more unfortunate time. I was able to discuss and listen to the pros and cons without any ill-feeling from my friends, who ranged from Inspectors and enginemen, to fitters and cleaners. I must confess that my feelings were very mixed. They certainly had an axe to grind, especially so if compared with those in industry, and indeed many cases of unskilled labour, but their action had long-reaching effects which I believe marked the beginning of the end, at least on the Cambrian.

The union concerned was ASLEF, whereas the NUR did not come out. A few locomotivemen, who were members of the latter union, managed to keep the merest of skeleton services operating and in fact, one mixed traffic train was able to work in and out of Aberystwyth throughout the stoppage. Naturally life had to go on, and alternative modes of transport were sought. The original trade for the railways was never to be recaptured, whilst the powers of command were given the opportunity to review the entire system on a more economical basis. A large question mark had previously hung over many unviable lines, so the Cambrian thus became a sitting duck for pruning or complete slaughter.

At that time, Aberystwyth locomotivemen were not enjoying the best of turns, but their action lost them the 'paper train', previously a nice 'double home' working to Oswestry. On Saturdays, a 'Dukedog' with an Aberystwyth crew would double-head the 'up' 2.35 p.m. first mail train to Oswestry, returning the following Sunday morning with the paper van running ahead of the 'down' mail train. Both are now things of the past. Gone was the valuable schools traffic, which had helped to swell the 'down' 8.10a.m. passenger from Machynlleth and the 'up' 5.15p.m. in the reverse direction. These were two of the most profitable and popular local trains of the day but, far worse, many past passengers now shared the cost of running a car as the latter increased in numbers annually. This equally hit road motor services, as they to were beginning to feel the pinch.

Within a short space of time, railwaymen struck yet another blow to their security; the NUR came out on strike and this time, the locomotivemen had their hands tied behind their backs due to the total stoppage. The ultimate result of this action was even more far-reaching, with further losses in revenue. The writing was well and truly on the wall, and it was with no surprise that traders lost confidence and virtually everything went over to road haulage. Branch lines started to vanish, with the pruning of the Cambrian getting well under way.

Suddenly, from out of the blue, British Railways announced its modernisation programme; the rapid withdrawal of steam traction, dieselisation as a stop gap and, finally, electrification of viable lines. The Chairman stated that it was to be the end of dirty Emmett like steam trains, that clanked along from station to station. The taxpayer was promised a new, cleaner and slicker service — bold words, although, naturally, railwaymen were concerned, especially over job losses. Our railways were now well and truly nationalised and their debt had been written off; the old four companies no longer existed — competition within a system had gone and rightly so, and now Dr Beeching was called in to reshape the railway system and to cut out the dead wood.

When his hurried proposal eventually became known, local councils, non-railway passengers, railwaymen and various bodies, including railway enthusiasts, threw up their hands in despair. Back on the Cambrian, with no surprise, the Mid-Wales and Carmarthen branches were listed for the axe, while even the coast line from Dovey Junction to Pwllheli had been sentenced; Dr Beeching was a very unpopular figure. However, a Cambrian Coast Preservation Society was formed and, after endless deputations, they succeeded where others had failed and today the line is still operative. Inevitably, the Mid-Wales line had to go whilst Mother Nature, in the form of floods, swiftly finished off the Ruabon to Barmouth and Carmarthen branch lines. Previously, to add to the complications, once again there were regional changes; the Cambrian was transferred to the London Midland Region.

At that time, the LMR were placed high on the table of revenue returns and, very naturally, were not overjoyed to be burdened with a lame duck. At first, the change of control was not noticeable, with steam continuing for a few years, but once complete dieselisation was established, wholesale slaughter took place — double roads and innumerable stations vanished within the space of one year. To the true Cambrian enthusiasts, it was a tragic spectacle, but what alternative had the LMR? Even if the powers that be had left the system under Western Region administration, a similar form of surgery would have taken place.

Dr Beeching's reign in office was nearing an end, whilst changes in Government and ministerial intervention diluted his original proposal for streamlining our national railway system. Possibly it was a case of well begun, but only half done. Extra road passenger services were installed as an alternative. Crosville Motor Services operated over the Mid-Wales route from Newtown to Brecon, but the service was not patronised and was soon withdrawn. Today, the Cambrian is but a ghost railway of the past, and the wheel of ill-fortune has alarmingly almost completed its full cycle.

To whom and where does one point a finger for this unmistakable decline of the Cambrian? Having lived alongside her tracks for four and a half decades, rightly or wrongly, I have recorded my personal impressions, each of which must indicate the proportion of blame contributing to the final picture. Freight has been lost for ever, whilst the railway no longer has the facilities to cope with such traffic in Mid-Wales. From the passenger aspect, road passenger services had already stabbed her in the back, but the pendulum of fortune in turn has already swung against the former. Crosville is one of the largest of our national provincial bus companies, whose routes stretch from the outskirts of Manchester to Carmarthen in South Wales. Many of its country services in rural Wales have now been slashed, depots have been closed and, indeed, a dark and heavy cloud hangs over its future.

However, in spite of the various contributors to the railways' downfall, I am convinced the real culprit or 'nigger in the woodpile' was, undoubtedly, the private motor car, today a household essential. Of course, British Railways themselves are not blameless, but one must not forget the fact that they had an immense burden on their shoulders trying to keep an unremunerative system operational and, at regular intervals, it would appear that even the Almighty was not on their side.

As recently as January 1976, the hungry sea, backed by ferocious winds, once again played havoc with stretches of the Cambrian lines which were exposed to the coast and tidal waters. The Dyfi Estuary was subjected to a most fearful onslaught, with even the massive GWR reinforcements being swept away like shingle. At the time, it was feared that South Cambria would never see a train again.

We have already seen how the elements accelerated the impending closure of the Aberystwyth to Carmarthen and Barmouth to Ruabon branches, whilst more recently, the famed wooden Barmouth Estuary railway bridge was closed for a considerble period due to an attack on its timbers by a form of marine wood-worm. Possibly the elements are the master, being one of the railway's greatest enemies who, in the end, could prove to be final.

The real plight of the Cambrian was brought home to me recently on one of many visits to Wales. It was during a short out of season break, made primarily with the intention of climbing some of the lesser commercialised peaks and playing a few holes of golf on the seaside links of North Wales. However, fate was not on our side, and indeed it became a landslide of disasters and sorrow.

En route, my wife and I paid a few hours' visit to Aberystwyth, and it was very apparent that this seaside resort had severe parking problems. It was quite impossible to find a parking space, and where parking was permissible there were endless rows of cars; a sign of the times! However the most alarming feature was the lack of support for public transport, a very different picture to that to which I had been accustomed in the past.

Later, as we headed north for the rocky crags of Snowdonia, the heavens opened and continued to stay open throughout our visit. The mountains looked black and angry, whilst white-capped waves lashed the shores of the inland lakes. Our intended activities were washed away with the torrents of water that cascaded down the cwms and mountain sides, but the wrath of the wind and rain failed to dampen my ardour. My salvation, once again, lay in steam, with yet another visit to one of the famous 'Great Little Trains of Wales' locations — on that occasion the Ffestiniog Railway at Portmadoc.

It was no surprise to find an immaculate train, complete with buffet car, waiting at the harbour-side terminus, but I was amazed at the number of passengers; virtually every seat was occupied, in spite of the adverse weather conditions. It was not the best day to appreciate the majestic scenery of the Vale of Ffestiniog; low racing white clouds obliterating everything as the little train snaked its way up the valley to the Meolwyns. Once again, as frequently as in the past, I was given the opportunity to appreciate these renowned little trains run on professional lines. Certainly 'Old King Coal' still reigns supreme, while the appetite for steam grows annually — alas BR's lost opportunity.

If only they had had the foresight at the time to retain three steam locomotives at Machynlleth, to work the coast line from Dovey Junction to Pwllheli during the holiday periods, the cost would have been a mere drop in the ocean. A glance at the map indicates the number of little steam lines it taps and, indeed, the line is unique in that respect. Consider the tourist trade it would have attracted, apart from helping to fill the diesel multiple units from Shrewsbury to the west on the main line. The line cries out for this sort of injection. Today, at the eleventh hour, it is too late, and doubt would arise if a light locomotive would be permitted to cross Barmouth railway bridge with its present restrictions.

Later in the day, as we returned by road to our base at Dolgellau, tragedy befell. Our wretched motor car developed a serious defect, so much so that we were compelled to leave it behind and return, at the end of our short break, to England by rail.

The real gale had abated and settled down to a steady drizzle when we eventually set out for Machynlleth to board the train. There's a Welsh saying; 'We'll keep a welcome when you come home again to Wales', but I was begining to doubt its sincerity, especially so on reaching the outskirts of Machynlleth to find the River Dyfi spitefully out in flood. Those mythical dragons were not on our side, and we were compelled to race around an almost twelve mile detour to reach the railway station.

In spite of the inconvenience of travelling home with half of our weekend gear left behind, there was the slight consolation of once again riding Cambrian metals to Shrewsbury. Alas, little did I expect the shocks which were in store. Our train, locally referred to as the 'Cambrian', was a very grimy and outdated two car diesel set, grossly overheated and devoid of comfort. We rattled along at a jogging pace, reminiscent of the old 'pirate' buses of the 1920s. It was impossible to see through the misted-up windows, and when a weather-worn orange curtain caught my eye, the temptation to utilise it to get a glimpse of Talerddig Bank was very strong. However, the last thing I wished for was the accusation of causing damage to railway property — especially on the Cambrian, so it was a case of sit and suffer. On arrival at Newtown the train emptied,

and for the rest of that tedious run to Shrewsbury, we were the sole occupants, in spite of calls at Welshpool and Westbury (crossing point only). When running along the bank of the River Severn, the main motor road runs parallel to the railway in many places, so armed with a discarded newspaper, I set about the task of cleaning the window, and immediately spotted streams of road traffic, which included heavy lorries, tankers and private motor cars, moving in both directions. These were the real culprits in the downfall of the Cambrian. The few stations we passed appeared empty and run down, and Welshpool, apart from the station entrance, was deserted and boarded up. What were once tracks and platforms were now piles of, I presumed, condemned sleepers; there was a smell of a dying system everywhere. On arrival at Shrewsbury I never thought the day would come when I would be thankful to get off a Cambrian train. Later, seated in the comfort of an Inter-City coach, to continue our journey to the South of England, it was possible to relax and ponder over what I had seen.

My previous suspicions as to where the real enemies of the Cambrian lay were now confirmed. Modernisation had not meant progress for its system, but a step backward into the dark ages, with those immaculate 'Cambrian Coast Express' trains of the old steam days gone for ever. Ah yes, that was yesterday.

Later, further research on my part brought to light that the ills of the modern Cambrian go far deeper than many or even I would suspect. Miles of track need to be replaced, and in spite of enormous subsidies, the coffers are empty, with the result that this essential work is just a 'patch up' affair; in fact, it is a case of robbing Peter to pay Paul. To my mind, way back in the horse and cart age, the railway opened up remote districts and later, in competition, road passenger services completed the picture. Today, both would appear to have outlived their function, certainly in rural areas, whilst the internal combustion engine, in the form of the motor car, is one of the major culprits. Of course, there were other collaborators which I have already tabulated, all of which have combined to produce this sombre image.

As I put pen to paper, British Rail is in the deepest overall trouble. If and when the dust settles, many minor lines will have to be axed, and only a miracle will reprieve the Cambrian. Finally, may I be so bold as to state that if the line did cease to exist, probably the only hardship to be felt would be by the men who work its system. Of course, there would be mourners, and I for one would lead the procession. Perhaps the 'Great Doctor's knife' did not penetrate deep enough originally to shorten this prolonged agony of what remains of the Old Cambrian.

Chapter 18
Reflections

Today, the sounds and scent of steam on our railways are lost and gone for ever. Daily, via the media, one reads alarming reports and proposals for the future of British Rail. If trustworthy, perhaps the younger generation could well recollect that railway lines one existed in their lifetime. Therefore, I rejoice that I had the good fortune to witness steam in the true Cambrian days, although some of the finer aspects are excusably cloudy. In sharp contrast, the GWR era up to nationalisation is far clearer, whilst the trials and tribulations of state ownership on her system remain paramount.

Probably I was a spectator of a span which saw the organisation range from a reasonable degree of prosperity to that of virtual bankruptcy, yet her changing fortunes provided me with a chapter of steam that can never be disputed. Of course, the demise of the latter form of traction was one of the sadder events in Cambrian history, but was inevitable. Its death was already indisputable, while retention would not have been practical and, at the time, would have been undeniably expensive. It was the bringing down of the curtain on magnificent machines and the breed of men who worked them. In spite of not only being an onlooker, but one privileged to ride such an assortment of locomotives working the ex-Cambrian lines, undoubtedly my greatest prize lay in the companionship of the men themselves. Without their friendship, it could well have become just another length of railway line.

In far away days, Lewis Rees had set my lifelong fascination in motion, whilst later, the men of the banking engines at Bromsgrove had kept the flame alight, with my post-war companions up and down the line helping to compile one of the happiest chapters of my life.

Of course, there were personal lost opportunities; an example being my failure to ride some of the fascinating branch lines, such as the Abermule—Kerry line and the Tanat Valley branch line. There was also my appalling lack of foresight in allowing the 'trains book' at Aberystwyth Shed to slip through my fingers. That massive ledger was an encyclopedia of steam workings stretching way back into GWR days, a priceless piece of steam information which sadly ended up on the rubbish heap. Even more painful was my stupidity in allowing a similar register to suffer the same fate at Machynlleth. However, in spite of those lost jewels, the boys rescued many souvenirs on my behalf, all being constant reminders of those happy past days.

Today, unfortunately, some of the remaining nostalgic stations would appear out of context alongside the modern matchbox development that has since arisen, yet the march of time and progress has still not completely overtaken the railway. Many a mile of track still exists which is Cambrian to the core. Throughout her existence, in spite of changes in ownership, it has always been the Cambrian, and as long as the tracks remain, will always be so.

Prior to my departure from Cardiganshire, a senior railway officer, addressing me by my christian name, said, 'We are going to miss you. You were never a railwayman by trade, but you are now an adopted Cambrian one.'

As I grow older and stiffer in limb, those magnanimous words often come to mind and have the greatest depth of meaning. In spite of the distance which now separates me from my native heath, my thoughts frequently drift back to those far away childhood days, especially in the dead of night when sleep refuses to come my way, and those revealing lines of Wordsworth come to mind:

'For oft when on my couch I lie
In vacant or in pensive mood,
They flash upon that inward eye
Which is the bliss of solitude,
And then my heart with pleasure fills,
And dances . . .'

Not always with his golden daffodils, but once again with the sea and the skies. The roar of the breakers and the rattle of the shingle as each wave retreats. Those offshore booms and waves that shatter the silence like the crack of a rifle. Lonely sand dunes, the song of the lark, the cry of a curlew and the distant sound of a steam whistle. That was the Ynyslas I like to recall.

Reflections; Ynyslas Station in steam days showing ex-GWR Mogul No. 6335 on the 'Cambrian Coast Express'.

P. Dalton

Ynyslas as it is seen today. No buildings now remain and the crossing gates have been replaced by automatic flashing lights.

P. Dalton

Carrying a double chimney, No. 75004 pilots No. 7806 *Cockington Manor* at the head of a summer evening special to the Midlands, and is seen leaving Borth.

P. Dalton

No. 82033, a BR 2-6-2, shunts with a Machynlleth crew on board at Aberystwyth after the shed at Aberystwyth had closed. At this time, April 1965, the 'up' and 'down' goods trains and the 'Cambrian Coast Express' was still steam-hauled.

P. Dalton

A view from the footplate of No. 73094 as it passes through Swansea Bay Station (now closed) on a 'down' run from Shrewsbury via the Central Wales line. Note the sand on the track and on the platform.

P. Dalton

Ex-LMS 8F No. 48735 stands at Llanwrtyd Wells as No. 73094 approaches the station with a 'down' train.

P. Dalton

As No. 73094 passes Builth Road Junction on the 'down' run to Swansea, an Ivatt 2-6-0, on shed, is seen from the footplate. At this point the Cambrian Mid-Wales line passes beneath the Central Wales line.

P. Dalton

Passing Llandre signal box and entering the station with a summer Saturday local train to Shrewsbury is No. 7811 *Dunley Manor*.

P. Dalton

Ex-GWR Mogul No. 6355 stands at Carmarthen at the head of the 10.45 a.m. 'down' passenger train.

P. Dalton

A fine study of the 'down' 'Cambrian Coast Express', with 'Manor' class 7823 *Hook Norton Manor* in charge at Glandyfi.

P. Dalton

The last in the class, No. 7829 *Ramsbury Manor*, backs on shed after having worked a 'down' passenger train from Carmarthen.

P. Dalton